M000211735

Invisible Children

Invisible Children

Reimagining International Development at the Grassroots

Maya Ajmera with Gregory A. Fields

Maya Ajmera
Society for Science and the Public
Washington District of Columbia,
USA

Gregory A. Fields
Philanthropy Directions International
Manassas, Virginia, USA

ISBN 978-1-137-57837-2   ISBN 978-1-137-57838-9   (eBook)
DOI 10.1057/978-1-137-57838-9

Library of Congress Control Number: 2016937982

Cover illustration © halil ibrahim kurucan / Alamy Stock Photo

Printed on acid-free paper

This Palgrave Macmillan imprint is published by Springer Nature
The registered company is Macmillan Publishers Ltd. London

To Talia Hollander, Michael Fields, and all children around the world who have the right to grow up and become productive caring citizens of the world.

Acknowledgments

This book would never have come into being without the support, encouragement, and insights of so many people equally committed to changing the lives of marginalized children across the globe. Their wisdom and experiences have fed this book's themes and made me far wiser in the writing of it than I was when it was first conceived.

I have been fortunate to teach motivated and curious international development students at the Paul H. Nitze School of Advanced International Studies (SAIS) at Johns Hopkins University. For three years they have challenged the assumptions that govern this field and asked the difficult questions that have helped define the issues in this book. I am especially grateful to my first class of students: Jemila Abdulai, Liz Decker, Regis Dock, Clare Dreyfus, Caitlin Galliker, Silvia Homberger, Dana Huff, Abhilaksh Likhi, Felix Lung, Laura Sennett, Hanyoun So, Daniela Solano, Sameera Syed, and Julia Wallin. They made my first year of teaching one of the most joyous intellectual experiences I have had.

My first research assistant, Saudamini Dabak, a graduate student in the International Development Program at SAIS, conducted hundreds of hours of interviews with leaders of community-based organizations around the world. Her interviews provided the backbone of this book. I am grateful to her for diving into the unknown when we began this project.

My research assistants and former students, Julia Wallin and Daniela Solano, spent countless hours sifting through documents, compiling interview transcripts, and digging deeply into the topics profiled throughout this work. I am grateful for their amazing commitment to this project and for their meticulous, professional diligence in building the book's factual foundation. Madeleine Gleave worked tirelessly to compile the analysis of USAID's child-focused funding. We are grateful to child rights advocate Tom Lent who provided his expertise at the beginning of this project.

Greg Fields and I are especially indebted to Clare Dreyfus, our lead researcher, who coordinated the entire project. A graduate of SAIS and former student, Clare managed deadlines and kept us all on task while providing critical original research. Her keen eye eliminated syntactical errors, flagged awkward phrasing, and ensured a consistent text. And despite the constant demands that we heaped on her, she never lost her smile or sense of humor. This book is as much Clare's as it is ours.

We are also indebted to Amy Mendez, Executive Assistant at the Society for Science & the Public, who provided excellent administrative support at the tail end of getting the book to Palgrave Macmillan.

Palgrave Macmillan's commitment to supporting public discussion of international development and children's issues made them the natural home for this work, and from the beginning we felt that there could be no more appropriate publisher. We have been fortunate to work with editors of exceptional professionalism and integrity. Our thanks go to Christina Brian, Ambra Finotello, and Amber Husain who have guided this work through Palgrave Macmillan and helped make it real.

We also want to express our deepest thanks to all the scholars and leaders in the children and international development field who were interviewed for this book. Their stories and scholarship were vital in shaping this book.

My colleagues at SAIS have been a constant source of encouragement, especially Cinnamon Dornsife of the International Development Program. She and the former dean, Jessica Einhorn, offered me the chance to become a visiting scholar at SAIS during my sabbatical. Cinnamon believed in this book project from the start. Dr. Deborah Brautigam, director of the International Development Program, has been generous with her time and insights, as well as my faculty colleagues Dr. Tanvi Nagpal, Dr. Melissa Thomas, and Dr. Bill Douglas who provided me guidance and support. Ada Ho and Robin Washington contributed thorough and professional administrative support at each step.

I also want to thank Nancy Birdsall of the Center for Global Development (CGD) who gave me the opportunity to spend six months at the CGD at the beginning of my sabbatical where I was inspired to begin thinking about this book.

The Smith Richardson Foundation and 5 51 5 Foundation provided essential funding for the research and development of Invisible Children: Reimagining International Development at the Grassroots. Greg Fields and I are grateful for their confidence in this important book.

This book would never have come into being if it were not for Dr. Bill Ascher, my graduate school advisor at Duke, mentor, and founding Chairman of The Global Fund for Children (GFC). Bill was captured by my idea of founding GFC over 20 years ago, and I was captured by his confidence in it. I am also grateful to several individuals who have provided support and enthusiasm for this book over the past three years—Adele Richardson Ray, Suzanne Duryea, Dave Hodgson, Stacey Keare, Mark McGoldrick, Pat Rosenfield, Juliette Gimon, Esther Hewlett, Sonal Shah, Cheryl Dorsey, Betsy Station, and the 2011 Henry Crown Fellowship Class.

GFC has been a passion for both Greg Fields and me. Its elegant model of driving support efficiently to the community level instills hope that there are ways to surmount the immense problems facing children and young people from the ground up. I am grateful to the entire GFC team, who offered their expertise, experiences, and wisdom, and especially to Katie Bell, Debra Burke, Victoria Dunning, Hoa Duong, Elsa Fan, Mitchell Fenster, Michael Gale, Susan Goodell, Monica Grover, Vineeta Gupta, Jerry Irvine, Tamar Lechter, Solome Lemma, Kristin Lindsey, Katy Love, Sandra Macias del Villar, Shawn Malone, Sarah Modica, Josephine Ndao, Cynthia Pon, Elizabeth Ruethling, Joan Shifrin, Anne Sorensen, and Jenny Tolan. I have learned a great deal from them.

I owe a debt of gratitude to my writing partner, Greg Fields. Greg and I have been colleagues since 2001 when he came to GFC to help build it into a truly global institution. He has shared the excitement of this book since the beginning. It only seemed fitting that he partnered with me on it. I look forward to working on our next book together.

Lastly, I thank my husband, David Hollander, who has been one of my most ardent champions and believer in my work. I am blessed to have him and our daughter, Talia. They are my North Stars

Washington, D.C.   Maya Ajmera

PREFACE

On a hot and dusty day in March 1990, I stepped onto a bustling train platform in Bhubaneswar, India. I was 22 years old, and I had been awarded a Rotary International Graduate Fellowship.

In one corner of the platform was a circle of children, perhaps 40 or so, learning to read and write. A teacher held up flash cards with letters and numbers, and the children laughed and shouted their responses. These young people were completely engaged and excited, and I became mesmerized.

The children were young, maybe six or seven years old. Some had baby siblings in tow. The teacher wore a bright, colorful sari and radiated confidence, passion, and delight as her students grasped what was on the flash cards. All of them were so focused on their lessons that the chaos, noise, and bustle of the train platform did not seem to bother them. They were in their own space, their own world, enchanted by the simple thrill of learning.

After the lesson, I approached the teacher and asked her what was going on. She explained that the children lived on and around the train platform. They worked, they slept, they begged, they played on the train platform, but they did not go to school. On the train platform, these children were not seen by the thousands of passengers running to catch a train, stepping around them, or looking the other way. But one teacher, Inderjit Khurana, did see them. She brought the school to the children. She was the founder of the Train Platform Schools of Ruchika Social Service Organization.

The teacher went on to explain that the school operated on about $400 a year, enough to support 40 children and 2 teachers. The school not only

taught the children but also fed and clothed them. Perhaps most importantly, it instilled in them a sense of self-worth. Throughout my travels in
South Asia, I had seen glimpses of local innovation—people in their own
backyards finding things that worked to improve the lives of people in
need. I had been intrigued by this creativity and resourcefulness, but to
this point I had only regarded it conceptually. On the Bhubaneswar train
platform, though, that concept became real.

I had had no coursework or exposure to international development.
As an undergraduate at Bryn Mawr College, I was a biology major. Still, I
was fascinated by the model of the train platform school, and I kept asking
myself two questions. Why were not there other platform schools at other
train stations across India? And quite simply, how can I help? This became
my Moment of Obligation.

After returning from India, I went on to Duke to get my masters in
public policy. I took courses in international development and economics. It was there that the idea of forming The Global Fund for Children
(GFC)—an organization that would make small investments to innovative community-based organizations working with the most marginalized
young people—came to life. Our very first grant in 1997 was to Ruchika,
the organization that runs the train platform schools. I came to see that
most of these remarkable community-based groups were undervalued and
undercapitalized, and that small amounts of capital for innovative grassroots organizations goes a long way.

GFC's model gained traction through the years, and, as it did so, I came
to realize more fully the plight of children throughout the world. The
stories attendant with every organization that GFC identified as potential
partners underscored the despair that visits the lives of too many children.

Since inception, GFC has invested nearly $40 million in more than
600 innovative community-based organizations in nearly 80 countries
touching the lives of over 10 million children. Each GFC partner has
supported the most vulnerable young people in their communities. They
work with children that other agencies and development efforts do not
see and cannot reach. In the mines, on the streets, in the most remote
and impoverished rural villages, living alone or scrambling for their very
survival, these children are consigned to the farthest edges of their societies until a community-based organization is able to find them and change
their lives.

It was at GFC that I recognized not only the immense breadth of these
children—they were hidden in almost every country—but also the genesis

of hope that their paths could be changed. I saw that this change could not come about by aid programs crafted by distant planners but through the efforts of leaders within the communities themselves—those who lived close to these children, who saw them, and who knew how to counter the forces that put them where they were.

GFC taught me that, in spite of the enormity of the numbers of vulnerable young people, there might be a way to change things. I realized that the best hope lay at the community level.

After 18 years of seeding, growing, and building GFC, it was time for me to take a sabbatical and reflect on what I had learned. Three important things happened between 2011 and 2013.

First, I became a Henry Crown Fellow at the Aspen Institute. I was part of a very small class, each accomplished in his or her career, and each committed to exploring the inflection point between "success" and "significance." Each class of Fellows comes together in a series of seminars to share insights, to learn from one another, and to stretch ourselves into a deeper engagement with the global community. At these seminars, we read excerpts from the works of Plato and Socrates, Martin Luther King, Jr.'s "Letter From a Birmingham Jail," Sophocles' "Antigone," and many other important texts.

At the first Crown seminar, I was called upon to read parts of a short story by Ursula Le Guin, "The Ones Who Walk Away from Omelas." I had not known this story, even though I knew of Ursula Le Guin's work. But when I read parts of the story aloud, I was horrified.

"Omelas" tells of an almost ideal society—peaceful, progressive, and with everyone having almost anything they could want. There was no need, no poverty, no contention. But, in one dark dungeon of this utopia, there was a six-year-old child, kept apart, kept alone, fed poor food once a day, mostly ignored, and when not ignored, verbally abused. Few spoke of this child, although most seemed to know of her. The prosperity and peace of Omelas was dependent upon keeping this child where she was. If she were to be released, brought into daylight and cared for, Omelas would cease to be a utopia.

Le Guin's story challenges our conscience. Her powerful allegory shows a society whose comforts are based on the silent despair of those whose existence is not acknowledged, and whose lives, even when seen, disturb our peace of mind but are ignored. She shows us a society that allows the neglect of its most vulnerable to perpetuate a way of life that is, in the end, false, and dearly bought.

Second, I was appointed as a Visiting Scholar at the Paul H. Nitze School for Advanced International Studies (SAIS) at Johns Hopkins University in Washington, DC. I was part of the International Development Faculty and it was a perfect place to reflect. I jumped at the opportunity to teach my first course on children and global poverty, the issues that impact marginalized young people, and the public policies and social factors that lead to marginalization. I was stunned that one of the world's premier international development schools did not have such a course, and even more stunned when I learned that SAIS was not unique.

As I was putting the course together, I was surprised to find that there was no single authoritative book on children's issues globally. There were solid, important studies of individual issues, profiles of certain demographics, explorations of the impact of poverty and underdevelopment, and some regional studies, but there was nothing that tied it all together or treated children as a distinctive, singular field of study. It seemed to me that children were an afterthought of global development, or, if not an afterthought, then a perpetual subset of something broader, like malnourishment or HIV/AIDS or extreme poverty.

As a result, I cobbled together what I thought to be an effective reading list, incorporating articles, news reports, monographs on certain areas of children's development, case studies, and other pieces that might shine light on the compendium of influences that make children invisible. I assigned the Le Guin story on the first day of class (and also on the last day), to the puzzlement of many of my students who did not expect to be reading literature in an international development course. But I could not assign a single book that covered the challenging topic of marginalized children. It simply did not exist.

And so I resolved to do what I could to correct this. The motivations for *Invisible Children* stem from my professional experience, exposure to the quiet heroes who devote their lives to changing the landscapes of marginalized children, and to a real desire to translate my past success into lasting significance.

But really there was more to it than that. In early 2014, I became a mother. When I looked into her eyes for the first time after giving birth, I realized how incredibly fortunate she was. My daughter tells me everyday what a child needs to have, and she shows me the potential that lies within each son and daughter. She does not know, nor has she seen, hunger, alienation, dispossession, or want.

But her mother has, and it is in recognition of those children who live very different lives, lives that we cannot or do not choose to see, that this book has been born. We owe it to them to see them. We owe it to ourselves as well.

Washington, D.C.   Maya Ajmera

CONTENTS

LIST OF TABLES

PART I

The Darkness of Obscurity

CHAPTER 1

The Sounds of Silence

One day in 2003, I was caught in typical congested Mumbai traffic, swarming with cars, pedicabs, scooters, and pedestrians, all ignoring whatever few laws governed the city's movement. It was a very hot day in Mumbai—humid, bright, and sunny. I was on Peddar Road, which is to Mumbai what Park Avenue is to New York: high-rise buildings for some of Mumbai's wealthiest citizens, and streams and streams of cars. My cab driver had stopped at one of the few traffic lights and turned off his engine to wait until the light turned green a mile ahead.

Suddenly, hearing a gentle tapping on my car window, I looked up from reading my newspaper. I saw a young boy looking at me with big brown eyes and a huge smile. Wearing round wired glasses and no shirt, I thought he was impersonating Gandhi. I rolled down my window. With a toothy grin, he pulled out *Harry Potter and the Philosopher's Stone* wrapped in cloudy cellophane.

"Harry Potter, very good book." His finger was pointing to the book with a huge smile on his face. I said, "Harry Potter?" and he kept on, "Harry Potter, very good book."

I was curious about him. After just coming back from visiting a grassroots organization working with children on the streets, I had to ask him, "*Aapko padhna likhna aata hai?*" (Do you know how to read and write?). He looked at me in hurried annoyance with his hands flailing, "*Padhna nahi aata hai, likhna nahi aata hai.*" (I don't know how to read or write.)

I looked at him and I smiled, "*Mann hai?*" (Do you have a desire?)

© The Editor(s) (if applicable) and The Author(s) 2016
M. Ajmera, G.A. Fields, *Invisible Children*,
DOI 10.1057/978-1-137-57838-9_1

And all of a sudden that smile went to a distant, wistful sadness. His eyes darted down and into the car, and then he looked at me. He made eye contact and he said, "*Mann hai, lekin mein kya karu.*" (I have a desire but what can I do.)

"*Aap kahan se ho?*" (Where are you from?), I asked.

"*Mein Bihar se hu.*" (I am from Bihar), he answered. That is why he understood my Hindi.

But then he grew impatient, sensing that he wasn't going to sell me a book. Cars were revving their engines as the light neared its change. He knew that the revving meant it was time to get off the street or he would be killed, and in a blink he disappeared.

He was visible one second, invisible the next. I did not even get a chance to learn his name.

But part of him stays with me still, as well as the realization that here was one of the most popular children's books of the twentieth century, and this boy could not read it. I thought this was a cruel joke. He was invisible to everybody on that street. In a part of the city where some of the wealthiest people live and businesses thrived, a young boy hawked pirated books that he himself could not read for the sake of a few pennies. He had abandoned his education, or perhaps had never even begun it. His world was a closed, narrow place where the only item on his daily agenda was surviving well enough to do it all again tomorrow.

We cannot discern what we do not see.

Hidden in shrouds of despair, hopelessness, and loss are the lives of hundreds of millions of children and young people. They occupy unseen corners in nearly every part of the world, and no society, no country, is exempt from their impact. For them, there is neither safety net nor safe haven. Their lives do not revolve around school, home, family, or play, as should the life of every child as defined by the United Nations Convention on the Rights of the Child. Their lives carry little wonder and are short on hope. But even though we do not see them, they are all around us.

They are invisible not because they are so few, but because their numbers are so overwhelming that we no longer notice. These are children who are outside the normal reach of social services launched from within their country or through the proliferation of foreign assistance programs targeting the people in poverty. No one finds them, and they live their lives outside any safety net.

They are the children trafficked for harsh labor or sexual purposes; those scavenging in dumps or living on the streets; those discarded, institutionalized, or abused because of physical or mental disabilities; and those suffering from cultural, ethnic, or gender discrimination. They are the children who die from preventable or treatable diseases and those who are conscripted or coerced to fight another person's war. They are the refugees and migrants who paid for their passage with their childhoods. They are the young men and women with no access to education, jobs, or stability, facing shiftless futures. They have become an accepted part of our global society, the white noise in the background of our constant quest for social and economic development.

But every day, if we choose to look, we can find glimpses in major media stories about dispossessed, brutalized, or forgotten children. We see stories in *The New York Times* about the harsh conditions children face in all parts of the world. Sometimes they pop up as feature stories in the Sunday magazine. We watch the BBC profile suffering in Africa and Asia, always with a personal story and usually with a name of someone too young to be heard and too far outside the reaches of compassion to be helped.

We can read the metro sections of every major newspaper, from the *Washington Post* to the *Chicago Tribune* to the *Los Angeles Times*, and see stories depicting the trauma visited upon young lives. Mainstream television news from CNN to PBS sends forth images of the catastrophes, the disasters, and the day-to-day anguish of marginalized children. When we turn on the radio, we hear stories of trauma and despair on NPR and Public Radio International, and when we scan online blogs such as *The Huffington Post*, we read stories that have become all too common.

And it is not just the journalists who bring forth the stories of the marginalized young. Local voices complement these journalists, and we see the perspectives of those who live close to the traumas. Khaled Hosseini, the award-winning author of *The Kite Runner* and *A Thousand Splendid Suns*, relates the anguish of child refugees from Syria, whom he terms "Syria's Lost Generation," in an April 2014 *The New York Times* opinion piece,[1] and Izidor Ruckel, who grew up in a squalid Romanian orphanage, now inspects the effects of such places on abandoned children in documentary films and guest editorials.[2] In an age of ready communication, witnesses to the despair of children and young people are everywhere.

We pick up periodicals and find advertisements for groups dealing with the hungry, the lost, the orphaned, and abandoned; their suffering eyes so sensational that the heartache behind it becomes a selling point rather than a rallying cry. And when we go to the websites of assistance and development organizations, we find the stories there as well, alive and real, but overwhelmingly present and emotionally numbing. We can easily become immune to it all and choose not to see the children and young people left behind by a fast-paced global society.

But simply because we choose not to see them does not mean that they do not exist.

I have seen these children, and 18 years at The Global Fund for Children has given me more stories than are comfortable to recall. But my stories only go so far. They are anecdotes, and only a sliver compared to the thousands of voices telling hundreds of thousands of stories from across the globe.

Variations of the Harry Potter book seller's story exist millions of times over if we choose to see them. Today more than half a billion children and young people around the world live in extreme poverty. These numbers will grow as economies and social systems continue to fall short of the capacity to address their needs. We ignore them at considerable social and economic peril, and, in so doing, risk violating the basic tenets of human security.

The United Nations Convention on the Rights of the Child eloquently speaks to the inherent responsibility of all societies to provide their children protection, safety, education, opportunities, free expression, and access to healthful living. The words of the Convention speak to an ideal that collectively we have not come close to approaching. Our failures have faces, and, as do all children, they have dreams. What they do not have, at least in sufficient measure, is a voice to call the rest of us to action. They remain in the shadows of our consciousness, in places we know to exist but choose not to visit. They are invisible.

Each of these young people has a name, each of them has a face, and each has a story. From these stories, we can identify the forces that rob children of their future while compromising their present. If we choose to look, we see lessons in these stories, and we can begin to discern the contours of who they are, and how they live.

In the *Financial Times*, Orla Ryan gives us the story of Joseph. Joseph grew up in a village in Ghana, near the central coastal city of Winneba. When Joseph was quite young, his father left his mother, leaving her to clothe, feed, and educate four children on her own, a common story when responsibilities and obligations overwhelm a father's strength to meet them. At the age of ten, Joseph abandoned his schooling, committed to helping his mother provide for the struggling family. His mother suggested that

Joseph go to work on Lake Volta, a vast expanse in eastern Ghana where young boys could get jobs fishing the lake. She had a contact, "Uncle Bob," who could arrange everything. If Joseph worked at Lake Volta for four years, the family would receive a lump sum along with earnings that would be given directly to his mother. Reluctantly, Joseph headed east.

His days there began before the sun rose and were spent paddling boats and hauling nets until late afternoon. There was no school but there were plenty of beatings, often with canoe paddles aimed at his head. Joseph accumulated his scars, both physical and emotional, living in virtual slavery for three years. In time, word of the abuse filtered back to his home village, and his mother traveled to Lake Volta to reclaim him.

Once home, Joseph resumed his schooling and sought to put away the memories of the lake. But the family was no better off than they had been three years earlier, and his mother's struggles continued.

Joseph's happiness at being home and safe proved to be short-lived. A few months after his mother had rescued him, she sold him again; this time for approximately $50. And while his new master was somewhat less abusive, he again was forced to work long, dangerous hours for no pay; his childhood nothing more than a commodity for sale.[3]

In *The New York Times*, Nicholas Kristof introduces us to an 11-year-old Kenyan girl named Flevian. She had faced years of sexual abuse by her grandfather who told her that he would cut her throat if she ever told anyone of his assaults. When she was eight, the grandfather was caught committing abuse, but the family did not quite know what to do about it. They treated Flevian with herbs and did nothing more.

Flevian suffered great physical harm from the assaults. After a particularly brutal turn with her grandfather, onlookers rushed to help her. She was too weak to walk, so they carried her to the police station. When she told the police that it was her grandfather who had done this, neighbors came forth and verified that this was likely so, indicating that they had known about the abuse for several years.[4]

PBS shows us an 11-year-old Afghan boy named Shafiq,[5] who is a *bacha bazi*, or "boy for pleasure." Shafiq is exploited as a sexual partner and often dressed up as a woman to dance at gatherings of wealthy Afghans. *Bacha bazis* are taken as young as eight or nine and kept until they reach puberty. Many of the men who abuse the boys are married, but because of traditional gender segregation, they take their boys and not their wives to social gatherings. The *bachas*, almost all of whom come from families in poverty, are viewed as property.

Shafiq was trained for several months by his handlers to sing and dance in the right way. All the while he lived in a separate house for the *bacha bazis* and his family received a small amount of money. He had little notion of what else would be entailed beyond the singing and dancing. In due course he ran away, but was returned to his handler. His family had no idea of what their son was doing to earn the bits of money they received. Shafiq was more fortunate than the vast majority of *bachas*. He eventually was rescued from the lifestyle by a man who used to manage *bachas* but had turned against the practice. Shafiq and his family were resettled elsewhere in the country, and the young boy began the long road back to a normal childhood by beginning school.[6]

Hamid was nine when he left his village in central Egypt to work in the limestone quarries near Al-Minya. There in a desert, where the afternoon sun regularly brought the temperature to 120°F, he would feed blocks of limestone into a crusher that ground them to powder to then be bagged for sale. The only shelter was a small shed, and the only drinking water was whatever they brought with them from the village. The pay for this work was not bad by regional standards, so families willingly sent their boys to the quarries. Hamid earned more than his village's schoolteacher, and he took most of his earnings back home with him on his days off to give to his mother. The family lived well and saw no issue with Hamid's work and the fact that he was not, and would never again be, in school.

But the window for these high earnings was small. Almost none of the boys survived past the age of 16, felled by lung disease from breathing the limestone dust, heat exhaustion, severe dehydration, or accidents involving the old crushers that worked as well on delicate limbs as they did on limestone rock. Others developed severe substance abuse problems, relying on stimulants to get them through the hot and dangerous days.

Hamid was one of the fortunate few. When he was 15, after six months in the desert quarry, an organization from nearby Al-Minya reached out to him and his fellow workers, offering them a shelter in town, basic literacy education, and training to become shoemakers. Only Hamid accepted, and, in so doing, earned the wrath of his family. The same week he came to the shelter, two of his friends who had elected to stay in the quarry were killed when the truck carrying bags of the limestone dust they had produced flipped on a curve and rolled on top of them.[7]

In rural India, a ten-year-old girl Meena and her 11-year-old brother have been orphaned for three years since their mother died of starvation. Their older brother left the village to work in a brick kiln, leaving Meena to take responsibility for her remaining sibling. She cooks, cleans, and tries to survive. In the three years since her mother's death, she has never been visited by any regional or national government agency. Meena gets by on her own.

That she has been able to do so for so long is remarkable, for both she and her brother are targets. Contractors look to impoverished rural villages to hire young boys for hard or hazardous labor, and young girls are sold to brothels or domestic worker agencies in the cities, from which there is rarely an escape. So far, Meena and her brother have avoided the notice of the traffickers, but such luck can only last so long. Said an official with a national child rights group, "Sometime in the next couple of years, while she's still a child, a (trafficker) may masquerade as an eligible groom and trick Meena's aunt into letting him marry Meena, and once she does he'll take her to Delhi and sell her off to a brothel or to an employment agency that will hire her out as a domestic worker, and she'll be treated like a slave.... He'll just whisk her away one night, and no one will notice, and by the time they do, she'll have vanished forever."[8]

Htun Htun Oo, 12 years old, was waiting for a train in Myanmar[9] to visit his uncle when a soldier stopped him to ask for his identification card. Because he could not produce one, the soldier took him off the railway platform and conscripted him into the Burmese army to fight the rebellious Karenni in the northwest provinces. He was paid $6 a month, for which he performed demanding manual tasks. "The Burmese officers would continually punish us and order us to do additional duties—we were no better than slaves."[10] Rarely given sufficient food to maintain his energy, Htun was regularly beaten when fatigue made him slow. Other "recruits" were sexually abused by their commanding officers. Htun ran away, roaming the jungles until he was given shelter and eventually repatriated by the same Karenni people he had previously been charged to kill.[11]

Srey was a seven-year-old girl selling umbrellas in a market in Cambodia to earn for her family. As the oldest of four children, with a sick mother, she felt obligated to do as much as she could. A man approached her in the market and told her he could find her a very well-paying job in Thailand. Srey's mother paid the man a considerable sum to take her daughter across the border, but once there, Srey was taken to the home of a wealthy family for whom she was forced to work as a maid for the next seven years. She was not paid, but she had few options. She was afraid of the family, the trafficker who had brought her there, and the Thai immigration authorities because her presence in the country was illegal. The family eventually sold her to another family, who put her in a brothel. She escaped with the help of another woman at the brothel, who in turn forced Srey to work as a maid on a houseboat, again without pay. When Srey finally escaped the boat, Thai authorities apprehended her.[12]

Jose Luis, 15, dropped out of school in the low-income Cerro Rico district of Potosí, Bolivia, when he was 11 to work in the tin, zinc, and silver mines that pocket the mountains there. He walks an hour to work in the morning, and then descends into the mine to work in spaces no more than four feet tall. He has seen dead bodies carried up the tunnels, and he lives with the constant fear of dying down there himself. So far, he has avoided the most dangerous jobs such as drilling, which kicks up dust that fills the lungs, often leading to infection and death. He might earn as much as $20 on a good day, but on many days he finds no minerals, and so is not paid. Luis does not consider himself exploited or manipulated: he does this by choice, the only avenue he can see out of a poverty that defines his limited options.[13]

In Haiti, which has received more than $6 billion in foreign assistance since the 2010 earthquake devastated the country,[14] 13-year-old Darline remains homeless. She and her family live in a makeshift shelter composed of old USAID grain sacks. Food is scarce, and Darline sometimes goes days between meals. She has never seen either a doctor or a dentist, and suffers from malnourishment. When her father died two years earlier, she had to drop out of school. Darline lives day-to-day and threats are all around. She is afraid to go to the outhouses behind her shack because two of her sisters were raped on their way to use them. "When I go to the toilet, men are scarier than the rats."[15]

Wilmer Villalobos Ortiz was orphaned in Honduras when he was eight. An aunt took him in, forced him to quit school, and put him to work in her pool hall and bar, where he would spend 17 hours a day doing menial chores. Members of a violent street gang frequented the bar and saw Wilmer as a prime recruit.

When he was 14, they asked him to join, and threatened to kill him if he refused. When he was 15, Wilmer escaped to the United States. To get through Mexico, he rode the tops of freight trains for more than a month. At one point, he saw narco-traffickers stop his train, club a woman unconscious, and snatch her young son from her arms. He witnessed a boy his own age stumble as he tried to hop a moving train and heard his screams as the boy's legs were cut off by the wheels. When he finally reached the United States, Wilmer was apprehended by the Border Patrol in Texas and faced deportation charges alone without access to legal representation.[16]

It would be a mistake to consider these stories as the province only of low-income countries[17] or societies beset by conflict or civil violence. No country is immune from circumstances that compromise the well-being of children and young people. Even the richest and most powerful players on the world stage are affected. Instances of violence or marginalization have in fact become so commonplace that they are often overlooked altogether, or dismissed as outliers. But this does a disservice to the children affected. We need to see these examples for what they are.

Orion Hamilton was placed into foster care shortly after her birth in Austin, Texas, United States, in late 2012. She was born with methamphetamine in her system, the result of her mother's drug use. After two months, Orion's care was transferred from a temporary foster home to the biological father's stepsister, who readily agreed to the arrangement, especially in light of the financial assistance provided by the state for serving as a foster parent.

The stepsister had a boyfriend who had been arrested four times previously, including twice for family violence, and was shouldering an accusation for child neglect when his own son was born with drugs in his system. The private agency contracted by the city to monitor Orion's foster placement knew of the boyfriend's presence but neglected to do a criminal background check or incorporate his presence into their monitoring of Orion's care. One day, when the stepsister was at work, the boyfriend crushed Orion's skull between his knee and a hard floor. A postmortem examination indicated that Orion had suffered other injuries consistent with earlier abuse. The young girl died before her first birthday.[18]

Dasani lives in a city-run shelter for homeless families in Brooklyn, New York, United States, in a 520-square-foot room with her parents and her seven brothers and sisters. The walls are moldy and they share the small space with roaches and mice. Incidents of sexual assault are common; violence is a daily occurrence. Through it all Dasani attends school, tends to her younger siblings, and dreams her dreams, such as designing a video game called "Live or Die," which focuses on an 11-year-old girl trying to stay alive in the shelter. Her shelter has no certificate of occupancy, so it is chronically overcrowded. Smoke detectors and fire alarms are in disrepair. Dasani is one of approximately 520 children living in the shelter.

Both her parents were the children of drug abusers, and each has had a run-in with the law for similar offenses. Dasani's mother sometimes panhandles on the streets to get enough money to buy food. Their small room at the shelter has been robbed, and their few precious belongings, including the ashes of Dasani's grandmother, are gone. Her life is unremarkable within the context of the 22,000 homeless children that live in New York City. But the constant, crushing problems of Dasani's homelessness resonate enough to warrant a five-part feature in *The New York Times*, written by Andrea Elliott, who characterized Dasani as an "Invisible Child."[19]

This book will bring the plight of these invisible children forward. But it will not seek to evoke pathos or sorrow other than to present the simple realities that marginalize these millions of young people. Instead, this book will explore why these children are where they are, what has failed them, and how we can collectively do better.

By identifying the ways in which the lives of children who have been beyond the reach of any assistance programs can be changed at the community level, the disturbing stories presented in these pages can eventually be retold with happier endings.

This is not an academic study in the traditional sense. While the points put forward are well researched, and some of the finest current minds in the field of international development have lent their thoughts, we have not sought to create another analytical study. What we have sought instead is to focus on the work being done on the ground, to put forward the views of practitioners rather than academics, and, in so doing, to begin to shine a light on the impact of small, localized efforts that taken together can help rewrite the futures of children that traditional approaches have yet to reach. In the process, we seek to give at least a small voice to those whose wisdom and strength are too often overlooked and whose stories are too often not heard.

NOTES

1. http://www.nytimes.com/2014/04/13/opinion/sunday/syrias-lost-generation.html
2. http://www.washingtonpost.com/sf/style/2014/01/30/a-lost-boy-finds-his-calling/
3. http://www.ft.com/cms/s/2/bb065486-37e8-11e2-b8d3-00144feabdc0.html#axzz2glA8AAYU
4. http://www.nytimes.com/2014/01/16/opinion/kristof-how-brave-girls-helped-crack-a-taboo.html?_r=0
5. Name changed by PBS to protect the child's identity.
6. PBS Frontline documentary transcript http://www.pbs.org/wgbh/pages/frontline/dancingboys/etc/script.html *Originally used: Washington Post,* 2012. http://www.washingtonpost.com/world/asia_pacific/afganistans-

dancing-boys-are-invisible-victims/2012/04/04/gIQAyreSwS_story_1.html

7. Trip report, Gregory Fields, Global Fund for Children, June 2005.
8. Sonia Faleiro, "Survival Without Adult Supervision, Stark Reality in Rural Bihar,"http://india.blogs.nytimes.com/2012/06/25/survival-without-adult-supervision-stark-reality-in-rural-bihar/
9. Until 1989, Myanmar was known as Burma. The Bamar ethnic group, which gave rise to the original name of Burma, is the largest of more than 135 ethnic groups in the country. Despite its name change, citizens in Myanmar are still commonly referred to as Burmese.
10. http://www2.irrawaddy.org/article.php?art_id=16620
11. http://www2.irrawaddy.org/article.php?art_id=16620
12. Hoa Duong Piyaka, Global Fund for Children, "Rehabilitation and Reintegration of Trafficked Cambodian Children," *On the Road Blog*, March 19, 2009, https://www.globalfundforchildren.org/rehabilitation-and-reintegration-of-trafficked-cambodian-children/
13. http://www.foreignpolicy.com/articles/2010/11/18/children_of_the_mines; http://www.vice.com/read/unaccompanied-miners-0000147-v20n11
14. Vijaya Ramachandran and Julie Walz, "Haiti: Where Has All the Money Gone?" CGD Policy Paper 004, Center for Global Development, May 2012, p. 1, http://www.cgdev.org/publication/haiti-where-has-all-money-gone
15. Nicholas Kristof, "Can Foreign Aid Help This Girl?" http://www.nytimes.com/2013/12/08/opinion/sunday/kristof-can-foreign-aid-help-this-girl.html?pagewanted=all
16. http://www.nytimes.com/2013/04/11/opinion/give-lawyers-to-immi-grant-children.html
17. The terms *low-income countries* and *high-income countries* are used to classify countries by the average income (GDP per capita) of their citizens. *Low-income countries* tend to have a lower standard of living and less-industrialized economies compared to high-income countries. These terms are used in an attempt to move away from more Western-centric classifications such as *undeveloped/developed* and *Global North/Global South*. It is important to note that these classifications are based on average income, and disparity between high- and low-income individuals exists in every country.
18. Andrea Ball, "State Punishes Austin-based Foster Care Agency in death of Orion Hamilton," Austin American-Statesman, December 19, 2013, http://www.statesman.com/news/news/state-punishes-austin-based-foster-care-agency-in-/ncQM8/
19. http://www.nytimes.com/projects/2013/invisible-child/#/?chapt=1

CHAPTER 2

Hiding in Plain Sight—Who Are These Children?

Invisibility is a lack of hope, a lack of opportunity, and the inability to access the basic elements that define a safe, productive life, including education, health care, housing, food, clean water, sanitation, and security. No child is born invisible. At the very least, a child issues forth from his or her mother in a spasm of consciousness and recognition that binds them to each other in that moment, that speaks of promise and life and hope.

But a child can become invisible any moment afterward. Within the first few weeks, babies can be lost to malnutrition because their mothers cannot feed them, to disease because medicines are unavailable, or to abandonment when there might be just too many mouths for parents to feed. They may be denied their very identity if their birth is not properly and officially registered. A child can be made invisible five or six years on, when he or she becomes the victim of emotional or physical abuse, or leaves education behind to work a job for long or dangerous hours to earn for the family. He or she might be trafficked or sold for sex or labor, entering an underground existence without identity or voice. By the time a child reaches the age of 12 or 13, she might run away from the poverty she has known since birth only to find new forms of desperation living on the streets. Or anger and despair may turn to violence, and he might join a street gang or be seduced into becoming a soldier. Invisible children survive in dark corners, unable to benefit from the extensive aid and development appropriations of governments, multilateral organizations, and the nongovernmental sector.

© The Editor(s) (if applicable) and The Author(s) 2016   15
M. Ajmera, G.A. Fields, *Invisible Children*,
DOI 10.1057/978-1-137-57838-9_2

No child is born invisible. Rather, they are made so through desperation and want, which can be prevented; through neglect, which can be ameliorated; and through brutality, which can be soothed. They become invisible because we have yet to find the collective solutions, to author the collective vision, which incorporates all children as contributors to a diverse, rich social fabric.

A child may become invisible in a number of ways and to various degrees. A spectrum of invisibility ranges from the state, which can fail to recognize a child legally; to a community, which might ostracize a child, fail to provide an education, or otherwise place the child on its edges; and to a family, whose economic or social circumstances might render a child unseen, uncared for, or, at worst, a commodity for sale. A child might be invisible to any of these institutions, or to all of them. We do a disservice to claim that one form is worse than another: any child, or group of children, whose life is unseen merits our concern. Joseph and Meena and Hamid and Dasani, along with every child whose story captures our attention and pricks our conscience, are real, sensate, complex individuals.

They are also not alone. Each personal story stands with hundreds of thousands of others to create an avalanche that can overwhelm our capacity to absorb it all. We can become exhausted by the immensity of the suffering, by the enormity of the issues. But if we look closely enough at the numbers behind the stories, we cannot deny the obvious—that marginalized children constitute an immense drain on our societal resources, that their abandonment carries huge opportunity costs, and that the futures of entire generations in all corners of the world, including those regions that can least afford it, are being wasted.

There are more than seven billion people in the world,[1] and more than 2.2 billion of them are children.[2] The United Nations (UN) through its Convention on the Rights of the Child defines children as anyone "below the age of 18, unless the laws of a particular country set the legal age for adulthood younger."[3] More than one billion of those children live in poverty, and half of these live in extreme deprivation.[4] They constitute, then, half a billion young people under the age of 18 whose very lives have been truncated and put in daily peril. Each day, for example, 18,000 children die from preventable diseases alone.[5]

Consider the impact of the global numbers: *50 million* infants born each year without proper registration, and hence, identity; more than *215 million* children engaged in hazardous labor; nearly *1.2 million* children trafficked each year in the sex trades; *38 million* displaced from their homes either by war or the lure of a better life across some romanticized border; more than *100 million* children living on the streets; and *27 million* each year, more than *400 million* on this planet right now, born into conditions of such extreme poverty that their lives are not inspired by hope or driven by dreams but governed by the most basic demands of day-to-day survival. In overwhelming numbers, we have marginalized massive parts of the generations that constitute our future and define the values of the present.

Let's view it graphically, including only those demographics with clearly delineated numbers.[6]

Table 2.1

And these numbers need not be compared to anything else to assess their impact. We do not need to calculate how many 9/11s, wherein 3000 people lost their lives and sparked a coordinated global response, are contained in these numbers, or how many tsunamis such as the one that devastated South Asia in 2004 it would take to reach these figures. These

Table 2.1 The demographics of invisibility

Demographic	Global snapshot
Unregistered children under five[72]	230,000,000
Under-five deaths annually[73]	6,600,000
Stunted or chronically malnourished children[74]	162,000,000
Children living in extreme poverty[75]	400,000,000
Street-connected children[76]	100,000,000
Children in hazardous or exploitative labor[77]	215,000,000
Children trafficked annually[88]	1,200,000
International migrant children[79]	33,000,000
Refugee and IDP children[80]	38,000,000
Children orphaned or living in orphanages[81]	18,000,000
Children living with HIV/AIDS[82]	3,400,000
Children involved in armed conflict[83]	300,000
Incarcerated children[84]	1,000,000
Children who have experienced rape or sexual violence[85]	223,000,000
Girls at risk for FGM[86]	30,000,000
Girls giving birth annually[87]	16,000,000
Children exposed to domestic violence[88]	275,000,000
Children living with a physical or mental disability[89]	150,000,000
Primary school-aged children not in school[90]	57,000,000
Illiterate youth[91]	127,000,000
Unemployed youth[92]	75,000,000

events became touchstones in the public consciousness, benchmarks by which to measure loss and sadness.

Accordingly, numbers cited to quantify the extent of any issue are necessarily inaccurate to some degree. There is, quite simply, too much overlap. Street-connected children[7] who are orphans and working in hazardous labor situations can be triple-counted in these statistics. A young girl who has no access to education and is subsequently sold by her parents to a trafficker can be double-counted. Migrant children can appear on the statistical records of more than one place. This is not, in any way, to minimize the impact of these numbers, for without question and in any evaluation, the numbers are vast. But we do well to understand that, as vast as they are, they may not be pure. The silos into which we tend to place these children and young people may satisfy our need for organization, but they hinder our understanding of the interrelated complexities of the issues impacting their lives. We must view their situations not in terms of the numbers they represent but as emanations of the immense personal, human, and societal costs they exact.

The development community has devoted considerable effort to quantifying the conditions of poverty, underdevelopment, and marginalization. The figures cited here are readily available and constantly updated. UNICEF's annual *The State of the World's Children* report carries immense value in understanding the range and depth of issues attending vulnerable children, and in fact has become the control "go-to" resource for those working in development and for those curious about the progression of the efforts to reach these children. While providing a wealth of statistics that are both global and country-specific, these annual reports also examine in some depth a key issue in children's development.

But statistics sometimes can be so overwhelming that they numb rather than enlighten. We can quibble about these statistics or how we cut the numbers. We can emphasize one group over another or think that the plight of trafficked children is somehow more pressing than those who are orphaned. We can point to Africa as more serious than Asia or South America. We can delude ourselves into thinking that these problems are the province of the developing world and do not touch Western Europe, Canada, or the United States.

But none of that matters. The plight of the world's children stands apart from any such comparisons. These numbers speak on their own, without embellishment, telling us without equivocation that something must be done to put a halt to the flood of misery, lost opportunity, and the despair in which millions of the children and youth we are collectively charged to protect find themselves.

Who, then, are these invisible children?

We can start by looking at some of the basic factors that hasten the path to invisibility. Most of these paths begin early in a child's life, and subsequently feed the negative social and behavioral influence that define their futures.

Unregistered Births

Some children are blessings only in the eyes of their mothers.

Each year across the world the births of about 50 million children are not registered, which translates to roughly one in every three live births worldwide.[8] This means that in the eyes of the government of their homelands, these children do not exist. Unregistered children lack a birth certificate, proof of their name, proof of their parents, and place of origin.[9] They become phantoms in the eyes of the state.

In 2012, only 60% of all babies born were properly and officially registered by their home countries. In some countries, the figures are stunning: only 3% of all births in Somalia are registered, 4% in Liberia, and 10% in Bangladesh. Eastern and Southern Africa had the highest regional incidence of unregistered births at 65%, closely followed by South Asia at 64%.[10]

Registrations are lowest in rural communities and in regions with low literacy rates. Many low-income countries lack the administrative structure to process birth registrations. In Bangladesh, registrations are the province of local governments, most of whom have few resources to do the job or to be present in remote communities. Countries with strong tribal traditions, such as Kenya, delegate the responsibility for registration to local chiefs. As a result, registrations at best are uneven, and at worst nonexistent.[11]

Societal pressures and customs can accentuate these rates. In Vietnam, for example, single mothers are reluctant to register the births of illegitimate children, while in many countries, such as Nicaragua and Nepal, the father's signature is required for proper registration. Children born to cross-border immigrants are often unreported as their parents seek to remain in the shadows of unwelcoming host countries.[12] In Indonesia, parents must present a marriage certificate to register their child.[13]

Even children who are registered face obstacles if they have no proof of that registration. Across the world more than one in seven registered children lack such proof. In some countries, fees for birth certificates place them outside the reach of impoverished families. Other countries, especially in sub-Saharan Africa, do not regularly issue certificates, leaving officially registered children absolutely no evidence of their standing.[14]

Without proper registration, options and opportunities, often already limited, evaporate. In many countries including Cambodia, Sudan, and Yemen, a birth certificate is necessary for a child to attend school. In Turkey, a certificate is needed to go beyond primary school, and in Sri Lanka, it is a basic requirement to take graduation examinations. In Mexico, a birth certificate is necessary for anyone to receive nonemergency medical treatment.[15] Unregistered children may not access health care in Kyrgyzstan, and in Palestine access to health and welfare services is limited to those possessing documentation. In China, children without proper registration are not able to attend school or draw upon the state's health and social service programs.[16]

Article 7 of the UN Convention on the Rights of the Child declares that all children "shall be registered immediately after birth and shall have the right from birth to a name, [and] the right to acquire a nationality."[17] Those children born without access to birth registration begin the descent into invisibility from the moment they draw their first breath.

The First Five Years

Despite recent decreases in infant mortality rates, the first 28 days of life remain the most perilous for the world's most marginalized babies. In 2012, nearly 44% of all under-five deaths occurred during the neonatal period—a staggering 2.9 million deaths a year, with about one million of those occurring in the first day of life.[18] Under-five mortality continues to claim the lives of children in poverty at alarming rates. In 2012, 6.6 million children died before their fifth birthday, a rate of 12 deaths per minute, or 18,000 each day.[19] Since 1990, 216 million children have not reached the age of five—more than the current total population of Brazil, the world's fifth most populous country.[20] Death comes through various doorways, but preventable, curable diseases claimed roughly one-third of these children. Pneumonia killed more than 3000 under-fives each day in 2012, constituting 17% of all deaths and making pneumonia the single largest killer. Diarrhea and malaria followed close behind.[21]

Major inroads have been made against long-standing pandemics such as polio and tuberculosis, thanks in large measure to both the financial investments and the multilateral coordination of the Bill & Melinda Gates Foundation. The End Polio Now campaign of Rotary International has been a vital partner in this effort as well, mobilizing awareness and support across the globe. And in spring 2014, the World Health Organization officially declared India, which as late as 2009 reported nearly half of the world's total polio cases, to be polio-free.[22]

But despite these successes, polio is reemerging as a global health concern. Pakistan and Syria have confirmed cases, and the disease has crossed into their neighboring countries of Afghanistan and Iraq. Total global infections more than doubled between 2013 and 2014.[23] As of August 2015, Africa has gone a full year without any recorded cases. This is a significant milestone thanks to the intensity of vaccination campaigns over the last several years, but experts remain cautious calling the situation 'fragile' due to the risk of unrecorded cases persisting in remote areas. The continent will need another two full years without incident before it could be declared *Polio-free*.[24] Tuberculosis persists as a major problem in many countries, ranging from Vietnam, Myanmar, Kenya, Mozambique, and the Democratic Republic of Congo (DRC), to stronger economies like India, China, South Africa, and Russia.[25]

Other less visible diseases, which have yet to be the focus of global eradication efforts, also take their toll. Congenital syphilis, which is passed from mother to child, is responsible for an estimated 500,000 deaths annually. That is slightly more than the number that succumbs to malaria, making it the fifth leading cause of deaths for under-fives. The disease was responsible for approximately 200,000 stillborn births in 2008, with another 91,000 neonatal deaths and another 151,000 children who survive infancy but still risk deformities or death. Treatment for congenital syphilis is simple—penicillin does the trick, administered either to the mother during pregnancy or to the child any time after birth. But there is no way to reverse whatever damage was already done before treatment. And few cases are detected and treated in low-income countries because awareness does not exist, diagnosis is poor, and the symptoms themselves often look like those of other diseases. Congenital syphilis is not prominent on the global health agenda because it is hard to describe, classify, and count in the usual categories of public health, which obscures the high morbidity and mortality associated with the disease. Congenital syphilis is not a priority disease globally and gets relatively little attention, yet exacts a considerable cost on vulnerable young lives.[26]

Survival to the age of five is only the first hurdle. Malnourishment is pervasive, with vast impact. Nearly 870 million people worldwide are malnourished, and among them, more than 100 million children under five are considered underweight.[27] A diet lacking adequate vegetables, fruits, and proteins has lifelong consequences. Between 250,000 and 500,000 children are considered to be at risk of becoming blind each year from vitamin A deficiency, which could be easily remedied through access to leafy green vegetables.[28]

Stunting—the condition of low growth where a child's height falls far below standard measurements for his or her age—is estimated to affect as many as 28% of children under five in low- and middle-income countries—162 million children in 2012.[29] Stunted children often appear proportionately normal, but they are generally much smaller physically, and can suffer from both physical and mental development issues. Stunting starts before birth and is caused by poor maternal nutrition, poor feeding practices, poor food quality, as well as frequent infections which can slow growth. Stunted children have weakened immune systems, and so are much more likely to contract serious illnesses. They are five times more likely to die from diarrhea than normally developed children. And the effects of stunting on mental and physical development are irreversible.[30]

Wasting, related to stunting, is where a child's weight is far below standards for his or her height. In 2011, UNICEF identified 52 million children under five who were moderately or severely wasted. In South Asia, up to 16% of children fall into this category, more than 25 million of whom are in India.[31]

Both stunting and wasting are functions of acute or chronic malnutrition, which weakens immune systems and precludes normal development. The conditions replenish themselves: undernourished mothers are far more likely to give birth to stunted or wasted children, who, if they survive to maturity, perpetuate the cycle. These conditions are preventable through well-established interventions, including the improvement of women's nutrition, early and exclusive breast-feeding, improved food security, and micronutrient supplements.[32] A growing body of research in India has also demonstrated that adequate sanitation systems are essential to reducing exposure to bacteria and illness that keep even well-fed children malnourished because their compromised immune systems are working overtime.[33] But as effective as these steps might be, they have a narrow window. Once a child turns two, the impact of early malnutrition is most often irreversible.[34] This robs them of any chance of reaching their full intellectual, physical, and social potential.

GROWING UP IN EXTREME POVERTY

Poverty, regardless of its origins, exacts a huge toll on the young. Each year, more than 27 million babies are born into extreme poverty worldwide. No continent is spared. Extreme poverty exists in the savannahs of sub-Saharan Africa, in the crowded, sprawling slums of South Asia, in the *barrios* of Latin America, the hovels of the Caribbean, and the squalor of North American cities and towns. Poverty is not the sole province of either urban or rural populations; we can find children on the bare margins of survival in the North African deserts as well as the Cairo slums, in the Mississippi delta as well as the streets of Chicago. What children born to poverty share, regardless of their setting, is limited educational opportunities, reduced access to quality health care, higher rates of abuse, a greater risk of exposure to violence, and reduced physical, emotional, and mental development. Annually, we consign millions of children to these struggles.

The impact of extreme poverty on the lives of the children born into it is comprehensive, touching upon indices measuring educational access, health, sanitation, and physical development. Most of the under-five mortality figures cited earlier are derivative of the conditions of extreme poverty, and the correlation between poor economic indicators and poor under-five mortality indices is clear.

Dangers imposed by the conditions of extreme poverty take many forms. A lack of safe drinking water, open defecation, and poor hygiene are significant threats to child survival.[35] Even through the best efforts, immunizations fail to reach at least a fifth of all vulnerable children, who are inaccessible by any broad-based assistance program.[36] Cycles of poverty are difficult to break. Studies have shown irrefutably that children born to mothers without a basic education are at greater risk of dying before age five.[37]

Children in extreme poverty are vulnerable to many diseases that can be prevented or mitigated through well-established vaccinations and treatments. For example, rheumatic heart disease is caused by a common streptococcal virus, the same family that triggers strep throat, and can be treated with antibiotics. Failure to do so causes the heart to deteriorate, often resulting in heart failure. Children who cannot access these antibiotics pay a steep price: as many as 15 million are affected by the disease, which can require hospitalization and corrective surgery. More than 230,000 die annually. Up to 1% of all school children in Africa, Asia, the Eastern Mediterranean, and Latin America show signs of the disease.[38]

Intestinal parasites, such as roundworms, hookworms, and whipworms, are a fact of life for too many children, with profound consequences. Parasites are readily ingested from contaminated food or infected soil, and can undermine a child's nutritional status, affecting his or her cognitive processes; induce tissue reactions, such as granuloma; and provoke intestinal obstruction or rectal prolapse. These conditions reduce school attendance and can lead to death. And all of this could be prevented through improved sanitation, health education, and simple low-cost drug treatments.[39]

Quantifying the number of children caught in extreme poverty, defined as living below $1.25 per day, is difficult at best. Indices compiled by the World Bank indicate the percentage of people living in extreme poverty in the developing world has fallen by less than one-third over the past three decades, but most of that reduction has stemmed from gains made in the fast-growing economies of India and China. Factoring out those two countries, indices are almost identical to what they were 30 years ago. In fact, excluding those two countries, the absolute number of people living in extreme poverty in the developing world actually increased by 103 million during this period. Half of all children in low-income countries live in extreme poverty, and more than one-third of all people living in extreme poverty globally are under age 13—that is over 400 million children.[40]

Nor is the developing world the sole province of the conditions of extreme poverty. In the 35 richest countries, more than 30 million children are caught in the deepest levels of poverty.[41] Among these 35 countries, the United States has the second highest level of children living below the poverty line—23.1%—encompassing more than 16 million children and second only to Romania at 25.5%.[42]

One of the most insidious impacts of extreme poverty is the effect on a child's likelihood to go to school. Currently, there are an estimated 57 million primary school-aged children who are not in school. This number has dropped from higher estimates of 120 million ten years ago. While this improvement is welcome, it cannot obscure the problems that remain, especially among the most marginalized who constitute the overwhelming majority of this 57 million. In 2011, 137 million children began school worldwide. Of this total, at least 34 million are projected to drop out before finishing primary school. This translates to a dropout rate of roughly 25%, the same level as in the year 2000. Clearly, although progress has been made in introducing young people to schools, much is left to be done to keep them there.[43]

The rates reflecting lack of access to and attendance at secondary schools are significant. Only 60% of secondary school-aged children globally are currently enrolled, and this already low figure is buttressed by high rates in wealthy countries. In sub-Saharan Africa, less than one-third of all secondary school-aged children are attending any type of school, and this rate is worsening rather than improving.[44] In Eastern Europe, Roma children are only one-fifth as likely as others to transition from primary to secondary education.[45] In all, more than 71 million young people of lower secondary school age are not in school. Literacy rates in areas where secondary schooling opportunities are limited run low. Of the 127 million illiterate youth in the world, 90% live in South Asia or sub-Saharan Africa.[46]

Extreme poverty is itself a gateway to the many manifestations of abuse, neglect, and marginalization that make children invisible. A child in poverty may drop out of school to become a bonded laborer, or he or she might run from a family unable to provide nourishment and care, and so become a street-connected child. A rural young girl in poverty might be sent to the city by her parents to earn money, and so end up trafficked for sexual purposes. A child in poverty might seek to dull his or her despair by sniffing glue or learning to drink before learning to read. And uneducated, unemployed young people with nowhere to go and nothing to do might act out their despair in anger and violence. Poverty itself weaves together conditions of desperation that ensnare millions of children in all manner of ways.

Family Breakdown

It is no secret that children thrive on stability. Ideally, the core of stability for any child is his or her family; however that family might be defined or comprised. But social and economic conditions among low-income areas have broken down families, often leaving children and young people with a minimal support system through their struggles.

Several factors contribute to this disintegration of family units. Migration from impoverished rural areas to larger cities, with their lure of economic opportunity, has compelled many families to migrate. Some move intact, but others leave their children behind as one or both parents seek what the city might offer. In China, one in five children, or roughly 61 million, is growing up without at least one of their parents who have migrated in search of better work. Of these, 30 million have no parent living with them at all, and another two million are left completely alone without any adult supervision.[47]

For various reasons and causes, over 153 million children worldwide are labeled as orphans, having lost one or both parents.[48] Of that, 18 million have lost both parents.[49] Millions more have been abandoned.[50] But, of the eight million children now living in orphanages, as many as 90% by some estimates are not truly orphaned. Institutionalization occurs because their families lack the resources to care for them, one parent might be dead, the child has a disability, has suffered abuse, or is from an oppressed ethnic minority.[51]

Some studies have emerged in recent years indicating that children in institutionalized care as a whole suffer no more than orphaned or abandoned children in community-based care.[52] At best, this is damning with faint praise. Some countries, such as Colombia, place a high premium on their quality of care for orphaned or abandoned children. Institutions in these countries tend to raise the curve in generalized studies. But other countries have neither the resources nor the will to provide nurturing care for those without parents or stable home lives. It must be noted, too, that there can be a marked difference between government-run institutions, private institutions, and community-run institutions.[53]

The HIV/AIDS crisis has created millions of orphans. In many cases, children are being raised by grandmothers, older siblings, or friends in their communities in makeshift family structures that only approximate what they had before. Many of the families taking in children are impoverished themselves, and so extra responsibilities of care can become overwhelming burdens. Grandparents, who care for as many as 60% of AIDS orphans, depending on the region, are called upon to raise children again as they grow older and require support themselves. With their adult children lost to HIV/AIDS, their own support system for old age vanishes while they care for increasing numbers of grandchildren. As these aging caregivers themselves die off, the already flimsy social safety nets become more frayed. Family and community resources get stretched too thin to handle the millions of orphans needing places to live and grow. In an orphan crisis without historical precedent, regional poverty deepens under the combined factors of fewer earners, too few caregivers, and still more in need of support.[54]

In some cultures, fatherhood is marked by the number of children sired rather than the attention and affection directed to those children. Children growing up without a father are more likely to become substance abusers, to drop out of school, and to become involved in criminal activity.[55] Fathers leave, sometimes to find work, sometimes simply to escape from the weight of responsibilities they cannot readily meet, and when they do, the children left behind lose an important rudder.

Antisocial behaviors contribute to family breakdown as well. When a parent is incarcerated, children are often left on their own, or, in some cases, live with their parent in a jail cell. As a result, children of incarcerated parents are six times more likely than other children to become incarcerated themselves at some point in their lives.[56]

As many as 2.7 million children in the United States have at least one incarcerated parent according to a 2010 study by The Pew Charitable Trusts. They have been termed the "silent victims of incarceration."[57] Their propensity to run afoul of the law themselves does not stem from seeing their parents' behavior and repeating it, according to Sharon Content, founder of Children of Promise, a group helping children cope with a parent in prison. "From my experience working with the population, the cycle repeats itself because of the lack of support that this young person now has after going through these traumatic experiences."[58]

In Kenya, hundreds of children under the age of four live with their mothers in that country's prison system. Almost all are confined with their mothers in their cells, lacking the stimulation and outlets that create healthy children. There is no educational access, no playtime with friends, and little recreation.[59] In Mexico City's high-security prisons, numerous children live with their mothers.[60] In Bolivia, more than 1400 children are housed in prison with their mothers.[61] In India, children under five stay with their parents in prison because they have no place else to go.[62]

Parental addiction leads to family disruption; foster care systems throughout the world are filled with children who require support because substance abuse has prevented parents from being parents. In the US state of California alone, almost 60,000 children and youth are in foster care, and, of these, 90% come from environments impacted by substance abuse.[63]

Poverty in itself is a stressor and contributes heavily to family breakdowns. As parents struggle with the pressures of keeping a home together financially, frustrations can translate to negative actions impacting their children. Between 2000 and 2009, rates of hospitalization for children suffering physical abuse in the United States increased nearly 1% per year. Those children admitted for traumatic brain injury rose by more than 3% per year. Linking hospital admissions data for these children to indices for unemployment, mortgage delinquency, and foreclosures, researchers at Children's Hospital of Philadelphia determined that, for each 1% increase in the 90-day mortgage delinquency rate in metropolitan areas, there was a 3.09% increase in admission rates for child abuse and nearly a 5% increase in brain injury admission rates.[64]

In Chicago, a homeless woman's struggle to find work while shifting between shelters has exacted a hard toll on the health of her children. One was hospitalized for asthma a week after the family slept in the rain on a friend's back porch. Another has developmental and speech delays, and another spent a week in a psychiatric ward.[65] Throughout the United States, more than 1.6 million children are homeless. Included in this count are infants, young children, and teenagers living on the streets, in hotels, and in their parents' cars.[66] Family rejection of lesbian, gay, bisexual, and transgender (LGBT) youth feeds the conditions of homelessness. Although they comprise less than 10% of the total youth population, LGBT young people make up roughly 40% of those under 18 living on the streets in the United States.[67]

Parenting in any form carries its own stress and demands responsible reaction to those pressures. Those who respond poorly become poor parents, and it is their children that suffer—from abuse, from abandonment, even from being sold into slavery or trafficked. While we can understand the financial pressures on a low-income mother or father who cannot feed or house his or her children, the temptation to treat those children as commodities that can bring revenue as either young workers or products for sale is hard to justify under even the most severe circumstances.

But family breakdown is not solely rooted in poverty. Bad parenting can happen anywhere, and we have seen too many instances of comfortable, economically secure families breaking apart for various reasons, and their children left to suffer, experiencing physical abuse, substance abuse and addiction, abandonment, and the usual range of issues attendant upon the most marginalized. At some point, the issue of responsibility must come into play, in both strong and weak economies.

Anand Giridharadas, columnist for *The New York Times* and author of *The True American*, said "The inequality of access to good parents is by far the most important source of inequality in America."[68] Indeed, this is true for the entire world.

Children On the Move—A Global Crisis

Near the close of 2015, more than 60 million people—half of whom are children—have been displaced by war, civil conflict, or persecution. This represents the highest such total since World War II.[69] The Syrian conflict alone has generated more than seven million refugees, most of whom have headed toward Europe, but they are not alone in their flight. Tens of thousands of Rohingya refugees are fleeing ethnic persecution in Myanmar and Bangladesh, thousands more are fleeing the ongoing civil violence in South Sudan, Kurds continue to flee Iran, Karen refugees flock to the Thai border, the conflict in Ukraine has internally displaced whole towns and villages,[70] and violent gang activity has sent thousands of young people northward to the United States from Central America.

War rarely recognizes social class, and so these millions of refugees span the socioeconomic spectrum. Lawyers and laborers flee side by side with shopkeepers and engineers as entire regions are thrown into turmoil and flight becomes universal.

The migrations following World War II were propelled by a global conflict after which developed nations galvanized their resources to accommodate those who had been uprooted. But what the world faces now is quite different, spawned by dozens of separate upheavals and impacting nations ill-equipped either financially or politically to settle those who cross their borders. The result is an ongoing global crisis that shows few signs of abating.

As a result of this crisis, 30 million children, either with their families or on their own, are at risk. Physically vulnerable, deprived of social, educational, and cultural stability, and placed into situations where their futures cannot readily be determined, they embody the human toll that forced migration compels. And they do so in numbers we have not seen in generations, with no easing of these numbers in sight.[71]

Refugee status can be anything but temporary. Palestinians on the West Bank and the Gaza Strip long to return to their homeland even after five decades, while some children born in the DRC have only known life in a refugee camp. The slums of southern Bogota are jammed with children uprooted from a civil conflict that is unwinding only now after 25 years.

And so what will happen to 30 million children deprived of a secure home and whose very identity is jeopardized? As the world grapples with what to do to accommodate, absorb, or repatriate them, the future of these young people will remain at best in limbo and at worst subject to the most negative social influences, violence, despair, and disillusion.

The collective uncertainty of 30 million children on the move is staggering. What comes next for these children? Who are they going to become?

Notes

1. US Census Bureau, International Database, http://www.census.gov/population/international/data/idb/region.php?N=20Results%20&T=13&A=aggregate&RT=0&Y=2014&R=1&C=
2. UNICEF, "State of the World's Children 2005: Children Under Threat," 2005, http://www.unicef.org/sowc05/english/sowc05.pdf
3. http://www.unicef.org/crc/files/Guiding_Principles.pdf
4. UNICEF, "State of the World's Children 2005: Children Under Threat," 2005, http://www.unicef.org/sowc05/english/sowc05.pdf
5. The UN Inter-agency Group for Child Mortality Estimation (IGME), 2013. *Levels and Trends in Child Mortality: Report 2013*, UNICEF, New York, p. 1.
6. These numbers provide a snapshot by category, but they do not provide a comprehensive or accurate total of all children who are marginalized or at risk. Many children are double- or triple-counted between categories, and many others, because they are truly invisible and beyond the reach of any counting, are missing altogether.
7. In a definition provided by Sarah Thomas de Benitez for the UN Office of the High Commissioner for Human Rights (OHCHR), a *street-connected child* is "a child for whom the street is a central reference point—one which plays a significant role in his/her everyday life and identity." This term is used as an alternative to *street children*.
8. UNICEF, 2013. Every Child's Birth Right: Inequities and trends in birth registration, p. 14.
9. UNICEF, 2013. Every Child's Birth Right: Inequities and trends in birth registration, p. 6–7.
10. www.who.int/pmnch/media/news/2013/birth_registration/en/
11. UNICEF, 2013. Every Child's Birth Right: Inequities and trends in birth registration, p. 12–13.
12. UNICEF, 2013. Every Child's Birth Right: Inequities and trends in birth registration, p. 12–13.

13. UNICEF, 2013. Every Child's Birth Right: Inequities and trends in birth registration, p. 12–13.
14. www.who.int/pmnch/media/news/2013/birth_registration/en/
15. UNICEF, 2013. Every Child's Birth Right: Inequities and trends in birth registration, p. 12–13.
16. UNICEF, 2013. Every Child's Birth Right: Inequities and trends in birth registration, p. 12–13.
17. http://www.ohchr.org/EN/ProfessionalInterest/Pages/CRC.aspx, Article 7.
18. The UN Inter-agency Group for Child Mortality Estimation (IGME), 2013. *Levels and Trends in Child Mortality: Report 2013*, UNICEF, New York, p. 12–13.
19. UNICEF, 2013. Committing to Child Survival: A Promise Renewed, Progress Report 2013, p. 3.
20. UNICEF, 2013. Committing to Child Survival: A Promise Renewed, Progress Report 2013, p. 3.
21. UNICEF, 2013. Committing to Child Survival: A Promise Renewed, Progress Report 2013, p. 24–25.
22. Moni Basu, "India Beats the Odds, Beats Polio," CNN, March 27, 2014.
23. Donald McNeil, "Polio's Return After Near Eradication Prompts a Global Health warning," *The New York Times,* May 5, 2014.
24. Donald McNeil, "A Milestone in Africa: No Polio Cases in a Year," *The New York Times,* August 11, 2015.
25. World Health Organization, "Global Tuberculosis Report 2013, http://www.who.int/tb/publications/global_report/en/
26. Jesse Bump and Nicole Salisbury, "Under the Radar: Why is a leading child killer invisible on the global health agenda?" PATH, March 4, 2014; and Dr. Jesse Bump, email message to Clare Dreyfus, July 8, 2014.
27. http://www.fao.org/news/story/en/item/161819/icode/
28. UNICEF, *Children and Young People with Disabilities Fact Sheet,* United Nation Children's Fund, New York: UNICEF, 2013, p. 27.
29. http://www.who.int/mediacentre/factsheets/fs342/en/
30. http://www.unicef.org.uk/UNICEFs-Work/What-we-do/Issues-we-work-on/child-hunger-stunting/
31. UNICEF, "Improving Child Nutrition: The achievable imperative for global progress," 2013, p. 7–13.
32. UNICEF, "Improving Child Nutrition: The achievable imperative for global progress," 2013, p. 7–13.
33. http://www.nytimes.com/2014/07/15/world/asia/poor-sanitation-in-india-may-afflict-well-fed-children-with-malnutrition.html
34. UNICEF, "Improving Child Nutrition: The achievable imperative for global progress," 2013, p. 7–13.
35. UNICEF, 2013. Committing to Child Survival: A Promise Renewed, Progress Report 2013, p. 30.

36. UNICEF, 2013. Committing to Child Survival: A Promise Renewed, Progress Report 2013, p. 30.
37. UNICEF, 2013. Committing to Child Survival: A Promise Renewed, Progress Report 2013, p. 29
38. World Heart Federation, "Rheumatic Heart Disease," http://www.world-heart-federation.org/press/fact-sheets/rheumatic-heart-disease/#.U3qgZQobQUc.email
39. World Health Organization, http://www.who.int/topics/helminthiasis/en/
40. Pedro Olinto et al., "The State of the Poor: Where Are the Poor, Where is Extreme Poverty Harder to End, and What is the Current Profile of the World's Poor?" Economic Premise, World Bank, October 2013, no. 125, p. 3.
41. Poverty in this context is measured in relative terms as living below 50% of a country's median income level.
42. Peter Adamson, "Measuring Child Poverty: New league tables of child poverty in the world's rich countries," Innocenti Report Card 10, UNICEF Innocenti Research Center, 2012, p. 3, referenced in: Knafo, Saki, 2012. "US Child Poverty Second Highest Among Developed Nations" *Huffington Post*, May 30 2012.
43. http://www.unicef.org/education/bege_61657.html
44. UNICEF, 2012. Progress for Children: A Report Card on Adolescents, p. 13–14.
45. UNICEF, 2012. Progress for Children: A Report Card on Adolescents, p. 16.
46. UNICEF, 2012. Progress for Children: A Report Card on Adolescents, p. 13–14.
47. http://www.cnn.com/2014/02/04/world/asia/china-children-left-behind/index.html
48. Thielman, N. *et al.* (2012). *Correlates of Poor Health among Orphans and Abandoned Children in Less Wealthy Countries: The Importance of Caregiver Health.* PLoS ONE 7(6): e38109.
49. UNICEF Orphan Estimates, 2013, cf. http://www.cnn.com/2013/09/16/opinion/international-adoption-tarikuwa-lemma-stolen-children/
50. Thielman, N. *et al.* (2012). *Correlates of Poor Health among Orphans and Abandoned Children in Less Wealthy Countries: The Importance of Caregiver Health.* PLoS ONE 7(6): e38109.
51. Mulheir, Georgette, CEO, Lumos, www.wearelumos.org/the-problem
52. Kathryn Whetten et al., 2009. A Comparison of the Wellbeing of Orphans and Abandoned Children Ages 6–12 in Institutional and Community-Based Care Settings in 5 Less Wealthy Nations. PLoS ONE, Volume 4: Issue 12, December 2009; and Denise Grady, "Study Suggests Orphanages Are Not So Bad," *New York Times*, December 18 2009.

53. Denise Grady, "Study Suggests Orphanages Are Not So Bad," *New York Times*, December 18 2009.
54. Kerry Olsen et al., "From Faith to Action: Strengthening Family and Community Care for Orphans and Vulnerable Children in Sub-Saharan Africa," Firelight Foundation, 2008, p. 2–3.
55. Simon Antrobus, "Why Growing Up Without a Dad Can Store Up Future Problems," *The Guardian*, May 21, 2012.
56. Zadock Angira, "Hundreds of Children Under Four Live in Prison With Their Mothers," *Nairobi Daily Nation*, February 21, 2012, http://www.nation.co.ke/News/Hundreds+of+children+live+in+prison+with+their+mothers+/-/1056/1332402/-/5qri99z/-/index.html
57. http://www.cnn.com/2012/11/26/world/cnnheroes-prison-children/
58. http://www.cnn.com/2012/11/26/world/cnnheroes-prison-children/
59. Zadock Angira, "Hundreds of Children Under Four Live in Prison With Their Mothers," *Nairobi Daily Nation, February 21, 2012.*
60. http://www.nytimes.com/2007/12/31/world/americas/31mexico.html?pagewanted=all
61. http://content.time.com/time/world/article/0,8599,1890642,00.html
62. http://news.bbc.co.uk/2/hi/south_asia/4354712.stm
63. http://www.kidsdata.org/topic/20/fostercare/table#fmt=16&loc; cf. California Department of Social Services, http://www.cdss.ca.gov/cdss-web/PG59.htm
64. Nicholas Bakalar, "Childhood: More Abuse Seen in Areas of Fiscal Stress," *New York Times*, July 23, 2012.
65. Meribah Knight, "Homeless Families in Illinois Walking a Hard Road," *NewYork Times*, December 10, 2011.
66. Craig Blankenhorn, "Young and Homeless, Sunday Review, *New York Times*, August 31, 2012.
67. http://williamsinstitute.law.ucla.edu/press/americas-shame-40-of-homeless-youth-are-lgbt-kids/
68. Anand Giridharadas, Interview at Aspen Institute, Washington, DC, April 29, 2014 (David Brooks, interviewer): http://www.aspeninstitute.org/video/new-york-times-columnist-anand-giridharadas-his-new-book-true-american-david-brooks#
69. Jake Silverstein, "Displaced: An Introduction", *New York Times Magazine*, November 5, 2015.
70. Patrick Boehler and Sergio Pecanha, "The Global Refugee Crisis, Region By Region", *New York Times*, August 25, 2015.
71. Jake Silverstein, "Displaced: An Introduction", *New York Times Magazine*, November 5, 2015.
72. UNICEF, 2013. Every Child's Birth Right: Inequities and trends in birth registration, p. 6, http://www.unicef.org/publications/index_71514.html

73. The UN Inter-agency Group for Child Mortality Estimation (IGME), 2013. *Levels and Trends in Child Mortality: Report 2013*, UNICEF, New York, p. 1, http://www.childinfo.org/files/Child_Mortality_Report_2013.pdf

74. http://www.who.int/mediacentre/factsheets/fs342/en/

75. Siteresources.worldbank.org/EXTPREMNET/Resources/EP125.pdf., p.3

76. http://streetchildren.org/about/street-children/

77. Orla Ryan, "FT Seasonal Appeal helps thousands of vulnerable children," *Financial Times*, November 27, 2012. http://www.ft.com/cms/s/0/2bb4cea8-47c7-11e3-9398-00144feabdc0.html

78. http://www.unicef.org/protection/57929_58005.html

79. Covell, Katherine and Becker, Jo (2011). Five Years On: A Global Update on Violence Against Children, NGO Advisory Council for Follow-up to the UN Study on Violence Against Children, p. 24; and www.unicef.org/socialpolicy/files/UNICEF_Factsheet_Children_and_Adolescent_Migrants_May_2012.docx

80. UNHCR. (2011). *UNHCR Statistical Yearbook 2011.* 8. Retrieved October 26, 2013, from UNHCR: http://www.unhcr.org/516285b89.html

81. UNICEF. (2013). Orphan Estimates. New York: UNICEF

82. http://www.who.int/hiv/topics/paediatric/en/

83. BBC, Children of Conflict: Child Soldiers page: http://www.bbc.co.uk/worldservice/people/features/childrensrights/childrenofconflict/soldier.shtml

84. UNICEF, 2007. 'Children in Detention: Calculating global estimates for Juvenile Justice Indicators 2 and 3', Programme Division, UNICEF, New York. Cited in: UNICEF, 2009. *Progress for Children: A report card on child protection*, Report No. 8, UNICEF, New York, p. 20

85. *World Health Organization, Geneva, 2004*

86. http://purposefullyscarred.com/2013/07/22/unicef-report-125-million-survivors-of-fgm/

87. http://www.who.int/mediacentre/factsheets/fs345/en/

88. Covell, Katherine and Becker, Jo (2011). Five Years On: A Global Update on Violence Against Children, NGO Advisory Council for Follow-up to the UN Study on Violence Against Children, p. 24

89. www.unicef.org/sowc06/profiles/disabilities.php

90. http://www.unicef.org/education/bege_61657.html

91. UNICEF, "Progress for Children: A Report Card on Adolescents," April 2012, pp. 13–14: http://www.unicef.org/lac/PFC2012_A_report_card_on_adolescents%281%29.pdf

92. "The Lost Generation," *The Economist*, May 1, 2013; http://www.economist.com/blogs/freeexchange/2013/05/global-youth-unemployment; and http://www.un.org/en/ecosoc/about/employment.shtml

CHAPTER 3

Why Should We Care?

Every day we are exposed to images of suffering. The stories and statistics presented here reflect the human dimensions of that suffering, the tremendous toll exacted upon children and young people around the world. Western society in particular does not shrink from showing the images that back up these stories. We see them, if we choose to look, in every news cycle. These images even permeate our entertainment—a film depicting extreme poverty and abandonment in India, *Slumdog Millionaire*, wins an Academy Award for Best Picture, while other films of varying levels of creativity depict drug addiction, children in war, trafficking, life in the slums, and dozens of other variations.

We become inured to what is pervasive. The scope of suffering endured by children and young people has become so vast that we tend to catalog it as part of the definition of a global society, that development is uneven, that young people are disproportionately impacted, and that that's the way it is because that's the way it has always been. Compassion fatigue becomes quite real.

But the plight of marginalized children is more than a function of compassion, and our response to it all must transcend the emotional. Conditions confronting marginalized children provoke a response on several levels. A moral imperative crosses almost all cultures, religions, and values, wherein the welfare of children holds high standing. Children are our legacy, our sustainability, and the hope for a better society. They merit our attention and protection.

© The Editor(s) (if applicable) and The Author(s) 2016   35
M. Ajmera, G.A. Fields, *Invisible Children*,
DOI 10.1057/978-1-137-57838-9_3

WHAT TYPE OF SOCIETY DO WE WANT TO BE?

The plight of marginalized young people must also be viewed as a human rights issue, articulated eloquently in the United Nations Convention on the Rights of the Child (CRC), which speaks to the inherent responsibility of all societies to provide their children protection, safety, education, opportunities, and access to healthful living. Moreover, the ways in which we either preserve or curtail the well-being of our youngest and most vulnerable in large measure define the type of society we create.

The CRC makes this case quite clearly in outlining 41 articles that, taken together, provide a basis for the integration and protection of children in complex societies. The CRC specifies rights of survival, including nutrition, shelter, and health care; rights of development, including education, play, thought, and religion; rights of protection; and rights of participation, including freedom of opinion and expression.[1]

Significantly, the United Nations has seen fit in its collective judgment to segment the rights of children as meriting particular protection. The nature of the articles within the CRC identifies with some clarity where the threats to children lie, and how a responsible society must respond. Sadly, though, the CRC is not a living document for many of its signatories, instead filling a useful public relations role but not creating the framework for effective enforcement of the rights so clearly enumerated.

But questions defining human rights within complex, pluralistic societies are not the province of modern man, nor a recent departure from issues of social definition. Such questions go back more than 2500 years to the writings of the Greek philosophers. Hidden, and often overlooked, in these discussions is the place of the youngest, most vulnerable members of society. Too often the rights of children have been compromised through systems that regard their conditions as collateral.

The Greeks, whose thinking has provided much of the foundation of modern civilization, saw the need to protect society's children. Poets, lawgivers, and philosophers saw social justice in the civic bonds that provided benefits for the comfortable and protections for those in need. The writings of Homer extolled the virtues of protection of the weakest and most vulnerable,[2] and Epicurus asserted that justice demanded mutual protection, which advanced the well-being of even the most marginalized.[3] Plato emphasized that each child should be educated to play a productive role in his society and that the state had a responsibility to secure each young person's education and well-being.[4] And while Plato's thoughts had as much to do with the welfare of the state as it did the welfare of children within that state, he nonetheless illustrated a universality concerning child protection. Pliny the Elder noted 2100 years ago, "What we do to our children they will do to society," and so the cycles of poverty, neglect, and disregard continue.

Regard for children permeates the thinking of every major world religion. Judeo-Christian philosophy has traditionally placed a high value on the safety and care of children. Ancient Judaic texts identify and appreciate the distinct stages of childhood, including infancy, adolescence, and youth. Rituals affiliated with these various stages, such as *bris* and *bar* or *bat mitzvahs*, attest to the spiritual importance of the transitions from birth to adulthood. Philo of Alexandria, a first-century CE Jewish philosopher, articulated clearly the importance of caring for all infants, asserting that children were a "divine command."[5] Coupled with Judaic practices of Tzedakah, which translates from the Hebrew as "justice" or "righteousness" and is commonly applied as providing support for the neediest in the community,[6] the rights of children and young people have been well honored within Jewish tradition.

Christian thought has similarly embraced the importance of protecting and nurturing the young. The New Testament is filled with Jesus' references to children, including his raising a child from the dead. His exhortation that his followers "become like little children" has entered Christian thought through the centuries as justification for the protection and care of the young. Often quoted in various contexts within Christian traditions is Psalm 127: "Children are a heritage from the Lord, offspring a reward from him. Like arrows in the hands of a warrior are children born in one's youth. Blessed is the man whose quiver is full of them," and Matthew 18:10: "See that you do not despise one of these little ones. For I tell you that their angels in heaven always see the face of my Father in heaven."

Today, the Catholic Church has no fewer than 17 patron saints for children and childhood protection. Saint Nicholas of Myra, upon hearing that a man had fallen upon such hard times that he was about to sell his three daughters into prostitution to support the family, threw three bags of gold through the man's window, thereby providing an early example of generosity that helped grow the culture of St. Nicholas, or "Santa Claus."[7] Saint Bathilde was sold into slavery as a child in the seventh century. After escaping, she worked in the French court, married King Clovis II, and used her position as queen to help those in poverty, especially children in peril of slavery, abuse, or neglect.[8] Protestant and Evangelical traditions have been no less virulent in their regard for the role of children.

Like Christianity, Islam also views children as sacred gifts from Allah that are to be cherished and respected. Through the teachings of Mohammed and passages in the Koran, Islamic tradition has derived that all children must be fed, clothed, and protected; that they must have respect and love from their parents; and have a right to an education.[9] Mohammed himself had seven children, an adopted son, two grandsons, and three granddaughters, and Islamic tradition is filled with stories of his gentle interactions with children, his encouragement of their parents, and his reverence for young people as an emanation of Allah's grace. Furthermore, in addressing social inequalities of his time, Mohammed stressed the equality between male and female children. Aisha, Mohammed's wife, did the same, and is historically regarded as an example of the Islamic view of the young through her continual emphasis on the great reward in rearing children.[10]

Even Buddhist thought, which is commonly identified with renunciation of material goods and the longings that they instill, has carved a special niche for the young. Nonattachment to material goods does not, in Buddhist philosophy, equate to poverty. Buddhist ascetics maintain a simple life but still require sufficient food to alleviate hunger and sustain good health, clothing, shelter, and health care. These simple necessities must extend to all members of society. The rights of children are to be protected, and all children merit respect and compassion because they have *Buddha-nature*[11] and can attain nirvana, thereby confirming their integrity as living beings. In an enlightened society, all relationships will be fair and peaceful, underscoring a sense of social justice and opportunity for all members of any society.[12]

Hinduism, with an emphasis on rebirth, views life from the perspective that current existence is part of a continuum of lives, both preceding and succeeding this one. Children, then, are gifts from the gods and products of previous karma or the energy and behavior of those lives. Hindu law specifically protects the rights of illegitimate children. According to Gautama Sutras, sons of unmarried women are still to be recognized by their fathers with the same legal and social rights as the sons of married women[13] One of the four stages of life according to Hinduism is *Grihastahshram* (living with wife and children), instilling the need for protection and care. Traditional Hindu thought places the role of parents and teachers next to that of God.[14]

Observers and social thinkers through the centuries have continued to refine a definition of society that incorporates engagement of the young and care for those caught in poverty, violence, or abandonment. The weight of statistics today, showing that we have failed at least a billion young people in honoring the most basic tenets of the rights that pertain to all men and women—protection, safety, opportunity, and health—cast a societal definition that falls well short of the ideals espoused by the Greeks and embraced conceptually by most major civilizations through the modern day.

In the last analysis, caring for this world's children is an issue of decency, defined across cultures, across philosophies, and across religions. It is indecent for a child to go hungry. It is indecent for a child to forage for survival or be bound to another for sexual purposes. It is indecent for a child to live amid violence and brutality. It is indecent for a child to grow up uneducated. It is indecent to have the normal vibrancy and health of youth compromised by preventable illnesses. It is indecent for a child to be nothing more than someone else's commodity.

Gandhi wrote that, "A nation's greatness is measured by how it treats its weakest members." No society can call itself civilized if it does not seek to address the current needs and the future hopes of its marginalized young people.

THE HISTORY OF CHILD PROTECTION

Concern for the plight of marginalized children is not a modern phenomenon. Efforts to protect the poor, the vulnerable, the exploited, and the abused go back centuries. As far back as the Enlightenment in the 1700s, philosophers such as Locke and Rousseau argued that childhood seeded the development of the individual, and therefore should be protected and nurtured.[15] Harsh social conditions in the nineteeth century spawned vigorous child protection movements in both England and the United States. Sparked in some measure by the writings of Charles Dickens, England in the mid-nineteenth century passed a number of laws governing child labor and working conditions in factories. England's Factory Act of 1833 specified that children below the age of nine could not be employed, and that those under the age of 16 could work no more than 16 hours a day.[16] It was a beginning, often ignored because of the demands of stark poverty, but a beginning nonetheless.

Concurrently, in the United States, the first law mandating that all children receive free public education was passed in Massachusetts in 1851. England quickly followed suit with mandates for free day schools, reformatory schools, and industrial schools.[17] In 1889, England adopted the Children's Charter, the first measure to prohibit cruelty to children. Parents found mistreating their young could be arrested and imprisoned.[18]

The rise of child-focused relief organization evolved with some energy following World War I. Eglantyne Jebb drew attention to the plight of children impacted by the sanctions imposed on the losing side after World War I, leading to the establishment of Save the Children, whose work continues vigorously to this day. Her advocacy helped generate the Geneva Declaration on the Rights of the Child in 1924, which informed the United Nations 1989 CRC.[19]

The social and political landscape of the twentieth century provided impetus to continue expanding protections for children. Movements for universal education, rising largely in the 1930s, impacted all parts of the globe, and today some form of education is required—at least theoretically—in almost every country on the planet.[20] The devastation of World War II energized child rights activists, and the United Nations Children's Emergency Fund, known today as UNICEF, came into being in 1946 and became a permanent part of the United Nations system in 1953.[21] The Indian Child Development Service (ICDS), launched in 1975, exists to provide nutrition, immunizations, and nonformal preschool education to millions of children in India.[22] (Although critics of this effort have complained that ICDS is more concerned with increasing coverage rather than providing quality services, thereby limiting their impact,[23] this is not an uncommon assessment for any group basing its work on numbers served rather than the impact on those they serve.)

Despite the growth in the momentum to improve the plight of the marginalized young, millions of children fall outside the reach of any public awareness. If we view history as a series of progressive steps moving in a definable direction, then it becomes obvious that the laudable efforts of those who authored the initiatives that have brought us this far still have much more ground to cover.

DEMOGRAPHIC CHALLENGE: DIVIDEND OR DISASTER?

Most high-income societies view children as a resource, as a dividend for the future. But when young people fall outside a society's most basic level of care, they assume a different role. As the number of vulnerable young people grows, negative impulses ensue and the potential dividend of a vibrant youth sector becomes less clear.

Societies seek to replenish themselves through their children. In the best instances, growing numbers of young people contribute to and sustain a society's forward motion. They fill jobs, and they create new economic opportunities both as consumers and as producers of youth-oriented goods. They feed into schools and emerge with societal insights, complemented by the youthful energy to employ those insights in productive ways. Young people become doctors that heal the sick, attorneys that protect human rights, manufacturers that produce the goods that make life easier, and scientists that find new clues to manage the ever-changing world around us. They sustain family units and the stability that accompanies them. They become writers, musicians and poets, painters, and sculptors, transforming the wonder they find in their young, unfolding lives into works of art that inspire and compel self-examination. Young people seed our cultural, social, and economic evolution through new perspectives and through new questions. They drive us forward.

But when great numbers of children are born into desperate circumstances, they create neither progress nor resource, but stress. Their collective dividend becomes diluted, and the sheer weight of their numbers can threaten societal stability and societal health.

For various reasons, including some success in bringing down infant mortality rates and combating infectious diseases, the number of young people in low-income countries has increased over the past two decades. Quite simply, there are more people between the ages of 15 and 24 than ever before, and, in regions where economies are stuttering and educational infrastructures are weak, these young people are often left with little in the way of vocational or social alternatives. They are the Youth Bulge.

When the proportion of young people in any population increases significantly compared to other age groups, those young people create, among other things, a surplus of labor. Indeed in most low-income countries, the majority of the population is under 25 years of age. More than 200 million young people are unemployed and idle, with high concentrations in Africa, Asia, and the Middle East.

In 2011, almost 75 million youth globally between 15 and 20 were seeking work. Africa has the world's youngest population, where youth make up 37% of the working age population and 60% of the unemployed. In all, nearly 25% of the world's young people are economically inactive, pursuing neither education nor engaged in the work force.[24]

At 1.2 billion, the number of young people in the world is at an all-time high. Within the next decade, another one billion young people will come of working age, and they will be seeking jobs.[25] Those who remain unengaged will face huge risks for stress, stigma, unrest, drugs, crime, and the sex trade for jobless youth who already face too many risks.

The world's population is growing disproportionately between high- and low-income countries. According to UNICEF, the world's under-18 population will grow only marginally through 2025, but there will be graphic shifts in the composition of this demographic, which will only accelerate over time. While Western Europe is projected to see a slight decrease in population over the next three decades, populations in lower-income regions will grow by as much as a factor of six before 2050.[26] Most of this growth will be in the number of children. Africa, for example, will double its population by that date, and 43% of that growth will be below the age of 15. By mid-century, one in every three births will occur in Africa, and nearly one in every three people under the age of 18 will live in sub-Saharan Africa. By contrast, that ratio was one in ten in 1950. The top ten countries that will see increases in the percentage of child populations are all low-income sub-Saharan nations.[27]

In India, where 76% of a population surpassing 1.2 billion lives on less than $2 a day, projections indicate that there will be more than 400 million people 15 or younger by 2050. Because the largest demographic increases will be in areas where economic and social development are lagging, the numbers of vulnerable children and youth will skyrocket without proper mitigation strategies and a more comprehensive response. Accordingly, UNICEF projects that by 2050, one in every five deaths of those under the age of 18 will occur in India.[28]

Compounding this demographic explosion, focused on low-income regions, is the concurrent shift in demographics among high-income countries whose populations are aging. The United States is projected to be the only wealthy nation that will see an absolute increase in the number of its young people by 2050, but it will also see its average life expectancy rise to nearly 80 and find the number of its citizens over 75 jump markedly to 102 million, up from 46 million in 2000. This pattern will be echoed in Brazil, Indonesia, Western Europe, and especially in China, which will have half a billion citizens 75 and older by 2050.[29]

The burden of caring for aging populations in the high-income countries will add further stress to any agenda for addressing the needs of young people, whose numbers in impoverished parts of the globe will rise dramatically.

A further demographic shift heightens the problem of available resources. Population growth in strong economies will likely be concentrated upon those social segments near the bottom of the socioeconomic scale. In the United States, child poverty has reached record levels, and children of color[30] are disproportionately in poverty. Yet for the first time in 2012, the majority of children in the United States under the age of two are children of color, and by 2019 the majority of all children nationwide will be children of color. In one of the world's strongest economies, poverty is becoming more concentrated at younger ages, and, as that poverty is largely centered on children of color who will increase in number over time, the percentage of children in poverty will continue to rise.[31]

Some cultures view children as assets, and parents, especially fathers, may strive to sire as many as possible. Each child carries the hope of a new wage earner for the family, or more hands around to help maintain a household, care for siblings, and ease the burden of parents coping with their own stresses. There are currently 222 million women in low-income countries who want but do not have access to modern contraception, and this unmet need is a serious threat to the physical, social, and economic well-being of women and children living in poverty around the world. Extending coverage to these women would have prevented 100,000 maternal deaths and 1.1 million infant deaths in 2011 alone.[32]

But the demographics of the next several decades promise to threaten this traditional way of thinking. High birth rates in low-income regions coupled with declining birth rates in strong economies and aging populations that will siphon off much-needed resources will accentuate existing social conditions in these economically stressed regions. These demographic concerns provide an additional layer of complexity in addressing the situations that already marginalize millions of young people. More people in low-income countries and fewer people in stronger economies with an aging population will limit resources available for children in poverty. Things stand to get worse.

HUMAN SECURITY: CHILD PROTECTION AND SOCIETAL PROTECTION

Ingrained in human nature, as it is with every species, is the instinct to protect our young. Yet when children are marginalized by economic or social conditions, their odds of being subjected to emotional, psychological, or physical harm rise markedly. We have seen that children working in the limestone quarries of Egypt, for example, rarely live to see the age of 16, while young people in Kolkata's worst slums, who live by begging and foraging for food and shelter, are subject to complex physical illnesses, an absence of self-esteem, and a lingering sense of despair. Their lack of personal security compromises any future trajectory.

At the simplest level, children require protection. The smallest, most vulnerable members of any society, they merit safe places to develop physically, to grow emotionally, and to come of age intellectually. The instances of violence recounted in these pages show the failures of societies and systems to offer the most basic protections to children. Economic systems that regard human beings as commodities find another product in young people, and the vast numbers of the young engaged in hazardous labor testify to their marketability. States that equate the legal status of young people with that of adults too readily place them in dangerous or stifling situations, either in jails or in deportations that send them back into the jeopardy and despair they sought to leave. Domestic violence claims young victims every day in all parts of the world, in both strong and weak economies.

Child Protection

Different players have responsibility for protecting children—parents and caregivers, the state, legal systems, schools, and communities. When one of these actors fails, the others must step up to ensure the safety of the child. But failures exist at every level. In Chap. 1, we saw how the state system failed to see Dasani and compensate for her mother's inability to provide adequately. Children living on the streets in effect live outside their communities and derive no support from community structures. Those consigned to foster care often face uncertain environments, sometimes with tragic results, as with Orion Hamilton's death before the age of one.

UNICEF has advanced a position on child protection that calls to action government, civil society, parents, caregivers, families, and other community structures to create a systems approach that implements a wide range of interventions to ensure the safety of children in various situations. This approach shifts the focus from "particular groups of children in need of protection, to the achievement of more sustainable, comprehensive and long-term responses to child protection issues."[33]

The obligation to protect the young exists as splendid theory, but the reality of these instances of failure on the part of states, economies, and families in enacting that high sentiment exacts an immense toll in reality. Millions of children face each day with either an overt or a subtle threat of violence, inflicted by dysfunctional systems, by families, and by strangers from whom they are not protected.

Societal Protection

But the plight of vulnerable children is also an issue of societal security. The United Nations Development Program has stated that human security entails both "freedom from fear" and "freedom from want," arguing that the social and economic impacts of hunger, disease, and lack of opportunity have cost global society more than the combined impact of wars, acts of terror, and natural disasters. The lack of human security among young populations is, then, especially destabilizing, and creates a weak foundation for countries' futures and their economic and political development. Moreover, vast numbers of indigent young people with nothing to do and no hope for the future provide a fertile field for destabilizing social unrest.

In particular, the plight of marginalized boys and young men creates a huge potential for social destabilization. In recent years, increased attention has been paid to issues impacting girls and young women. But while girls matter, so do boys. Demographic studies have shown that the distinctive problems of boys and young men exert impacts beyond their gender. In some countries, boys drop out of school at a higher rate than girls. For example, dropout rates among boys in Cambodia, Chad, Nicaragua, the Central African Republic, Ethiopia, and Uganda far exceed those for girls, and each of these countries has suffered in recent years, or continues to suffer, from significant internal violence.[34] In the United States, one-third of all African–American and Latino young people will not graduate high school. With heightened poverty rates within these demographics, coupled with increased rates of violent crime and incarceration, the elements for aggressive socially negative behavior are profound.[35]

Boys comprise a disproportionate part of the negative consequences of the "youth bulge." They are unemployed, not in school, and their idleness sparks an additional range of social problems. Idle young men become a fertile recruiting ground for violent activities, including the more extreme politically or religiously motivated movements, social unrest, and dissolution. As well, the attitudes of boys and young men toward the opposite gender, often based in societal or cultural traditions, assumptions, and prejudices, deepens the vulnerability of girls and young women in many contexts.

Moreover, demographics in such populous countries as India and China indicate a rise in gender disproportion, so that, over time, these distinctive problems will be accentuated.[36] Where males outnumber females by notable margins, social structures can be affected in unhealthy ways. In Asia, there are 104.4 males for every 100 females,[37] and birth ratios in the region point to this disparity increasing in the near future. In India, the ratio of boy births to girl births is 113, and in some areas as high as 156. In China, the ratio is 119, peaking at 135 in some regions.[38] By 2020, up to 15% of men in these two countries will not be able to marry or build a family because there will not be enough women to do so. The Chinese refer to these men as "bare branches"—family tree branches that cannot bear fruit but may be useful as clubs. Criminal rates for unmarried men in these countries are much higher than for married men, and so an element of social instability stands to deepen.[39] Economists project 30–40 million more young men than women of marriageable age in China and India by 2020. A 2007 statement by the Central Committee of the Communist Party of China and the State Council deemed the growing number of "bare branches" a "hidden danger that will affect social stability."[40]

An inequality in basic nutrition and health care exacerbates this gender gap. Nobel Laureate Amartya Sen has advanced the notion of "missing women," those who are not here because they have not received adequate nutritional, health, and social service support. In India, for example, the death rate for women is consistently higher than that for men well into their late thirties. Sen estimates that there are at least 100 million "missing women," indicative of inequality and neglect that contributes to excess mortality for women and girls.[41]

The prevalence of child soldiers and children in conflict stems from the objectification of children for political ends, feeding long-term instability that does not end when the shooting stops. While children might be the currency at hand for fighting wars of rebellion, their trauma transcends any war, and those who take part often spend the rest of their lives struggling with trauma, incapable of readapting to peaceful society, or plagued by addiction to the drugs and alcohol forced upon them during their wars.

A rising manifestation of civil violence is the proliferation of "ungoverned spaces," those areas that are beyond the control of any governmental authority where insurrections and violent political movements have created conditions nearing anarchy. We see this in the eastern provinces of the Democratic Republic of Congo (DRC), where ethnic separatist movements have broken down almost all societal structures, including law enforcement, schools, and health care. In Uganda, the Lord's Resistance Army has had a similar impact on vast regions of the countryside, with government forces unable to reestablish control. Portions of Colombia during the recent civil conflict there were under the control of neither the rebel FARC organization nor the Colombian government.

The result in such situations is even more drastic levels of violence perpetrated by actors who fear no repercussions nor have any restraint on their actions. Children, of course, are at primary risk. Boko Haram's impact on the ungoverned regions of northern Nigeria gives testament: in addition to their kidnapping of hundreds of school girls, the group burned children alive in a locked schoolroom, massacred people indiscriminately at a soccer game, and killed boys while they slept at a boarding school.[42] Children in these ungoverned spaces live outside any systemic protection beyond the whims of the violent forces that have broken down authority and control. In essence, children in ungoverned territories meet one of three fates—to be killed, to be soldiers, or to be abused.[43]

In Afghanistan, a 17-year-old suicide bomber was stopped by security forces on the edge of Kabul just before he could finish his work detonating a minibus laden with explosives. When the police detained him and took away his bombs, he asked if he could go home. His school exams were the following week, and if possible he would like to pass them. The young man was drawn to an extremist act because his family was desperate, and in return for his suicide they would have received some money to buy the essential things that kept them all alive.[44]

A demand for education that far outstrips the government's capacity to provide it can become a breeding ground for violence among young men. Those left out can become embittered. Where schools are accessible, quality becomes an issue. Poor learning outcomes translate to a lack of skills, including an understanding of citizenship and community. Schools that do not prepare young men for future work and participation in their society create a frustrated recruiting pool for militants.[45]

In Rwanda, the Hutu *Interahamwe*, the local militias that were the foot soldiers of the genocide that killed up to one million Tutsis and moderates, were comprised almost entirely of young men, and a few young women, under the age of 25. With little education and few economic opportunities, these young people were easily manipulated into a killing frenzy by radical Hutus using state media to issue calls to exterminate the Tutsis.[46]

Idle young men in India have been responsible for an upturn in that country's incidents of rape and sexual assault. In the northern Indian state of Haryana, a 16-year-old girl was brutally raped by at least eight men, perhaps more, who threatened to kill her if she told anyone. As a Dalit, the lowest caste in Indian society, the girl had little recourse, and kept silent. The young men who committed the assault took cell phone photos and videos, circulating them around the village until one found its way to the girl's father, who, out of shame, committed suicide. Rapes and sexual assaults have risen sharply in India over the past six years, up as much as 25%, although it is difficult to know for certain because most rapes go unreported.[47]

Several countries in Western Europe have witnessed outbreaks of rioting and social unrest by immigrants from North Africa or Eastern Europe who have too few social services to assist their assimilation and far too few economic avenues. The children of these immigrants are regularly subjected to prejudice, discrimination, and sometimes violence. Riots sparked by young immigrants have occurred in France, Italy, Spain, and Russia, all of whom are struggling to bring these recent arrivals into their social mainstream. In response, counter-riots have occasionally broken out, targeting the immigrants and bringing outcries for rigid new immigration laws or a shutdown of immigration altogether.[48]

THE VALUE OF OUR CHILDREN AND THE COST OF IGNORING THEM

In his book, *The Cost of Inaction: Case Studies from Rwanda and Angola*, Sudhir Anand, Professor of Economics at Oxford, argues that the economic costs of ignoring the plight of the world's children will dwarf any costs associated with ameliorating their conditions. While Dr. Anand's conceptual framework is applied only to two countries impacted by war and civil conflict, he nonetheless concludes that the failure to develop a society's children leads to preventable situations such as malnutrition, morbidity, and premature mortality, all of which carry immense social and economic costs. With support from Dr. Amartya Sen, Dr. Anand has advanced the notion that we pay dearly and in diverse ways for that which we do not do to nurture the youngest and most susceptible.

Children's issues have a vast economic impact on societies that must address the consequences of vulnerable young people who live in poverty, whose earning potential is compromised or eliminated, or who are denied a positive social role. Not addressing these needs in turn creates opportunity costs which are virtually incalculable. Research clearly shows that investing in children—especially early childhood—and youth have measurable economic and social returns that far surpass their costs.[49]

The HIV/AIDS pandemic, which is merely one part of the overwhelming range of issues facing marginalized young people, provides a microcosm of the costs inherent with failing to address adequately these complex problems. The pandemic's demographic impact translates into basic economic issues which are especially acute in low-income countries. Because the majority of those infected with the disease are between 15 and 49, prime working years, increased mortality and morbidity rates create a reduced supply of labor. Long periods of illness associated with the disease reduce productivity for those who are still able to work. And lower productivity can reduce a country's export capacity while it must find ways to import and distribute expensive treatment medications. Healthcare structures must be adapted to accommodate new protocols for a growing patient segment. As a result of these and other impacts, economies where HIV/AIDS is prevalent totter. As far back as 2003, the World Bank projected that HIV/AIDS would lower the Gross Domestic Product (GDP) of a country with a high infection rate by 2–4%.[50] This rate is not inconsequential: a 1.5% decrease, for example, means that a country's GDP would be 31% lower in 25 years' time than it would have been without the pandemic.

But this impact goes well beyond the economic, and in fact feeds upon itself. Take the education sector. School enrollment drops in areas of high HIV/AIDS infection. Children leave school to care for family members, or to work, and some may contract the disease themselves. Studies have shown that children with little or no education are far more likely to contract the disease. At the same time, teachers are not immune from infection, and some areas have had to close schools because of a lack of teachers.[51] As a result of these compounding factors, some areas have had a very difficult time mitigating the impact of the disease even with a reliable supply of effective medicines and treatments. The damage to the social structures affected by HIV/AIDS is not easily or quickly mended.

Recent developments in the ongoing battle to eliminate polio as a global disease provide economic lessons concerning the cost of such efforts and the potential dangers in not paying those costs. Vaccinating children in the most remote locations of countries such as India and Indonesia presents incredible logistical challenges. Villages are isolated and up to three vaccinations are needed to ensure immunity. Bill Gates, whose investments have fueled much of this work, remarked, "I can say without reservation that the last mile is not only the hardest mile, it's also much harder than I expected."[52] And so it would be logical to question why go to the expense of universal vaccination, especially when that elusive goal carries with it huge financial costs. Gates goes on to explain his thinking, "There is no such thing as keeping polio at its current low levels.... If we don't keep investing, cases will shoot back up to the tens of thousands annually in dozens of countries."[53] If that were to reoccur, the world would face a financial impact well beyond the cost of vaccinating children in remote locations.

Child trafficking carries with it enormous social and economic costs. The World Bank has estimated that trafficking worldwide generates profits in excess of $31 billion, or roughly $13,000 monthly for each trafficking victim.[54] This is big business. But the human costs associated with this sour trade, reflected through conservative economic projections, make the scope of this business even more staggering. In 2009, the International Labour Organization (ILO) estimated that the financial costs suffered by the victims of trafficking exceeded $20 billion. These costs include the opportunity costs of wages generated for others rather than oneself, lost income due to unpaid or withheld wages, and recruiting fees paid by victims or their families.[55] And, as sophisticated as the World Bank and the ILO might be, even they readily admit that there is no way to judge with precision the economic costs of the trade in humans because so much of it is hidden, underground, or even sanctioned by host governments. These figures are, by all accounts, low estimates.[56]

The costs of allowing children to be born into and subsist in extreme poverty are likewise immense. Given the layers of societal and community factors, the corollary costs of health care, the costs of law enforcement and prosecution in low-income communities, the incredibly elusive equations of lost potential earned income, and dozens of other variables, it is extremely difficult, if not impossible, to quantify the economic effects of children in poverty. Nonetheless, a group of scholars from Georgetown University and the University of Chicago tried to gage poverty's impact in the United States. They concluded that the aggregate costs of childhood poverty in the United States amounted to 3.8% of the country's GDP, or $500 billion annually. Specifically, they extrapolated that reduced productivity and economic output cost 1.3% of GDP, raised the costs of crime by 1.3% of GDP, and increased health expenditures by 1.2% of GDP.[57] These figures reflect an impact on one of the world's largest and strongest economies. What they do not begin to illustrate is the annual economic impact globally, drawn from societies where poverty is more the norm than the exception.

Providing opportunities for girls is also smart economics. The World Bank concluded in 2012 that India loses $383 billion in potential lifetime income due to four million adolescent girls who become mothers each year. If girls in Kenya completed high school, the economy would gain $27 billion over their lifetime. In Nigeria, if women had the same employment rate as young men, the country would add $11.7 billion to its economy annually.[58]

While these figures are noteworthy, they do not come close to capturing the range of social costs attendant upon marginalized children. In the United States, for example, studies have shown that poverty raises direct expenditures on health care by a minimum of $22 billion each year.[59] And in the UK, where an estimated 12.1% of children live in poverty,[60] total expenditures for health care for people in poverty approach £10 billion, or $16.8 billion.[61] And in low-income countries, health care for young people suffering from malnourishment, preventable diseases, or developmental issues adds millions of dollars to public budgets.

Marginalized young people have a greater tendency toward crime, with considerable financial implications. In the United States, which has the highest prison population in the world, more than $5.7 billion is spent annually on incarceration of those 18 and younger.[62] With an average annual cost of about $100,000 to incarcerate each young prisoner,[63] compared to the annual per-participant costs of socially positive programs such as the Boys and Girls Clubs (approximately $60), or even the average tuition and fees at a fine private university, the empirical costs of young people running outside the law are astronomical. The cost to society of dealing with a 14-year-old with a penchant for breaking laws can run as high as $3.2 million over the course of his or her lifetime.[64] And beyond the financial costs are the immense social costs of young lives locked away in places that breed resentment, despair, and sometimes radicalization.

Such costs are not the sole province of high-income countries with well-developed prison systems. Rwanda has the world's third highest rate of incarceration, owing in large measure to the 1994 genocide, the aftermath of which filled its detention centers. Because many of the perpetrators of the genocide were young men, thousands have spent their most fruitful years in prison camps, which are overcrowded and harsh. Disease is rampant, especially HIV/AIDS, and educational opportunities are extremely limited.[65] Rwanda's national budget for prisons is so limited that the prisons themselves need to produce their own revenue through the sale of cultivated crops, handiworks, and community labor.[66]

While we can argue about methodologies or parse the figures in different ways, we cannot deny the nature of these costs to our collective societal well-being. In times of limited government resources and sluggish economic growth, arguments abound against directing resources to deeply embedded social problems impacting children and young people. We too often measure the impact of programs and projects in immediate gains or quantifications that can point to numbers served, cost-per-beneficiary, or efficiency ratios. But the economic and social costs of not addressing these complex issues systematically far outweigh the financial expenses of prevention programs, including the support of organizations that can effectively address the root causes of marginalization.

The Negative Outcomes of Growing Up Invisible

Children struggling with conditions of poverty, hopelessness, and marginalization develop reactive mechanisms to help cope with the ongoing stresses of daily survival. The tendency to embrace self-destructive behaviors runs high, with devastating impacts that are not commonly considered as part of the traditional international development model. Whenever children are siphoned away from productive, positive activity by actions that threaten their health and debilitate their social roles, then society as a whole is poorer. Poverty compels negative personal outcomes that hinder societal participation, health, and individual development.

Toxic Stress

While stress can take many forms, including some stresses that are in fact positive and can facilitate a child's normal development, toxic stress—defined as "prolonged activation of stress response systems in the absence of protective relationships, usually from strong, frequent and/or prolonged adversity"[67]—can weaken developing brains. Frequent or continual stress on young children lacking adequate protection mechanisms and support from adults increases the risks of lifelong health and social problems.[68]

In the 2012 book *How Children Succeed*, Paul Tough raises the notion that childhood stress impairs a young person's ability to develop an adaptive resiliency. He states that early stress affects the development of that part of the brain critical to self-regulatory behavior. "The part of the brain most affected by early stress is the prefrontal cortex, which is critical in self-regulatory activities of all kinds, both emotional and cognitive. As a result, children who grow up in stressful environments generally find it harder to concentrate, harder to sit still, harder to rebound from disappointments and harder to follow directions."[69]

Constant serious adversities can overwhelm a child's tendency toward resilience, and negative behaviors can ensue as young people struggle to cope with the negative circumstances of their lives. Self-destructive behaviors can result, with addiction to various substances or behaviors too common. Depression, low self-esteem, and a sense of hopelessness parallel these behaviors. In the extreme, suicide is a possible consequence: the World Health Organization estimates as many as 250,000 suicides committed by those 25 and younger each year.[70]

Violence and Criminal Activity

Violence permeates a life on the streets, a life governed by poverty and devoid of hope. People in poverty suffer disproportionately from violent acts brought about by desperation. The murder rates in South Africa's townships, for example, are among the highest in the world, and few of these murders are systematic or planned. They are most often the result of anger, frustration, and loss, acted out when triggers are tripped and emotions erupt.

While hundreds of thousands of young people are engaged as child soldiers, the ILO estimates that twice as many are involved in illicit criminal activities, including the production and distribution of illegal drugs, the production of pornography, and prostitution.[71] As small and relatively inexpensive "employees," children are an attractive market for criminal labor.

In Mexico, the Children's Rights Network estimates that 30,000 children work for the drug cartels. Generally, girls repackage quantities of narcotics for sale on the streets and boys work as lookouts. Some children, however, are asked to be couriers or assassins.[72] In Afghanistan—which supplies much of the illicit global market for opiates—hundreds of children reportedly labor in the poppy fields, preventing their schooling and exposing them to significant risk including drug addiction.[73]

Gang membership codifies criminal behavior through affiliation with a substitute "family" that enforces discipline while providing a sense of belonging often absent in children's daily lives. In El Salvador, where estimates of youth gang membership range from 10,500 to 39,000, initiation for new gang members can involve beatings. Female recruits may be given the option of choosing between being beaten and having sexual relations with members of the gang.[74] In Cape Town, South Africa, gangs in the growing townships attract children as young as 12.[75]

Young people in poverty unaffiliated with gangs are still at risk of violence. In their book *The Locust Effect*, Gary Haugen and Victor Boutros contend that there is nothing shielding people in poverty from violent people and violent acts. Rape, police abuse, theft, and countless acts of everyday violence block development and extinguish hope, thereby perpetuating cycles of violence as young people with no alternative fight back in the only ways they know how.[76]

Toxic Substances—Tobacco, Alcohol, and Drugs

Bad behaviors are interrelated—despair can lead to substance abuse, which in turn can lead to risky sexual behavior, violence, or suicide. Separating cause and effect within these behaviors is inexact, even though evidence exists to suggest that the incidence of self-destructive actions among young people in low-income societies is considerable.[77] But it is clear that the use of toxic substances among the poorest of the poor contributes to cycles of despair.

While tobacco consumption in the United States has continued to decline over the past decade, tobacco production has never been higher, with products exported vigorously to the developing world. Exported with the products are the considerable negative health impacts of tobacco use.

Over the next 25 years, the number of smokers globally is projected to increase 45%, from 1.1 billion to more than 1.6 billion.[78] Every day between 82,000 and 99,000 young people begin smoking, most of whom are in low- or middle-income countries. Some are younger than ten.[79] The impact of their new habit is graphic. In the lowest-income families, scarce resources are often used to support the addiction rather than food, thereby making tobacco a contributing factor to hunger and malnutrition.[80] Poverty is accentuated and perpetuated when tobacco-related illnesses disable or claim the lives of primary breadwinners.[81]

Alcohol consumption among young people has risen steadily. In 2011, 71 of 73 countries participating in the World Health Organization's survey of alcohol usage reported increased consumption among those younger than 18. The highest rates of consumption were in economically fragile countries, including Uganda, Zambia, and Namibia. Also, the countries of the former Yugoslavia, beset by the social and economic residue of years of conflict, showed high usage as well.[82] In these countries, heavy alcohol consumption has been linked to suicide, especially among the young.[83]

Similarly, drug use has expanded rapidly and is now concentrated among those under the age of 25.[84] Because drugs cost money, young people in need often resort to acquisitive crimes such as petty robbery, shoplifting, and thieving to procure their drugs, leading to higher crime rates in areas of high usage. The cost of drug-related acquisitive crimes in the UK approximated £13.9 billion, or $23.4 billion, in 2004.[85] This, of course, does not factor in the human costs. And survey after survey has confirmed that drug use is much more rampant in areas with high inequalities in income distribution and high unemployment, particularly among those under 25.[86]

Drug use in the United States continues to exact a steep financial and personal toll. According to a study by the Center on Addiction and Substance Abuse (CASA) at Columbia University, 46% of all high school students currently use addictive substances, and 12% meet the clinical criteria for addiction.[87] The immediate costs per year of teen use include an estimated $68 billion associated with underage drinking and $14.4 billion in substance-related juvenile justice programs.[88]

The emergence of crystal methamphetamine as a drug of choice for young people has affected both rural and urban communities, but young people between age 18 and 25 in the smallest rural areas use meth at a rate that is nearly twice the rate of young urban adults (2.9% vs. 1.5%).[89] In Idaho, a largely rural state, of more than 2000 female offenders with a substance abuse problem, over 80% claim meth as their drug of choice. This small state spends approximately $66 million per year housing adult male inmates who admit to having a meth problem. California's Department of Alcohol and Drug Program echoes Idaho's problems. Meth is now the most commonly reported drug problem in the state, surpassing alcohol.[90]

Other drugs have left their mark as well. Heroin use claimed more than 3000 lives in the United States in 2010, 88% of whom were white and more than 20% under the age of 24. Heroin deaths of teenagers and young adults tripled during the 2000s. Abuse of painkillers, including OxyContin, claimed even more lives, nearly 16,000 in 2010.[91]

In the Horn of Africa and the Arabian Peninsula, people have been chewing khat,[92] grown in the highlands, for thousands of years. In Yemen, up to 90% of men and 50% of women chew khat three to four hours a day, and as many as one-fifth of all children under 12 chew khat daily. Khat imparts euphoria, followed by depression. Regular chewing can lead to sleepiness and low productivity. Chewing is a social act in many communities, and a refusal to chew can lead to ostracism. Families sometimes deprive their children of essential foods so that they can spend their limited income on khat.[93] Jamal Al-Shammi, head of a Yemeni nongovernmental organization (NGO) known as the Democratic School, identifies impacts of khat that go beyond the consumer's body. "Khat chewing … breaks down immediate family ties. Men chew alone, women chew alone and children are eventually left alone to do as they please with no adult supervision."[94]

Among children in poverty around the world, glue-sniffing provides a cheap high to help them forget their daily despair. Throughout Central and South America, street-connected children and the extremely marginalized turn to toxic inhalants, including glue, gasoline, lighter fluid, propane, and kerosene. In Kenya, thousands of street-connected kids sniff glue, most often sold to them by women drug dealers in Nairobi, many of whom are mothers trying to earn a living for their own children.[95] Glue costs very little, is readily available, and the high lasts for hours. But the high also carries with it the risk of respiratory failure, brain damage, and death.[96]

RESILIENCE

What we see in these marginalized children is not just the stresses that define their daily existence. We see with it enormous reservoirs of strength and resilience that allow children and young people in destructive circumstances to carry on. In the mid-1970s, the study of resiliency in young people emerged as a formal discipline, carrying with it the definition of resiliency as behavioral adaptation when encountering significant adversity, trauma, tragedy, threat, or stress.[97] Resiliency is more than just the ability to cope. It is, rather, the opportunity and capacity of children to draw upon psychological, social, cultural, and physical resources to navigate pathways through tensions and trauma.[98]

Academic studies centering on demobilized child soldiers, street-connected children, urban poverty, and other demographics of marginalized young people have identified the characteristic of resiliency in clinical terms,[99] and stories of young people overcoming immense odds to find some level of success, peace, or security are not hard to find. We take comfort in these stories and characterize the resiliency shown by these young people as heroic.

Yet clinical definitions fail to capture or adequately categorize the extreme conditions faced by the young people highlighted here and the hundreds of millions like them whose adversities strike to the heart of survival itself. Through it, all these marginalized young people find the mechanisms to survive, to reach out and interact with those around them, and, if strong enough, to keep dreams alive. This remarkable quality alone merits respect and mandates action on their behalf.

A RISING TIDE DOES NOT LIFT ALL BOATS

Conversely, a school of economic thought has proposed that the best approach to alleviating poverty on a global basis is to create a suitable environment for comprehensive economic growth, and that funds spent on social programs are better directed to programs spurring economic activity in all sectors. In this construct, a strong economy is the ultimate resolution of the miseries impacting marginalized children and young people.

But recent economic indices have shown continuing disparities in the distribution of wealth between high- and low-income countries, and between high- and low-income people globally. In 2011, the Organization for Economic Development and Co-operation (OECD) reported that, "over the two decades prior to the onset of the global economic crisis, real disposable household incomes increased by an average 1.7% a year in OECD countries.[100] In a large majority of them, however, the household incomes of the richest 10% grew faster than those of the poorest 10%, widening income inequality."[101] Mining these figures even more deeply, the level of disparity between top and bottom has not closed, and, in many countries has widened, in some considerably more so.[102] The idea that a growing economy lifts even the poorest sectors is, at best, untested, and, at worst, unsubstantiated.

A close look at these indices shows that the most marginalized are not benefiting equally from these material gains. While absolute poverty is falling, inequality persists, leaving many of the most marginalized outside this trend, unable to access the mechanisms that ease poverty. And many of the measurable outcomes impacting children continue to lag behind global averages.

For example, between 2002 and 2011, school enrollment in Ethiopia improved by 11%, a significant jump for that country. The commensurate 1% increase in child literacy countrywide, though, stemmed from stronger improvements in urban areas and better-off households in neighborhoods where schools were present. Literacy among the poorest sampled quintile in Ethiopia actually declined by 6%.[103] In the landmark longitudinal study *Young Lives*,[104] run by Jo Boyden at the Department of International Development at Oxford University, research shows that child literacy within the poorest quintile of those sampled in Peru increased by 5.7%, while that increase among children in the wealthiest sample quintile was 12.7%. These disparities grow wider as children grow older. The study showed that marked differences in the rate of school enrollment between urban and rural children, between those in low- and high-income neighborhoods, with corresponding differences in literacy rates, became more pronounced as children reached the age of 15.[105]

Despite general gains in income in the developing world, inequality of distribution remains very high, with debilitating impact on children and young people. An increase in average daily income from $1.00 to $1.25 per day may help daily subsistence, but it cannot adequately address the long-term development needs of the most marginalized. Large disparities in income equality have been linked to poor health indicators, increased political instability, and minimized social mobility.[106] The needs of those at the bottom of the social order point to food, health, and shelter as opposed to aspirational needs, such as education or vocational training. As a result, the people in poverty often remain mired in low social stations despite regional or national increases in income. And those on the lowest rung of the economic ladder are far more vulnerable to economic downturns, unforeseen challenges (such as the death of a family member), natural disasters, or any other event which might compromise the structure of their lives. In such circumstances, poverty becomes a lasting sentence.

These disparities have a multidimensional impact, and there is a ready correlation between lagging income, health, literacy, and educational access. In the Indian province of Andhra Pradesh, for example, the number of children who were physically underdeveloped in the lowest-income group sampled increased by 2.1% between 2002 and 2009, with a corresponding 6% decrease in their literacy rates. By contrast, those children in the wealthiest sample saw their rates of physical underdevelopment decrease by more than 10% while their literacy rates rose slightly.[107]

Limited access to health care, poor nutrition, and unreliable water and sanitation systems lead to high incidents of illness that further compound a young person's capacity to advance him or herself. And while improvements in health care in low-income countries have been well documented, those who cannot access those improvements are no better off. For example, fewer households in the poorest quintile of those studied in *Young Lives'* assessment were able to access improved water and sanitation between 2002 and 2009, despite general regional improvements.[108] High child mortality rates in low-income regions are seen to be a direct result of this lack of access. Most deaths caused by this healthcare gap were due to treatable or preventable infectious diseases.[109]

All children dream dreams, and children in poverty are no exception. Of those with the lowest income who do attend school, many aspire to paths they ultimately cannot follow, including a university education or a professional career. Compounding the economic challenges are more subtle cultural factors, such as the stigmatization of poverty and gender gaps that often obstruct girls and young women from following nontraditional pursuits. Children growing up in poverty often lack the self-confidence and affirmation to pursue what is, given their social and economic circumstances, a difficult course. Young girls in many cultures are the currency of marriage, and anything that diverts them from that traditional subservient path is anathema.

As a result, young people often regard the already narrow pathways to education and upward mobility as beyond their grasp, inconsistent with their experience and defying the expectations that their communities place upon them. Ambitions change, and the need to help provide for their families in desperate, vulnerable circumstances too often trumps their desire or ability to vault themselves forward.[110]

Those at the very end of the socioeconomic spectrum are largely untouched by the steady improvements in global economic, education, health, and social metrics. Progress is uneven, and some benefit more than others. For those children and young people who do not benefit at all, poverty, despair, and desperation remain the currency of their sad realms.

THE MAKING OF A GOOD SOCIETY

Marginalized young people exact a civic and political cost. If society fails to care for its young, then the very nature of society, defined from our earliest civilizations as noted above, becomes compromised. Beyond the philosophical imperative, though, there are practical consequences in allowing large numbers of young people to exist outside societal limits of care.

Vulnerable children constitute a political segment that lends itself to mobilization. While we are often inspired to see young people engage in the world around them, marked by a genuine hope to make things better, too often such mobilizations are not positive, and populations who lack quality information can be subject to manipulation. They can be viewed as a security threat on both national and regional levels. Other developments in recent years, such as the rise of gangs in Brazil's *favelas* or the huge levels of violence in South Africa's townships, underscore the volatility of disenfranchised young people.

Fragmented communities cannot by definition act cohesively. Rural villages that have seen adults migrate to the cities to find work have become splintered, leaving sons and daughters behind with jerry-rigged care structures for children. These villages have lost some of their most productive workers, and so life within the villages themselves will suffer. In the future, countries whose communities are disintegrated will be at a competitive disadvantage both economically and socially as they interact with their neighbors, seek profitable trade and cultural relationships, including educational exchanges, and otherwise strive to maintain pace with the increasing speed of a global village. For a complex, pluralistic society to function well, all its segments must maintain a positive momentum. When one segment is left behind, a society must direct part of its resources to ameliorating the conditions that cause a gap in development. If it cannot do so, through either a lack of resources or a lack of will, then its entire social fabric becomes weakened.

A sound society, with all parts respected and engaged, and able to ensure the most basic human rights of all its members, comes neither quickly nor cheaply. But in evaluating the human, social, cultural, security, and economic costs exacted by the plight of marginalized young people, the toll of inaction is immensely greater. And this toll will continue to drain the strength of future generations.

NOTES

1. http://www.ohchr.org/EN/ProfessionalInterest/Pages/CRC.aspx
2. Homer, *The Odyssey,* New York: Simon and Brown, 2012, Book 23.
3. Epicurus, "Principle Doctrines," no. 31, translated by Robert Drew Hicks, cf http://classics.mit.edu/Epicurus/princdoc.html and http://www.epicurus.net/en/principal.html

4. Plato, *The Republic of Plato.* Trans., Francis Macdonald Cornford. New York: Oxford University Press, Book 2, p. 376.
5. Philo, *The Works of Philo: Complete and Unabridged, New Updated Edition,* C.D. Yonge, translator, Peabody, Massachusetts, 1993.
6. Maimonides, *Mishneh Torah,* "Laws Concerning Gifts for the Poor," 7:5.
7. http://saints.sqpn.com/saint-nicholas-of-myra/
8. http://saints.sqpn.com/saint-bathilde/
9. I. A. Arshed. "Parent-Child Relationship in Islam", Islam 101, Retrieved, April 5, 2010 http://www.islam101.com/sociology/parchild.htm
10. Saheeh Bukhari, as quoted by http://www.islamreligion.com/articles/3584/viewall/#_ftn21343
11. *Buddha-nature* is concerned with ascertaining what allows sentient beings to become *Buddhas* or reach the state of enlightenment. In Buddhist thought, this is the fundamental nature of all beings.
12. Birnbaum, Raoul, *The Healing Buddha,* Boston, Shambala Press, 1979.
13. Gautama Sutras 28:33–34 accessed at http://www.hinduwebsite.com/sacredscripts/hinduism/dharma/gautama2.asp#ch28
14. http://hinduismfacts.org/
15. Dr. Katherine Carlson, "The Bildungsroman Projet: Childhood in the enlightenment," Chapel Hill, NC, 2014; http://bildungsromanproject.com/childhood-in-the-enlightenment/
16. http://www.nationalarchives.gov.uk/education/resources/1833-factory-act/
17. Carpenter, Mary (1851). *Reformatory Schools: For the Children of the Perishing and Dangerous Classes and for Juvenile Offenders.* London: C. Gilpin. pp. 38–39.
18. http://www.legislation.gov.uk/ukpga/1889/44/pdfs/ukpga_18890044_en.pdf
19. http://www.savethechildren.org/site/c.8rKLIXMGIpI4E/b.6354847/k.2DD5/The_Woman_Who_Saved_the_Children.htm
20. http://en.unesco.org/themes/education-21st-century
21. http://www.unicef.org/about/who/index_history.html
22. http://wcd.nic.in/icds.htm
23. http://timesofindia.indiatimes.com/city/varanasi/ICDS-has-had-only-limited-impact/articleshow/9881755.cms
24. "The Lost Generation," *The Economist,* May 1, 2013; and www.unicef.org/socialpolicy/files/Global_Crisis_and_Youth_Bulge_-_FINAL.pdf
25. "Global Youth Unemployment: A Ticking Timebomb," *The Guardian,* March 27, 2013.
26. http://www.unicef.org/media/files/Generation_2015_and_beyond_15_Nov2012_e_version.pdf., p.3.
27. http://www.unicef.org/media/files/Generation_2015_and_beyond_15_Nov2012_e_version.pdf., p.10.

28. http://www.unicef.org/media/files/Generation_2015_and_beyond_15_Nov2012_e_version.pdf., p.7.
29. http://www.un.org/esa/population/publications/worldage-ing19502050/pdf/80chapterii.pdf., p.1.
30. In the United States, *children of color* are defined as children who identify as African–American, American Indian, Asian and Pacific Islander, Latino, or two or more races. This term is being used as an alternative to *minority children*, in order to recognize the changing demographics in the United States, where *children of color* no longer represent a minority of all children.
31. http://www.unicef.org/protection/57929_57990.html; cf. *The State of America's Children 2014*, Children's Defense Fund, p. 4. http://www.childrens-defense.org/child-research-data-publications/state-of-americas-children/2014. Kids Count Policy Report: Race for Results, Annie E. Casey Foundation http://www.aecf.org/KnowledgeCenter/Publications.aspx?pubguid={5B863B11-62C7-41EC-9F7F-6D12125C4DC2}
32. Singh, Susheela, and Jacqueline Darroch. Adding it Up: Costs and Benefits of Contraceptive Services Estimates for 2012, Guttmacher Institute, June 2012.
33. UNICEF, "Adopting a Systems Approach to Child Protection: Key Concepts and Considerations," January 2010, http://www.unicef.org/protection/files/Adapting_Systems_Child_Protection_Jan__2010.pdf.
34. http://www.uis.unesco.org/Education/Documents/unesco-world-atlas-gender-education-2012.pdf, p.47.
35. Robert Balfanz, "Stop Holding Us Back," *The New York Times,* June 7, 2014; http://opinionator.blogs.nytimes.com/2014/06/07/stop-holding-us-back/?module=Search&mabReward=relbias%3Ar
36. http://data.worldbank.org/indicator/SP.POP.DPND.OL/countries?display=map
37. By means of comparison, the sex ratio in Europe is 93.1 boys for every 100 girls, and in Latin America that ratio is 98.
38. Valerie Hudson and Andrea Den Boer, "Missing Women and Bare Branches: Gender Balance and Conflict," Woodrow Wilson International Center for Scholars' Environmental Change and Security Program Report, Issue 11, 2005, p. 20–24.
39. Valerie Hudson and Andrea Den Boer, "Missing Women and Bare Branches: Gender Balance and Conflict," Woodrow Wilson International Center for Scholars' Environmental Change and Security Program Report, Issue 11, 2005, p. 20–24.
40. Jeremy Hsu, "There Are More Boys Than Girls in China and India," *Scientific American*, August 4, 2008.
41. Amartya Sen, "More Than one Million Women are Missing" *New York Review of Books*, December 20, 1990; http://www.nybooks.com/articles/archives/1990/dec/20/more-than-100-million-women-are-missing/

42. Eliza Griswold, "Can General Linder's Special Operations Forces Stop the Next Terrorist Threat?", *New York Times Magazine*, June 13, 2014.

43. Eliza Griswold, "Can General Linder's Special Operations Forces Stop the Next Terrorist Threat?", *New York Times Magazine*, June 13, 2014.

44. Qais Akbar Omar, "Where's My Ghost Money?" *New York Times*, 2013-04-04.

45. Rebecca Winthrop and Corinne Graff, "Beyond Madrasas: Assessing the Links Between Education and Militancy in Pakistan," Center for Universal Education at Brookings, Working Paper 2, 2010.

46. Fergal Keane, *Season of Blood*, London, Penguin Press, 1995.

47. Jim Yardley, "A Village Rape Shatters a Family, and India's Traditional Silence," *New York Times*, 2012-10-27.

48. http://www.bbc.co.uk/search/news/?q=immigration%20riots

49. http://developingchild.harvard.edu/index.php/download_file/-/view/67/

50. http://www.ncbi.nlm.nih.gov/pmc/articles/PMC1122139/

51. http://www.avert.org/aids-impact-africa.htm

52. Bill Gates, Richard Dimbleby Lecture, London, England, U.K., January 29, 2013.

53. Bill Gates, Richard Dimbleby Lecture, London, England, U.K., January 29, 2013.

54. Megumi Makisaka, "Human Trafficking: A Brief Overview," Social Development Notes, World Bank, Issue No. 122, December 2009.

55. http://www.ilo.org/wcmsp5/groups/public/DOUBLEHYPHEN-ed_norm/DOUBLEHYPHEN-relconf/documents/meetingdocument/wcms_106230.pdf

56. Megumi Makisaka, "Human Trafficking: A Brief Overview," Social Development Notes, World Bank, Issue No. 122, December 2009.

57. http://home.uchicago.edu/~ludwigj/papers/HolzerEtAlChildhood Poverty.pdf, p.1.

58. Jad Chaaban and Wendy Cunningham, "Policy Research Working Paper 5753: Measuring the Economic Gain of Investing in Girls: The Girl Effect Dividend," August 2011, p. 31–32.

59. http://www.americanprogress.org/wp-content/uploads/issues/2007/01/pdf/poverty_report.pdf, p.15.

60. UNICEF Innocenti Research Centre, 2012. Measuring Child Poverty: New league tables of child poverty in the world's rich countries, Innocenti Report Card 10, UNICEF, p. 3.

61. http://www.jrf.org.uk/sites/files/jrf/2313.pdf, p.5.

62. http://www.justicepolicy.org/images/upload/09_05_REP_CostsOfConfinement_JJ_PS.pdf, p.1.

63. http://www.mit.edu/~jjdoyle/aizer_doyle_judges_06242013.pdf cf. Nicholas Kristof, "'Jane' Didn't Get the Help She Needed: When the

Juvenile Justice System Isn't the Answer," *New York Times*, June 28, 2014.

64. Nicholas Kristof, "'Jane' Didn't Get the Help She Needed: When the Juvenile Justice System Isn't the Answer," *The New York Times*, June 28, 2014.
65. http://rwanda.usembassy.gov/criminal_justice_in_rwanda.html
66. http://focus.rw/wp/2010/10/national-prison-service-to-transform-penal-system/
67. http://developingchild.harvard.edu/index.php/resources/briefs/inbrief_series/inbrief_the_impact_of_early_adversity/
68. http://opinionator.blogs.nytimes.com/2013/10/30/protecting-children-from-toxic-stress/
69. Tough, Paul, *How Children Succeed,* Houghton Mifflin Harcourt, 2012; cf.   http://www.nytimes.com/2012/08/26/books/review/how-children-succeed-by-paul-tough.html
70. http://www.who.int/mental_health/prevention/suicide/country_reports/en/index.html;   cf.—http://www.who.int/mental_health/prevention/suicide/suicideprevent/en/
71. ILO, (2010). Accelerating action against child labour: Global report under the follow-up to the ILO Declaration on Fundamental Principles and Rights at Work 2010. Geneva: ILO. Cf: Covell, Katherine and Becker, Jo (2011). Five Years On: A Global Update on Violence Against Children, NGO Advisory Council for Follow-up to the UN Study on Violence Against Children, p. 29.
72. Jason Beaubien, "War turning Mexican kids into targets, killers," NPR, 1 May 2011, Cf: Covell, Katherine and Becker, Jo (2011). Five Years On: A Global Update on Violence Against Children, p. 29.
73. Afghanistan: Students play truant to work in Helmand's poppy fields," IRIN, 18 March 2008, Cf: Covell, Katherine and Becker, Jo (2011). Five Years On: A Global Update on Violence Against Children, p. 29.
74. International Human Rights Clinic, Harvard Law School, (2007), "No Place to Hide: Gang, State, and Clandestine Violence in El Salvador," February 2007. Cf: Covell, Katherine and Becker, Jo (2011). Five Years On: A Global Update on Violence Against Children, p. 36.
75. Ward, Catherine L., and Karlijn Bakhuis. 2010. "Intervening in Children's Involvement in Gangs: Views of Cape Town's Young People." *Children & Society* 24, no. 1: 50–62. *Academic Search Complete*, EBSCO*host* (accessed January 2, 2013).
76. Gary Haugen and Victor Boutros, *The Locust Effect*, Oxford University Press, 2013, introduction.
77. http://www.who.int/gho/alcohol/en/
78. Mackay J, Eriksen M, Shafey O. *The Tobacco Atlas*. 2nd edition. Atlanta, GA: American Cancer Society; 2006.

79. Mackay J, Eriksen M, Shafey O. *The Tobacco Atlas*.
80. Lando, Harry et al., 2010. "Tobacco is a Global Pediatric Concern," *Bulletin of the World Health Organization* 2010, 88:2–2.
81. Efroymson D, Hammond R. *Tobacco and Poverty: A Vicious Circle*. Geneva: World Health Organization; 2004.
82. http://www.who.int/substance_abuse/publications/global_alcohol_report/msbgsruprofiles.pdf, p.10.
83. http://www.who.int/substance_abuse/publications/global_alcohol_report/msbgsruprofiles.pdf, p.22.
84. http://www.unodc.org/documents/data-and-analysis/WDR2012/WDR_2012_web_small.pdf, p.4.
85. http://www.unodc.org/documents/data-and-analysis/WDR2012/WDR_2012_web_small.pdf, p.71.
86. http://www.unodc.org/documents/data-and-analysis/WDR2012/WDR_2012_web_small.pdf, p.88.
87. http://www.casacolumbia.org/addiction-research/reports/adolescent-substance-use
88. http://www.casacolumbia.org/addiction-research/reports/adolescent-substance-use
89. "Substance Abuse Among Rural Youth: A Little Meth and a Lot of Booze," Maine Rural Health Research Center, Muskie School of Public Service Research and Policy Brief, 2007.
90. http://www.crchealth.com/troubled-teenagers/teenage-substance-abuse/adolescent-substance-abuse/meth-use-among-youth/
91. Ben Garvin, "Heroin's Small Town Toll, and a Mother's Pain," *New York Times*, February 11, 2014; http://www.nytimes.com/2014/02/11/us/heroins-small-town-toll-and-a-mothers-pain.html
92. Khat (*Catha edulis*) is a flowering plant that is native to the Horn of Africa and the Arabian Peninsula. It contains a monoamine alkaloid called cathinone, an amphetamine-like stimulant, which is said to cause excitement, loss of appetite, and euphoria.
93. Bulletin of the World Health Organization, Volume 86, Number 10, October 2008, 737–816.
94. Bulletin of the World Health Organization, Volume 86, Number 10, October 2008, 737–816.
95. Anders Kelto, "Nairobi Glue Pusher Preys on Addicted Kids to Help her Own," Public Radio International, *PRI's The World*, 2012-10-29.
96. "Adolescent Inhalant Use and Selected Respiratory Conditions," Substance Abuse and Mental Health Services Administration, Department of Health and Human Services, 2010.
97. Luthar, Suniya S. "The Construct of Resilience: A Critical Evaluation and Guidelines for Future Work," *Child Development*, 2000, pp. 543–562.

98. Ungar, M., "Resilience Across Culture," *British Journal of Social Work*, 2008, pp. 210–235.

99. Numerous studies of the impact of trauma on these demographic groups exist, including Suarez-Orosco, C., Rhodes, J., Milburn, M., "Unraveling the Immigrant Paradox: Academic Engagement and Disengagement Among Recently Arrived Immigrant Youth," *Youth and Society*, 2009; Eggerman, M., "Suffering, Hope and Entrapment: Resilience and Cultural Values in Afghanistan," *Social Science and Medicine*, 2010; and Boothby, Neil, "When Former Child Soldiers Grow Up," *A World Turned Upside Down*, 2006.

100. The OECD has 34 member countries including the United States, Canada, most of Western Europe, and other wealthy economies, as well as emerging countries like Mexico, Chile, and Turkey.

101. http://www.oecd.org/els/soc/49499779.pdf, p.22.

102. http://www.oecd.org/els/soc/49499779.pdf, p.22.

103. http://www.younglives.org.uk/publications and Save the Children UK, *Young Lives: An International Study of Childhood Poverty*, Oxford, UK, p.5.

104. Young Lives is a longitudinal study of child poverty following the lives of approximately 12,000 young people over a 15-year period in four countries—Ethiopia, India, Peru, and Vietnam. The study follows groups of children born in 1994–1995 and 2001–2002 in each country, relying upon extensive household surveys and qualitative research.

105. http://www.younglives.org.uk/publications and Save the Children UK, *Young Lives: An International Study of Childhood Poverty*, Oxford, UK, p.6.

106. J.H. Lopez, *Pro-Poor Growth: A Review of What We Know (And of What We Don't)*, World Bank, 2004.

107. http://www.younglives.org.uk/publications and Save the Children UK, *Young Lives: An International Study of Childhood Poverty*, Oxford, UK, p.6.

108. http://www.younglives.org.uk/publications and Save the Children UK, *Young Lives: An International Study of Childhood Poverty*, Oxford, UK, p.23.

109. http://www.who.int/bulletin/volumes/87/3/08-052175/en/index.html

110. http://www.younglives.org.uk/publications and Save the Children UK, *Young Lives: An International Study of Childhood Poverty*, Oxford, UK, p.17.

CHAPTER 4

A Glass Half Full; A Glass Half Empty

On February 3, 2012, *The New York Times* reported that in Kabul, Afghanistan, at least 22 young children froze to death because the camp they called home had neither heat nor electricity. The city is a major center for the distribution of more than $3.5 billion in international humanitarian assistance and $58 billion in development assistance over the past decade, all administered by more than 2000 aid groups. But none of that assistance filtered to these children who perished from the predictable cold of a predictable winter.[1]

In December 2013, *The Times* reported again that more children were already starting to die for the same reasons as the previous winter.[2] In the intervening year, nothing, apparently, had changed. No lessons had been learned.

The Afghan children represent, sadly, a microcosm of systemic breakdowns that keep the marginalized on the margins. Efficient, effective, targeted programs to lift children and young people out of their despair have become exceptionally difficult to coordinate. Well-meaning bureaucracies impede the delivery of critical resources to populations that might not fit cleanly into preconceived guidelines. Program administrators of international nongovernmental organizations (INGOs)[3] and multilateral organizations, often underfunded and facing immense pressures to deliver aid in a timely fashion, too frequently do not look outside their immediate programmatic boxes to see the broader landscape.

© The Editor(s) (if applicable) and The Author(s) 2016
M. Ajmera, G.A. Fields, *Invisible Children*,
DOI 10.1057/978-1-137-57838-9_4

The scope and complexity of challenges facing children worldwide has generated its own range of responses. Millions of individuals and thousands of organizations are directing their work to alleviate these challenges. Yet clearly the whole of these efforts is less than the sum of their parts, and we are left looking at a glass that is only half full.

THE IMPACT OF FOREIGN AID—A GLASS HALF FULL

Since 1990 there has been drastic improvement in the outcomes measuring the general state of the world's children. Poverty alleviation efforts and health-based initiatives launched both by multilateral institutions and by individual governments have touched the lives of millions of young people, evidenced by a number of quantifiable facts.

For example, the absolute number of deaths of children under five has been reduced from 12.5 million in 1990 to 6.6 million in 2012, and under-five mortality rates have been reduced from 90 deaths/1000 live births to 48 deaths/1000 births.[4] There has been success, too, in combating the impact of individual diseases. Polio, as noted, has been almost completely eliminated, although pockets of the disease appear in societies disrupted by civil violence. Childhood death from measles declined 71% globally from 2000 to 2011, and new cases dropped 58%.[5]

Even HIV/AIDS, which has run rampant through low-income parts of the world for two decades, is being beaten back: in 14 of 17 countries surveyed, the number of pregnant women living with HIV has declined, and in seven of these countries the decline has been at least 25%.[6] In 2000, only 10% of all African children in need were able to access antiretroviral treatments. That figure had increased to 34% by 2012.[7]

Addressing mother-to-child transmission (MTCT) of the disease through an aggressive regimen of antiretroviral drugs administered either during pregnancy or immediately after birth has driven MTCT rates downward. Each year, nearly 1.5 million women living with HIV become pregnant, and without intervention their children run a risk approaching 40% of becoming infected with the virus. With treatment, though, this rate can run as low as 5%. Nevirapine (NVP) can be taken only once a day, an innovation that makes treatment much simpler. Since 1995, more than 350,000 children have avoided contracting the disease through these interventions.[8]

In all, 17,000 fewer children died each day in 2012 than in 1990, thanks to more effective and affordable treatments, innovative ways of delivering critical interventions to those in poverty, and a sustained political commitment. These and other vital child survival interventions have helped to save an estimated 90 million lives in the past two decades.[9]

Significantly, some of the biggest gains against child mortality have been made by some of the world's lowest-income countries, such as Bangladesh, Ethiopia, Malawi, and Nepal, all of which have reduced their child mortality rates by at least two-thirds since 1990.[10] A combination of political will, external resources, focused service delivery programs, and coordination of sectors has brought about these successes, although there remains much ground to travel. Even so, this data confirms the expectation that even the world's weakest economies can foster dramatic social improvements on behalf of their youngest citizens.

The Millennium Development Goals—A Good Start

At the United Nations Millennium Summit in 2000, member nations adopted eight Millennium Development Goals (MDGs) with the broad aspiration of reducing extreme poverty throughout the globe by 2015. Each goal carried with it specific targets and benchmark dates for meeting those targets. All 189 member nations, and 23 multilateral organizations, approved these goals and committed financial resources and human capital to reaching them. Never before has the world seen such a coordinated, well-articulated, goal-driven collective effort to address deep-rooted social complexities that lead to poverty and marginalization.[11]

Accordingly, the level of foreign engagement in low-income societies spiked since the adoption of the MDGs. Initial results reflect the impact of this coordinated action. MDG Goal 1 was the reduction of extreme poverty, including halving the number of people suffering from hunger between 1990 and 2015. Global underweight prevalence in children under the age of five has decreased from 31% to 26% by 2008, an early indication that children are getting more and better food.[12] And as part of this focus, the United States Agency for International Development (USAID) serviced more than 12 million children under five globally through its nutrition programs in 2012.[13]

MDG Goal 2 was the achievement of universal primary education, and the numbers to meet this goal are also moving in the right direction: The number of children out of primary school was reduced from 115 million in 2002[14] to 57 million today,[15] with almost 90% of children entering primary school remaining until their final year.[16] It is important to note, though, that huge gains in the major fast-growing economies of India and China have fueled most of this improvement. With those two countries factored out, the indices do not look as bright.

In June 2012, the governments of the United States, India, and Ethiopia, in conjunction with UNICEF, convened the Child Survival Call to Action.[17] The result was *A Promise Renewed*, an initiative to enhance efforts to end preventable child deaths. More than 175 governments and multilaterals have signed on, with commensurate pledges of financial support. *A Promise Renewed* focused on MDG Goals 4 and 5, reducing child mortality rates and improving maternal health, respectively.

The impact of HIV/AIDS and other infectious diseases has received much emphasis over the past two decades. MDG Goal 6, combating HIV/AIDS, malaria, and other diseases, has shown progress. The availability of antiretroviral treatments is expanding in Africa, and millions of treated antimalaria mosquito nets have been distributed. But just as encouraging is the increased reintegration of AIDS orphans into their societies. School attendance among AIDS orphans has nearly reached parity with nonorphans, an indication that programs targeting educational assistance to these orphans are having an impact.[18]

With the expiration of the original timetable for the MDGs in 2015, the evaluation of a post-2015 agenda became a high priority for the world community. Within this framework, the opportunity clearly existed for children's issues to receive a higher priority. The multilaterals and the INGOs lent their thoughts forcefully to these considerations as the successor to the MDGs—the Sustainable Development Goals (SDGs)—were evaluated and eventually adopted.

David Thomson of World Vision UK has stressed that new goals need to focus on the hardest to reach, committing to the full eradication of poverty, hunger, and abuse, with children at the center of this framework.[19] Save the Children has echoed this call for full eradication, adding the goals of all children receiving a quality education and that all children be protected from all forms of violence, including civil conflict.[20] Ban Ki-moon, UN Secretary-General, has said that these new development goals must be rights-based and emphasize women, young people, and marginalized groups through partnerships.[21]

The conversations among stakeholders from 88 countries in developing the SDGs were unprecedented, reflecting participation in the decisions and evaluations of what should be included and emphasized. Conferences, workshops, meetings, and online discussions brought immense amounts of information and viewpoints to the table.

The SDGs present a stronger platform for children than did the MDGs. Issues that the MDGs did not address, including reducing inequality, ending violence against children, and combating child poverty, are clearly stated in the SDGs. Many of the individual goals carry valuable applications to the plight of the most marginalized children: Goal 2—End hunger, achieve food security, and improved nutrition—specifically targets acute malnutrition, stunting, and wasting among children; Goal 3—Ensure healthy lives—sets targets for maternal mortality, newborn, and under-five death; and Goal 16—Promote peaceful and inclusive societies for sustainable development; provide access to justice for all; and build effective, accountable, and inclusive institutions at all levels—requires states to provide legal identity for all, including birth registration, the basis for legal recognition in countries throughout the world and, as noted in Chap. 2, something that 50 million children do not have.[22]

UNICEF

Among all multilateral efforts, UNICEF continues to play a leading role in impacting the lives of the most marginalized. UNICEF's mandate has always encompassed children on the edges of society, and they have developed interventions that have had demonstrable impact.

In 2011 alone, UNICEF's work provided vaccinations, deworming, and vitamin A supplements for more than 36 million children, treated more than 1.2 million children for malnutrition, and helped nearly a million children access child protection services in their home countries.[23] The organization also provided essential food and medicine to children in crisis situations, ranging from the drought in the Horn of Africa to floods in Pakistan. Their work necessarily focuses on countries with the greatest immediate needs, often sparked by natural disasters and civil conflicts. As a result, much of their energy has recently been devoted to countries such as Haiti, the Democratic Republic of Congo (DRC), South Sudan, and Syria.[24]

In an alliance with the World Health Organization and the International Council for Control of Iodine Deficiency Disorders, UNICEF has made huge inroads into iodine deficiency, which is the world's most prevalent cause of impaired cognitive development in children. Through a policy of universal salt iodization adopted in 1993 and in place ever since, 66% of all global households now have access to iodized salt. As a result, the number of countries where iodine deficiency is a public health problem is half what it was ten years ago. The World Health Organization projects that iodine deficiency is close to total elimination, an achievement which it believes would be as significant as the elimination of smallpox or polio.[25]

The UNICEF Innovation Unit, a special initiative since 2007, seeks to engage organizations and individuals from the public, private, and academic sectors to facilitate the development of new projects, models, and approaches based on the real needs of the most marginalized. Practical and effective projects have arisen through the Innovation Unit, including a major effort in Nigeria to improve birth registration through the use of SMS technology. In Uganda, the Innovation Unit sponsored a program called Ureport in which weekly questions are sent via SMS to 250,000 young people to gather information about what was happening in their communities. Collected information, and the implications that information sheds on the conditions of children at various social levels, is shared with parliamentarians so that policies could be evaluated and altered. In such a way Ugandan young people are now connected directly with their government.[26]

USAID

We cannot ignore other major actors that have been able to address long-standing conditions and bring needed change to the lives of the most marginalized children. The most significant of US agencies is USAID, established in 1961 and currently budgeted in excess of $20 billion annually.[27] USAID's mission is "to end extreme poverty and to promote resilient, democratic societies while advancing our security and prosperity."[28] Its work entails the major areas of disaster relief, poverty relief, and technical cooperation on global issues, including the environment, socio-economic development, and US bilateral interests.[29] USAID missions in 128 countries oversee and coordinate funded projects, implemented in partnership with national governments, multilateral organizations, and INGOs.[30]

In the war-torn DRC, children are regularly coerced into joining one of the fighting factions. Girls who are forcibly conscripted face high level of gender-based violence, including forced marriage and sexual slavery. Upon escape, reintegration for both boys and girls into their communities is problematic because families may reject them and communities distrust them or seek to hold them accountable for real or imaginary acts of war. A USAID program that burrows into these communities has helped these young people through door-to-door outreach and meetings with community leaders, counseling, family mediation, health care, education, skills training, and economic assistance. In its first year, 1905 young people, 1039 of whom were girls, repatriated safely to their home communities.[31]

Other examples are easy to find. USAID has saved roughly three million lives globally each year through its immunization programs,[32] and PEPFAR, the President's Emergency Plan for AIDS Relief, supported antiretroviral drug prophylaxis to prevent MTCT for nearly 750,000 women who tested positive for HIV, allowing approximately 230,000 infants to be born HIV-free.[33]

Other Actors

Good work is not reserved for government programs alone: In 2012, Save the Children helped more than nine million children through their emergency response programs, providing food, shelter, and health care to the victims of Typhoon Haiyan in the Philippines, in Syria, in South Sudan, and in East Africa's food crisis.[34] That same year, Save the Children provided health and nutritional support to more than 25 million young people and reached nearly 40 million through their HIV/AIDS programs.[35]

Responding to a growing awareness of the plight of vulnerable children and young people, governments, multilaterals, and international organizations have stepped up. Perhaps most encouraging in all of this is the coordinated, collective action of initiatives such as the MDGs, a recognition that the best actions are taken together and that the impact of foreign investments might best be leveraged in cooperative applications. There can be no minimizing the impact of these efforts. Millions of young lives have been positively changed, redirected, and saved by the aggressive interventions fueled by public monies directed to attack the debilitating conditions of poverty, exploitation, inequality, and disease.

Public–private partnerships pursuing innovative approaches to children's issues offer great promise. The GAVI Alliance, formerly the Global Alliance for Vaccines and Immunization, brings together host country and donor governments, the World Health Organization, UNICEF, the World Bank, the pharmaceutical industry, research and technical agencies, civil society, the Bill and Melinda Gates Foundation, and other private philanthropists to provide immunizations to children in the world's 73 lowest-income countries.[36]

GAVI widely distributes the pentavalent vaccine (Penta), a five-in-one immunization against tetanus, diphtheria, pertussis or whooping cough, Hepatitis B, and *Haemophilus influenzae* B, which causes pneumonia and meningitis. This combined approach has several advantages, including reducing the number of injections to combat these diseases from nine if they were approached singularly to a total of three Penta immunizations. Fewer injections mean less distress for children and parents. Shipping costs for the combined medicines are lower, and so the entire project is more cost-efficient than singular inoculations.[37]

Penta is currently being used in around 170 countries, and low-income children are increasingly being given the vaccine. UNICEF purchased 97 million doses in 2010, and that number had grown to 550 million by 2015.[38]

High-income countries have directed vast amounts of resources to humanitarian efforts, disease eradication, relief, rehabilitation, and reconstruction of damaged societies. Well respected and effective groups operating across a spectrum of situations have accomplished immense good. The efforts of organizations such as UNICEF, World Vision, Save the Children, American Red Cross, Catholic Relief Services, and many more have resulted in measurable improvements in infant mortality, child literacy, nutrition, and access to medical services. Their work—supplemented and supported by major governmental donors such as USAID and its counterparts in the UK, Norway, Ireland, and Sweden, with other bilateral programs—must remain a central aspect of any comprehensive strategy.

THE IMPACT OF FOREIGN AID—A GLASS HALF EMPTY

Despite these gains, though, we have not seen a "turning point" impact on the conditions of the majority of children worldwide. Time and again, we see how programs that may be effective in the moment lack sustainability once their sponsoring organizations shift focus, lose their funding for specific initiatives, or otherwise pull out of the arenas in which they are working. We see programs with delivery systems that fail to reach the children at the farthest edges, those who remain invisible. We see a glass half empty.

The MDGs and SDGs, Revisited

We have cited some of the remarkable gains measured through the MDGs. But the goals can be helpful too in measuring the depth of the continuing crises. For example, despite its gains, MDG Goal 1—eradicate extreme poverty and hunger—sputtered. Only half of all countries are on track to achieve the target for reducing underweight children, a key indicator. Children in rural areas in low-income societies are 1.5 times more likely to be stunted as urban children and twice as likely to be underweight. And in low-income countries only 39% of newborns are breast-fed within an hour of delivery, a factor which can reduce neonatal mortality by as much as 20%.[39]

The rapidly emerging economies of India and China have skewed many of the averages concerning development and the welfare of children. With huge populations, these two countries carry a disproportionate weight in all indices. Moreover, their strengthening economies have rewritten their demographics to an extent, and each country now has lower percentages of people in poverty than it did two decades ago. Pressing problems definitely remain in each country. But their sheer size, coupled with their economic expansion, skews many of the global indices used to measure progress against these issues.

Access to primary education, MDG Goal 2, has, as shown earlier, made good progress, but 57 million children worldwide still remain out of school. [40] More than half—52%—are girls. And again the geographic disparities are striking: in sub-Saharan Africa, only 65% of all primary-age children are attending school.[41] We can understand the depth of these disparities by examining the raw numbers. South Asia, with its massive populations in India and Bangladesh, has 33 million children out of school, while the less densely settled regions of West and Central Africa have 25 million.[42] Un-enrollment rates are bound to be erratic. And even if primary school is accessible, too often the educational road stops there. Excluding China, only 42% of children in the developing world are able to go beyond primary school to secondary school.[43]

And these figures do not speak to the quality of education provided. All schools are not equal, and many lack facilities, well-trained or motivated teachers, and educational materials. They are warehouses, keeping young people occupied in one place for part of the day, and so can be counted as "schools" even though those who attend them gain little from the experience.

Despite gains in child mortality rates, too many children under the age of five are still dying: 25,000 each day, mostly from preventable or treatable causes.[44] For too many, medicines and vaccinations are not getting through. In South Asia, only 18% of children under five suffering from pneumonia receive antibiotics, and in sub-Saharan Africa less than a third of those with diarrhea receive oral rehydration treatments.[45]

The accident of location goes a long way in determining a child's odds for survival: child mortality in Luxembourg is 2 per 1000 live births, while in Sierra Leone, the ratio is 182.[46] Sub-Saharan Africa and South Asia account for more than four out of every five deaths under the age of five. The problem in sub-Saharan Africa merits special attention. By mid-century, this will be the region with the single largest population of children under five, accounting for 37% of the global total and close to 40% of all live births. And, because it is the region making the least progress on under-five mortality, too many of these children will be born from their mothers' wombs into great jeopardy.[47] About half of under-five deaths occur in only five countries: India, Nigeria, the DRC, Pakistan, and China. Between them, India (22%) and Nigeria (13%) account for more than a third of all under-five deaths.[48]

The progress in reducing child mortality rates is markedly uneven. West and Central Africa is the only region not to have halved its rate of under-five mortality since 1990, and it is the only region to have seen virtually no reduction in the absolute number of children dying over the past two decades. That stagnant number still stands at approximately two million deaths annually.[49]

Even at the current rate of reduction in child mortality, the world failed to meet MDG Goal 4—reducing under-five mortality rates by two-thirds—by its 2015 goal. In fact, if current progress were to be maintained and not enhanced, that goal would not be reached until 2028, and 35 million more children will have died.[50]

The leading causes of death for those under five are rooted in poverty and a lack of adequate medical care. Pneumonia claims 17% of all under-five deaths, followed by preterm birth complications (15%) and complications during birth (10%). Diarrhea and malaria each account for slightly less than 10% of these deaths. Adequate medical care during pregnancy and access to simple and effective interventions would drive these figures down dramatically.[51]

Despite the attention directed to HIV/AIDS and infectious disease eradication (MDG Goal 6), vast problems remain. We can feel good about improved numbers and declining infection rates but we cannot lose sight of the millions who have yet to see the benefits of these trends. And there are indeed millions.

In 2008, of the 33.4 million people living with HIV, 4.9 million were between the ages of 15 and 24, and 40% of all new infections are currently in this age group.[52] In 2011, there were 3.4 million HIV-positive children younger than 15.[53] Despite vigorous efforts at public education, many young people are out of reach. In low-income countries, only 31% of young men and 19% of young women had comprehensive knowledge of HIV/AIDS and effective prevention practices.[54] Malaria and other diseases are far from memories of the past. In 2012, malaria killed an estimated 627,000 people, 90% of whom were in sub-Saharan Africa, and over two-thirds were children under five.[55]

MDG Goal 7, ensuring environmental stability, has also had its share of shortcomings. Despite gains, 884 million people still lack access to safe drinking water. The problem remains particularly acute in rural areas, where 84% still lack access, but it is not confined there. The poorest quintile in urban areas has significantly lower access to safe water than their fellow citizens.[56] Sanitation access shows similar concerns. Only 40% of rural dwellers in low-income countries have access to adequate sanitation, and at least 1.1 billion people worldwide are still practicing open defecation.[57]

Migration from rural areas to cities has strained already thin service systems in areas that have become slums. Those left behind in the rural areas often found themselves with fewer services as resources were redirected to the cities to try to cope with the burgeoning emigration.[58] These migrations have also helped bring about an urban–rural demographic divide. Over a billion children now live in cities and towns, and by 2050, 70% of the world's population will be urban. With infrastructures straining to keep pace with this growth, many more urban children will find themselves with inadequate water, sanitation, health care, or education. Even today, hundreds of thousands of urban children live close to schools and hospitals but have no access to them.[59]

The variables attendant upon international development and foreign assistance programs remain volatile. The last few years have seen global financial crises, food shortages, natural disasters triggered by climate change, rapid urbanization, and civil conflicts, all of which have had graphic impact on the issues affecting children and young people and the assistance programs that seek to reach them. The gains of the MDGs were clearly fluid and vulnerable to these influences, which thrust new variables into an already overly challenged development dynamic.

The MDGs have guided, and the SDGs will guide, much of the world's efforts to alleviate poverty and want, but it is critical to note that they are subjective goals, drafted by the consensus of a limited group of decision makers. They cannot, nor should they, be considered the absolute determinant for the work at hand. Poverty issues cannot be summarized in eight goals, no matter how well crafted or reasoned. Real problems impacting real children and young people have invariably been left out of these incomplete equations.

There is a reason that the original MDG goals pointed to poverty reduction rates of only two-thirds or three-quarters. Reaching those on the outermost edges of society is costly. The logistical challenges of finding and impacting the lives of children in the most abject circumstances drains the resources of those coming into a society from the outside, and the expenses of service delivery to these children, even if they are found, can be daunting. The MDGs at their best aimed for incomplete successes.

The transition from the MDGs to the SDGs received considerable study and went through numerous drafts. The preliminary draft of the SDGs received robust criticism from those who noted that, while the MDGs had eight goals with 21 target actions described in 374 words, this draft had 17 goals with 169 target actions encompassing 4369 words.[60] *The Economist* determined that implementation of these actions would require a $2–3 trillion investment over 15 years, or roughly 4 % of the world's GDP, even though Western governments have promised only 0.7 % of their GDP to these efforts and in the past delivered even less than that. They concluded that the SDG draft was the result of input from every conceivable lobby and special interest, and that including everything dilutes the setting of priorities.[61]

As sweeping as the SDGs might be, children and young people still remain largely outside the equation. In the final document, "child" or "children" appears just 24 times, "youth" 14 times, "girls" 16 times, and "boys" just five times.[62] Children were mentioned specifically in only 8 of the 17 goals, girls in only three, and boys in just one.[63]

But in reviewing the participants of the workshops whose input helped craft the SDGs, and in noting the composition of the leadership directing the development of this new phase, the presence of CBO leaders, grassroots organizations, and representatives of lower-income societies were notably thin. The intent of the SDGs is laudable, but their success will be contingent upon the work on the ground. The voices of those who are closest to the ground, who view every day what works and what does not, must be involved in devising any comprehensive strategy.

Money and funding does not ensure wisdom: wisdom comes best from the hard experience of working with children others have difficulty seeing. Without these voices, any strategy or set of goals will necessarily be academic and crafted with incomplete knowledge of the realities on the ground.

Financial Woes and Other Challenges

The global financial crisis spurred economic vulnerability worldwide, bringing with it higher unemployment, reduced or lost income, and eradication of financial reserves. Children in the lowest-income households absorbed more than their share of the burden. Aside from the tendency to bond children into labor situations, remove them from school, or displace them altogether from stable environments—all products of financial desperation—the crisis undercut the purchasing power of households across the globe and those in poverty suffered disproportionately.[64] Donor countries feeling their own financial constraints struggled to meet their financial commitments to foreign assistance programs. As a result, publicly supported multilaterals and country-based aid programs remain chronically underfunded.[65]

Despite the relevance of UNICEF programs in addressing the needs of the world's most marginalized children, and despite the collective response of governments to the MDGs, UNICEF often finds itself making do with underfunded budgets. In 2011, UNICEF's operating budget for all programs was approximately $1.6 billion, yet it received only $854 million from government donors. Many of its programs failed to reach their targets as a result. In the Philippines, for example, only 22,000 children were equipped for school, less than a third of their 75,000 goal. UNICEF's program in South Sudan made do with only 36% of its funding.[66] Much of UNICEF's funding is given in response to particular situations, including natural disasters, or is thematically or regionally restricted. The European Commission remains the organization's largest funder, with the United States and Japan relatively close behind.[67]

But financial hardships were just one of these destructive variables. Climate changes and drought led to diminished food supplies in some regions, in turn contributing to undernutrition and stunting. Beyond that, climate change has endangered people in extreme poverty because of their insufficient shelter, disproportionate exposure to pollutants, and inadequate sanitation. With poorer infrastructures and lack of sophisticated emergency systems, the developing world bears the brunt of the natural emanations of climate change, including flooding and major storms.[68] Low- and lower-middle income countries experienced 97% of all fatalities brought about by natural disasters in 2008, and that trend has continued through the most recent natural crises.[69]

Through it all, the data used for analysis of these conditions is itself subject to question. Most low-income countries do not have systemic data collection processes, and especially in marginalized communities populations are fluid. The children in these communities are often invisible, uncounted, and completely overlooked. Accordingly, it is exceedingly difficult to track uniform populations from year to year. It is also difficult to establish baselines, identify trends, and quantify impact with complete surety.[70]

The most marginalized often remain outside the reach of systemic interventions, and the data that tracks their impact. Most programs simply do not see them. Raj Panjabi, the founder of Last Mile Health, which provides community-based health care in Liberia, explained that the world celebrates a two-thirds reduction in child mortality but becomes complacent about the one-third that remains, the one-third for which nothing has changed: "the children at the last mile in remote villages, ...invisible children in slums... they don't count. They don't count in the analysis, they don't count in the intervention and they don't count in the way the intervention is judged for impact."[71]

Even if imprecise, the data tells us things. It tells us that the launch of sustained, collective foreign assistance programs, in coordination among governments, multilaterals, and private aid organizations, is having an impact on the numbers of children and young people living in desperate situations. It tells us, too, that the compendium of gains to date has still left millions of children beyond help and out of reach. While we can and should be pleased with the improvements in the lives of certain sectors of young people in low-income societies, we cannot be either satisfied or complacent with the results.

PROMISES AND FAILURES

The United States became involved in material aid to other countries for the first time during World War I. Beginning in 1914, the United States sent more than $387 million in assistance over the ensuing four years to the Committee for Relief in Belgium. Following the Great War, future president Herbert Hoover led the American Relief Administration, to oversee the distribution of food and medicines across postwar Europe. By 1925, the United States had become a leader in foreign assistance to devastated regions.[72]

Following World War II, the United States expanded foreign assistance as a diplomatic and humanitarian policy through its adoption of the European Recovery Program known as the Marshall Plan. This huge undertaking helped establish the potential and promise of foreign aid and, to this day, remains the bellwether of what strategic assistance can accomplish in rebuilding shattered societies. Over a four-year period, the United States disbursed approximately $12.5 billion in aid to war-torn European countries to rebuild infrastructure, spur economic recovery, and stabilize currencies.[73]

The perceived success of these early efforts, the Marshall Plan in particular, led to an assumption in US policy circles that foreign assistance could carry enormous benefits to both the recipients and the donor nation. The Marshall Plan had a graphic impact in the reconstruction of Western Europe. The infusion of dollars into societies whose economies and infrastructures lay in ruins, and whose populations had scattered, quickened the pace toward full functionality. Observers on both sides of the Atlantic saw Europe become itself again much more quickly than experts had anticipated.

Even so, the Plan's emphasis was on economic rather than humanitarian assistance, and it came with a heavily politicized agenda. Economic stability in postwar Western Europe, especially stability linked closely to US interests, kept recipient countries in the American orbit and staunched the westward march of the Communist bloc. Humanitarian relief was secondary to establishing a buffer against Soviet influence and stifling incendiary political movements that fed on deprivation and ruin. The Marshall Plan stemmed from a recognition that socioeconomic repair, as essential as it was, carried with it strong political benefits.[74]

A Donor-Driven Approach

In effect, US foreign assistance, and to varying extents the assistance offered by almost all donor nations, is tailored to the donor's perception of what this aid should look like rather than to the recipient's needs. Often there is a confluence between the two perceptions. If a recipient country has thousands of hungry children that need feeding, and a donor provides the means to do so, then assistance has a common basis. Even if the donor provides that assistance because of enlightened self-interest that improves its position within the recipient country, stabilizes the socioeconomic conditions of the country, enlists a political ally, or whatever form the self-interest might take, in the end, hungry children are fed.

But if a beneficiary community aligns its own structures to reflect the donor's perception, then an inherent tension arises. Aid becomes a tool of manipulation, and possibly exclusion. Recipients eager for assistance in any form may adjust their own priorities to suit the donor's preferences.[75] For example, a recipient country with thousands of hungry children may shift resources away from nutritional support in response to a donor's emphasis on education or health care. The children may remain hungry, although they might be receiving important vaccinations or have a new school building in their village. They may receive HIV/AIDS antiretroviral drugs, but they may still die from malnutrition.

Imposition of specific programs by donor countries can be seen as paternalistic, and at times out of touch with realities on the ground. Donors most often develop initiatives based on perceptions within their own circles. This in itself creates the potential for misallocation based on misunderstanding at best or, at worst, a desire to impose those perceptions on the recipient country. Based on this is the assumption that donor countries, through their programs, could supply all of the necessary conditions for development that recipient countries lack. Programs arrive wholly packaged, complete with implementation strategies, output measurements, and operational deadlines. In their conception nothing is left out. But what is often lacking is the input of the recipients.[76]

To be effective, development must be dynamic. Implementing a program is necessarily a first step in a process that ideally points to sustainability. The best programs adjust to circumstances that may have been unforeseen or arise from shifting social, political, or economic realities. Predrawn strategies from faraway organizations often lack this flexibility and their program administrators, who are not indigenous and are operating from general rather than culturally specific guidelines, often lack this dynamism. Such programs deal with the situation at hand, in prescribed and well-defined ways, but are not drawn with an eye toward long-range development. As such, these programs live in the moment, and when they conclude, the moment is done and nothing follows.

A Lack of Transparency

For much of its history, USAID has financed large-scale, top-down projects implemented by major INGO partners that followed traditional development schemas. But while USAID has devoted increasing attention, at least verbally, to the issues of marginalized and impoverished children, it is exceptionally difficult to determine the exact pathways that assistance has taken. Accuracy and accountability for USAID investments in children is in short supply.

While interagency reports on US Government Assistance to Children in Adversity indicate specific aid to children equaling $2.67 billion in FY2010 (the last reporting year), distributed through 1710 projects spanning various agencies, most of that assistance falls into top-down funding categories, such as food programs or disease mitigation efforts.[77] Roughly 70% of this total, or $1.8 billion, comes from USAID. The rest comes from other agencies, such as the Department of State, the Department of Labor, or the Peace Corps. Closer analysis of projects-level data from the same fiscal year, though, indicates that the US government directed more than $14 billion to roughly 6500 projects that referenced "children" or "youth" in their descriptions or guidelines (see Table 4.1).[78] The analysis based on information compiled by AidData, an independent

Table 4.1   Projects targeting vulnerable children, FY2010[122]

| Target populations | Children in adversity | AidData | |
| | 2010 report | | |
	No. of projects	No. of projects	Contributions (USD)
Affected by HIV/AIDS	702	1014	887,729,883
Poverty	556	96	5,444,867,992
Displaced & refugees	304	141	221,826,718
Violence/abuse	270	285	189,732,421
Natural disaster	158	6	26,272,082
Disabilities	128	234	357,909,532
Child labor	125	258	1,554,818,135
Armed conflict	121	110	87,813,963
Orphans	89	111	1,860,518,089
Child trafficking	78	189	171,746,572
Street children	54	5	234,393,781
Child marriage	28	16	59,023,046
Gangs	22	0	–
Child soldiers	12	2	8,665,463
Total[123]	1710	2995	7,289,181,951
Total containing "child"/"youth"/"adolescent"	6666		13,951,241,741

research group that seeks to improve development outcomes by making development financial data more transparent, indicates that this difference in volume stems in large part from major poverty-alleviation investments in countries such as Mexico, Kenya, and the Philippines, together total-ing nearly $6 billion. These social assistance programs include "children" in a broad list of tags but do not maintain a child focus.[79] Similarly, the largest concentrations of projects are those related to the massive US pol-icy emphasis and funding blocks for HIV/AIDS relief, including AIDS-affected children. Children's aid, then, is primarily issue-based rather than focused on children as a demographic.

What Does "Local" Really Mean?

In 2011, President Obama and former Secretary of State Clinton revised the mandate of USAID, calling on it "to support the institutions, pri-vate sector partners and civil society organizations that serve as engines of growth and progress for their own nations... through new models for public-private partnerships and increased investment directly to partner governments and local organizations."[80]

Rajiv Shah, USAID's former Administrator, endorsed this redirection: "This agency is no longer satisfied with writing big checks to big contrac-tors and calling it development. We've already accelerated our funding to local NGOs and local entrepreneurs, change agents who have the cultural knowledge and in-country expertise to ensure assistance leads to real local institutions and lasting, durable growth."[81] The amount awarded to large contractors fell from $9.6 billion in 2010 to $9.2 billion in 2013, while awards to local groups increased to $1.6 billion from $919 million dur-ing this same period. This small but hardly negligible shift away from its former funding pattern carried a measurable goal: by FY 2015, USAID hoped to direct 30% of its annual grants and contracts to local partners, three times as much as local procurement efforts from FY 2009.[82]

But the execution of these laudable intentions carries some inherent challenges. First is the definition of "local." In USAID's terms, local part-ners are those with an affiliation in the country in which funding will be expended. This does not define the partner's characteristics other than its location and site of governance. Partners may be multimillion dollar enterprises, and they may be sited in the capital far away from the most critical areas where assistance is needed. Indeed, in some cultures with deep ethnic or tribal identities, those from the cities may be considered outsiders by those in rural areas, even if they share the same nationality. Local partners are frequently country-wide organizations that may be just as bureaucratic and inflexible as major INGOs.[83]

Assistance programs that are crafted from the outside and implemented by administrators who are not indigenous necessarily exert some element of control over the communities in which these programs function. Control is power, which itself can be problematic and engender unanticipated resentments, especially in postcolonial societies where the legacies of Western imperialism have not yet completely faded. In many cases, foreign aid follows the pathways of empire. Belgium, for example, designates a portion of its foreign assistance for former colonies, such as the DRC, the Republic of Congo, and Rwanda. The UK Department for International Development (DFID) has a strong presence in East Central Africa and South Asia, both former colonial strongholds.

The distribution of assistance from what could be viewed as former masters reinforces traditional patterns of control. In the best cases, this control is ceded downward to the community level so that programs can be adapted and directed by those most closely familiar with the constituencies being served. In major national programs of foreign assistance, though, control of implementation is carefully guarded. [84] Even those programs with some participatory element, wherein program work is assigned to local staff, can fail to impel a sense of ownership. Participation, in the end, does not equate with either power or control. Such participation is little more than nominal and contributes too little to the design of on-the-ground work. The incentive to adapt and sustain such programs, then, is reduced. Foreign assistance, at least psychologically, can be just another form of empire. [85]

How much of this assistance ever reaches communities in need? USAID's investment models have long relied on "implementation partners," usually private contractors and large US-based nonprofit organizations. These implementation partners most often subcontract with other groups to perform tasks on the ground, and many times these are local or regional NGOs. But tracking information from this point becomes difficult, and it is impossible to say with any certainty what percentage of this funding burrows into the community level.

An analysis of AidData's information points to the conclusion that "The current flow of funding becomes invisible and unverifiable from an external perspective beyond a few steps along the chain. The lack of tracking suggests that if funding is trickling down to the community level, it is likely through a very top-down structure, with no direct accountability or decision-making at the lowest levels of implementation."[86]

In Malawi, for example, more than 20 different contractors carried out child assistance projects over the past two decades. [87] Many projects passed through multiple layers, with funding originated at USAID being directed to major players such as Catholic Relief Services, Abt Associates, or UNICEF, which in turn subcontracted to do the work (see Table 4.2). Only one funded project provided enough specific information to determine that it partners with community-based care centers. But even that project was contracted through Feed the Children, a major INGO. [88] The process of tracking all other funded projects stopped at the subcontractor level.[89]

Table 4.2   US projects to assist children in Malawi, 2000–2012[124]

Described as contracted through	No. of projects
Catholic Relief Services	29
USAID—unspecified	16
Government of Malawi	9
Abt Associates	7
Macro International	6
John Snow International	5
Jhpiego	5
Peace Corps	5
Academy for Educational Development	4
Population Reference Bureau, Inc.	4
UNICEF	3
World Learning	3
Management Sciences for Health	3
Creative Associates International Inc.	2
Futures Group Global	2
Save the Children	1
Concern Worldwide	1
Education Development Center	1
Health Net	1
IntraHealth International	1
JBS International	1
Johns Hopkins	1
The QED Group	1
Feed the Children	1
N/A	22
Total	134

Government data released in mid-2014 is slightly better than what came before. More agencies are included and more information about contracting partners is presented. But there is still no way to filter child-specific initiatives, and project descriptions remain limited, making analysis extremely difficult and deepening the conclusion that US government aid for children at the community level is nebulous at best.[90]

From all this, we can offer a final conclusion: "Ultimately, the picture of US assistance to children, particularly at the community level, is still an incredibly murky one. AidData and slowly improving USG reports are useful tools, but limited and inconsistent data make it difficult to know whom, how, and where funding is reaching and if it is working."[91]

The Best Laid Plans

Foreign assistance has traditionally been the work of *planners*[92] who view poverty as a technical problem to be solved through a series of formulas.[93] This approach is necessarily at variance with the fluctuations and fluidity of circumstances on the ground, which are commonly the product of complex factors spanning social, economic, institutional, cultural, and even historical influences. Except in the most general sense, intense, multilayered planning does not do well in situations beset by numerous variables constantly in motion. But much foreign aid is predicated on meeting predetermined outputs, which themselves are drawn from theoretical projections about what it might take to overcome a particular problem.

If, for example, a malaria prevention program in rural Kenya targets the distribution of 2000 antimalarial nets to children over a three-month period, then its success will be measured by its ability to disperse those nets and not necessarily by any changes in the rate of malarial infections. The distributions become the sole determinant of success. But there is no guarantee that the distributed nets will be for their intended use or to good effect. In some places, bed nets are used as fishing nets or rewoven into clothing. An initiative such as this, rooted in community-based variables, will face vulnerabilities that the best planners will be unable to anticipate through formulas and equations.[94]

Building a school provides a quantifiable output but that output is meaningless if the school is nothing more than a building that warehouses children without providing adequate foundational education. Programs that seek to bring marginalized children up to standard literacy and numeracy levels are by definition more nuanced, reflective of the cultures of the communities in which they operate and the specific conditions of the children they strive to educate. Evaluation of the impact of such programs is anything but immediate and can take years if an accurate assessment is to be made. This flies in the face of the demands of some donor programs who stress immediate results and measurable outputs, numbers which can easily be created by the construction of a new school building, even if the children within that building are no better off than they would be elsewhere.

Aid agencies are results-driven, focusing on short-term outputs, which are the products of planned program implementation, rather than long-term outcomes. Especially in an environment where financial resources are limited and multiple hands reach for the same pool of funds, output measurements become critical in establishing the validity of the efforts and justifying further investment. The foundation sector, beset by more requests from the aid community than it could ever fund, seeks the best possible return on its investment in development programs. Similarly, public sector programs must be able to quantify their results to funding authorities within their host governments. As a result, planners look for numbers.

Most of the time the numbers they seek are based on their interpretation of quantifiable factors, for example, the number of schools built, the number of children fed, the number of medicines distributed, cost per beneficiary, and so on. This can reduce the assessment of a program's impact, and subsequently its likelihood of continued funding, to a mathematical exercise, the creation of a checklist against which successes can be counted. Moreover, limited funding cycles can impair accurate measurement of an initiative's impact. A two-year grant may do well for that period, but its effect over the long-term, or its ability to develop sustainability, cannot be measured over so short a period.

In Myanmar, USAID facilitated a three-day Kayah Youth Forum at which Karenni youth, long marginalized and the target of state-sponsored violence, could discuss peace, reform, and local development. The forum was attended by governmental ministers and issued 41 specific action plans. The Kayah Youth Forum brought Karenni young people out of the shadows and gave them voice in the process of healing traditional social divides.[95] But it is only natural to ask what became of those action plans. USAID celebrated this quantifiable output, but what were the outcomes?

Development programs do not exist on controllable, homogenous playing fields. They seek to address the human element, variable under the best of circumstances, in conditions of great stress. Evaluation and outcome measurement would be more accurate if based less on a set of externally determined numbers and more within the context of the evolution of the groups being served. Incorporating feedback from the ground, from the beneficiaries themselves, would be an enhancement of most evaluation processes. Numbers matter, but so does the human element, particularly in situations where solutions to complex issues are best unraveled over time. Programs need to mature, and those who have the most at stake in any program's success should have the opportunity to be partners in its assessment.[96]

Safe Aid

A reliance on quantifying outputs exacts a price on creativity. Many assistance programs tend to be risk-averse and carry a fear of failure that becomes almost manic. In this context, support is most easily directed to programs that are safe options, which can assure some reasonable level of return while functioning in understandable and somewhat predictable ways.[97]

A satisfactory performance, though, only goes so far in addressing complex and intractable social issues. When old methods produce limited or marginal gains, especially after years of effort, new approaches must be considered. Risk becomes the driver of change and failure a necessary byproduct.

In eschewing the riskier pathways, aid agencies undersell their impact. If the net change of "safe" aid programs still cannot overcome the most intransigent problems of hunger and abuse and disease and violence, then agencies must move increasingly into more difficult, complex environments. In this interpretation, risk becomes something to be embraced rather than avoided, with setbacks marking the honor of the chances taken.

The pressure to make "safe" investments can in fact curtail efficiencies. Donors that rely on traditional, sometimes tangible, projects can limit the potential for significant, sometimes less tangible, outcomes. The World Bank estimates, for example, that the return on spending on instructional materials, supplies, textbooks, and educational enhancements such as new courses of study far surpasses the return on underwriting physical facilities. But donors have a tendency to build schools. What goes on inside those schools, and who teaches the children that attend them, is often ignored. We have seen an increase in the number of children attending primary school worldwide. But we have also seen continuing disparity in the quality of education across the world.[98]

This is not to say that foreign assistance needs to be reckless. The reality of limited resources precludes careless investment, and all programs need to be evaluated critically. But a focus, at least in part, on alternative types of programs—born from community inputs and functioning in areas of greatest need, and therefore greatest risk—can deepen funders' return on investment. Moreover, encouraging creativity at the local level strengthens the community's ownership of the solutions and generates self-worth, social identity, and entrepreneurial pride, all of which are difficult to cultivate through traditional top-down programs.[99] Risk can carry with it great reward.

Paved with Good Intentions

Economic development at its best is the emanation of a social ethic that embraces self-protection, self-reliance, and shared benefit. In most cultures, this ethic has evolved over time and become part of collective social behavior. Low-income societies, where children and young people often find themselves in situations of short-term desperation and long-term despair, do not have the luxury of an extended evolution. Solutions must come quickly, and they must be creatively adapted to the situations at hand. Experimentation then arises. Individuals and collectives are compelled to identify a problem's roots and causes, often invisible to outside programs, and experiment with new solutions.[100]

Foreign aid donors would do well to encourage this form of local creativity. In the end, money is perhaps the least effective tool a donor can employ. Critical to the development process are factors that enhance sustainability. These include networking, connections to other funders and program practitioners, and counsel concerning programmatic implementation. In this context, money is only one of a number of tools. Donors that focus primarily on financial support to the exclusion of this leveraging, and to the exclusion of locally engineered programmatic solutions, are missing essential components that can embed programs within the community at risk and enhance impact and sustainability. A donor's best contribution transcends the financial by helping recipient communities define their own needs and engineer their own solutions.[101]

Based on this reliance on financial contributions is the assumption that donors could provide all the conditions for healthy, sustainable social development. The paternalism in this assumption is offensive, and over several decades billions of dollars of foreign assistance was made less effective, or even squandered, by ignoring the thoughts, perceptions, reactions, and ideas of the communities involved. Development under these terms is static, not dynamic. Funds are delivered, programs are imposed, and the communities themselves become bit players, the repositories of good intentions without counsel.[102] When coupled with the insistence on output measurements that are essential in justifying public expenditures and used by donors to plan their next initiatives, creativity is stifled. Reliance upon the same methods, incomplete and undereffective, trumps the risks involved in devising new approaches.

At the same time, donors with established levels of funds to disperse face the expectation that those funds will find their way out the door within a given time frame. For many donors, the success of their efforts is measured at least in part by the size of their portfolios and not necessarily by how much of that portfolio makes its way into the support of effective programs. The emphasis on output measurements, referenced earlier, contributes to the conservative approach of some funders to find and continue to support programs of predictable, if not creative or maximum, performance. But further expectations related to size of disbursements and maintaining a set level of giving can have a similar effect. If a donor's emphasis includes equaling or surpassing a floor for investments, then the incentive to make those investments creatively is reduced.[103] And so development planners, armed with output requirements and investment budgets that need to be spent, set about the task of pushing funds outward for the sake of their own agendas and not those of the recipient communities. This dynamic creates a pressure to use these budgets thoroughly, if not wisely, and underscores traditional thinking that spending more against a problem is always better than spending smarter. In reality, under these circumstances, the potential for inefficient or wasteful investments, or investments that are squandered altogether, runs high.[104]

As noted above, the Marshall Plan helped define US policies on foreign assistance. By almost all measures, the Marshall Plan worked exceedingly well. But at its peak, its investments equaled no more than 2.5% of the GDP of its largest beneficiaries, France and Germany, and never surpassed 3% of the GDP of any of its beneficiary countries. That approach stimulated local economic development and placed the mechanisms of control in the hands of the indigenous population. The purpose of the Marshall Plan was never to flood Western Europe with money. Rather, it sought the strategic application of targeted funds that would be used in conjunction with and at the discretion of local authorities.

By contrast, Africa has been deluged with assistance money for a vast range of programs providing nutrition, vaccinations, education, health care, resettlement, and peace building, the overwhelming majority of which are driven by top-down initiatives administered by the donors. Currently, Africa receives assistance equal to approximately 15 % of its total continental GDP.[105] The economic engine in many countries is thus fueled by resources from the outside, over which they have little control and which, as noted earlier, are reflective of the priorities of the donors more so than the needs of the recipients.

An argument could be made, then, that in its traditional application contemporary foreign assistance does not build up the recipient society. It may provide temporary relief from crises or offer vital resources that might keep children alive, feed them, bring them to a healthy place, or even allow them to go school. But if the ownership of those programs and the funds that fuel them remain out of the hands of the recipients, then foreign assistance, for all its good, cannot build social capital. It cannot build sustainable social infrastructures that create lasting systemic change. By providing a flow of funds without local control, and thus local accountability, there is little pressure to improve efficiencies or to reform broken or corrupt institutions. By determining the programs to be implemented and how they will be funded, it can encourage a supplicating, obsequious attitude on the part of the recipients. And by swamping a locality with large amounts of programmatic funds that the community may not be able to absorb given a modest economic base, aid money can lead to corruption and waste. In the end, children on the margin still face each new day without what they need to build their lives in positive ways.[106]

The sum of all this is a perpetuation of a dynamic that places recipient countries in dependent relationships with donor countries. It is a dynamic that preserves the current flow of resources and the current mechanisms of control. In short, it is a dynamic which precludes systems change and the development of indigenous social capital. Within this framework, low-income countries are likely to remain low-income, and children within those countries will continue to lack long-term solutions to their vulnerabilities.

The Cost of Corruption

Development monies are often considered fungible by those receiving them. For example, a donor might fund an education initiative with the expectation that these funds will be used fully and exclusively for targeted educational programs. In the end, those funds are used exactly as directed, but the recipient country may well move the money it had already budgeted for education into something else that could be politically more desirable. In the end, nothing advances. If the recipient government has different priorities than the donor government, then this "replacement funding" becomes a real possibility.

Whether lost through waste, diversion to other projects or naked corruption, the impact of foreign assistance funds is too often diluted. Corruption as a mitigating factor cannot be ignored. The African Union has estimated that corruption in all its forms and sectors costs $150 billion annually, a figure well beyond the total levels of foreign assistance.[107] In Indonesia, government corruption in the form of embezzlements, bogus projects, inflated or fictional travel costs, and misappropriations amounted to $238 million in 2011.[108] Petty corruption in Bangladesh is estimated to equal more than 10% of that struggling country's annual national budget.[109] In Sri Lanka, 43% of those surveyed reported paying a bribe to the police within the past 12 months.[110]

On-the-ground corruption is big business, and its costs are considerable, whatever the measure. One of the debilitating side effects of this culture of corruption is a cynicism attendant on foreign investments in general. In light of corruption scandals and squandered funding, it becomes quite easy to characterize foreign aid as a bottomless pit that sucks in money and produces nothing of lasting value.

Transparency International, an independent nonprofit that monitors corporate and government corruption in international development, issues an annual report on perception of global corruption. Some of the weakest economies, all of whom have huge numbers of marginalized children, fall regularly at the bottom of the list.[111] For development assistance to be effective on any level, the recipient government must be motivated to actively participate in the process. Without that commitment, governments fall prey to a host of bad practices, wasteful spending, and corruption.

Fruits of Misguided Labors

Examples of misguided development efforts, fueled by ample funds and a lack of critical analysis, are easy to find. A study by the World Bank concluded that a huge percentage, perhaps as much as 85%, of foreign assistance lands in places where it was not originally intended. Often these funds are diverted to alternative initiatives, underwrite unanticipated costs, are wrongfully expropriated, or simply disappear.[112]

In 2004 in Chad, for example, the Ministry of Finance administered funding from the international community for a series of international health clinics. In surveying the impact of these funds following their disbursement, with the simple task of determining how much of this funding actually reached the clinics, it was found that less than 1% of these monies landed in the hands of the clinics they were intended to help.[113]

Despite PEPFAR's successes, not all has gone well. Uganda's drop in HIV infection rates in the late 1990s has been widely praised, but a recent study indicated that Uganda is now one of only two African countries, along with Chad, that has seen an increase in infection rates since 2005. During that time PEPFAR has spent $1.7 billion in Uganda to fight HIV/AIDS. PEPFAR's previous emphasis on abstinence and monogamy may in fact have driven these behaviors underground. Said Canon Gideon Byamugisha, a Ugandan AIDS activist, "We have messages confusing what is right with what is safe."[114]

Aid to Afghanistan takes many forms, including the construction of schools to improve access. But endemic problems in that country have yet to be solved by infusions of aid. Most schools are so overcrowded that they operate on split shifts, limiting class time. There remains a lack of teachers, too few textbooks, and shoddy facilities. UNICEF reports that in some rural communities, teachers with only tenth grade educations are teaching eleventh and twelfth grade students. USAID has given more than $934 million to educational programs, yet dropout rates are high and as many as half of all school-age children do not attend. Only 10% of all students graduate high school. Because schools' financing is based on enrollment figures, there is ample incentive to manipulate the numbers. In truth, most girls drop out between the sixth and ninth grades, and families often keep their daughters away from school because of Taliban threats and the traditional attitudes of local community elders.[115]

Haiti's earthquake unleashed a flood of global assistance, but the impact of this aid raises questions. Since 2010, nearly $6 billion in government assistance, and $3 billion in private donations to NGOs, have been directed toward Haiti's reconstruction. Most of these funds have gone through NGOs or private contractors performing government-financed work. As a result, Haitians are often left out of the equation: the Haitian government has only processed 1% of humanitarian aid, and only 15% of long-term development assistance, and Haitian firms have received less than 1% of USAID contracts ($9.45 million out of $1 billion) while more than 75% went to firms headquartered in DC, Maryland, and Virginia. Of the NGOs working in Haiti, 51% are headquartered in the United States, and only 21% are based in Haiti. Accordingly, NGOs and private contractors have built extensive distribution networks, often outside official accountability and sometimes less than transparent, answerable not to public authorities but to their own boards.[116]

In the earthquake's immediate aftermath, groups raced to the country to provide immediate relief. Fund raising appeals maximized the public outpouring of compassion, and the money flowed. But each organization most often pursued its own silo—emergency housing versus nutrition versus disease mitigation, and so on—and coordination between groups was spotty. Indeed, there is no strong central coordinating authority when disasters strike, and so organizations will try to meet what they perceive to be the strongest needs within their scope of work.[117] Overlaps are inevitable, as are gaps in service. Several years after the earthquake, more than 170,000 Haitians remain in temporary shelters, cholera continues to be a threat, and schools remain closed, even though more than 3000 NGOs continue to work in the country.[118] The Red Cross, despite raising more than half a billion dollars in response to the Haiti earthquake, built only six permanent homes in Haiti over the ensuing five years. Much of the money they raised was ultimately passed on to other groups to do the work on the ground, resulting in a dilution of the impact of those funds and a lack of quality control.[119]

A USAID grant to UNICEF was targeted in part to move children out of Georgia's institutional care system. The grant itself was part of a larger $1 billion aid package[120] that had some political motivations as a "thank-you" to Georgia for its position on an issue of conflict with Russia. Upon discovering that communities in Georgia had too few services for children with disabilities, UNICEF decided it would be easier to first deinstitutionalize those children without disabilities. When it came time to relocate the children with disabilities, though, the grant had run out. Instead, USAID and the US Department of Defense funded the construction of two new institutions for adults with disabilities, where children with disabilities in orphanages will be moved once they turn 18. In the end, USAID and the Department of Defense spent additional money to perpetuate a segregated system of care it had wanted to end, leaving children with disabilities institutionalized, likely for a lifetime.[121]

The rise in foreign assistance over the past two decades is, at its best, a manifestation of humanity's highest impulses—the desire to provide for those less fortunate, to save lives where needed, and to turn lives around where possible. At its worst, though, foreign assistance breeds inefficiency, corruption, and societal dependency. It binds low-income societies to systems of paternalism and stunts their capacity to develop their own solutions to their own distinctive, complex problems.

And so conflicting conclusions offer themselves in the assessment of the impact of foreign assistance over the past 70 years in general, and the past two decades in particular. Major indices capturing the health, education and well-being of children and young people have shown movement in positive directions. Through an influx of outside assistance, millions of lives have been touched for the better. Education has become more accessible, diseases have been pushed back, and more children are reaching the age of five.

Yet we cannot ignore the hundreds of millions of children that are not touched by this aid nor can we assume that all who benefit from donor efforts are left better off than they were before. Foreign assistance is a critical component in meeting the challenges facing the most vulnerable young populations. But it is just that—a component, one that requires constant evaluation, adaptation, and reimagination to be effective. Aid systems cannot solely rely on the formulas and timeworn processes that keep the means of financial and programmatic control solely in the hands of the donors. They cannot be the province of planners bound by budgets, guidelines, and target areas insulated from the input of the communities they reach.

Foreign assistance is hugely valuable, but its flaws become clear upon a close examination of how it works, the values at play, who it helps, and, most significantly, who it does not. Whether its glass is half full or half empty is up to the interpretation of those who consider it. But there can be no denying that the glass has vacant space. We must find ways to fill it.

NOTES

1. http://www.nytimes.com/2012/02/04/world/asia/cold-weather-kills-children-in-afghan-refugee-camps.html
2. http://www.nytimes.com/2012/12/30/world/asia/deadly-bite-of-winter-returns-to-ill-prepared-refugee-camps-of-kabul.html

3. An INGO refers to a large international nonprofit such as Save the Children, World Vision, and so on that often work in more than one country with its headquarters often outside the recipient countries. This term is used to distinguish international from national and local-level NGOs headquartered within their own country.

4. UNICEF, 2013. *Committing to Child Survival: A Promise Renewed Progress Report 2013*, p. 3.

5. http://www.who.int/mediacentre/news/notes/2013/measles_20130117/en/

6. UNICEF, 2009. The State of the World's Children Celebrating 20 Years of the Convention on the Rights of the Child, p. 15.

7. UNICEF, 2010. Progress for Children Achieving the MDGs with Equity, p.35;andhttp://data.unicef.org/resources/towards-an-aids-free-generation-children-and-aids-stocktaking-report-2013, p. 11.

8. http://www.avert.org/preventing-mother-child-transmission-hiv.htm and http://www.avert.org/who-guidelines-pmtct-breastfeeding.htm

9. UNICEF, 2013. *Committing to Child Survival: A Promise Renewed Progress Report 2013*, p. 3.

10. UNICEF, 2013. *Committing to Child Survival: A Promise Renewed Progress Report 2013*, p. 3.

11. http://www.un.org/millenniumgoals/bkgd.shtml

12. UNICEF, 2010. Progress for Children Achieving the MDGs with Equity, p. 14.

13. USAID, 2012. Global Health Programs Report to Congress FY 2012, p. 9.

14. UNICEF, 2009. The State of the World's Children Celebrating 20 Years of the Convention on the Rights of the Child, p. 16.

15. http://www.unicef.org/education/bege_61657.html

16. UNICEF, 2009. The State of the World's Children Celebrating 20 Years of the Convention on the Rights of the Child, p. 16.

17. The Child Survival Call to Action was a two-day conference held in Washington, DC, June 14 and 15, 2012. More than 700 leaders and global experts met to launch a concerted effort to save children's lives under age five.

18. UNICEF, 2010. Progress for Children Achieving the MDGs with Equity, p. 34.

19. http://post2015.org/2013/09/18/how-to-build-the-world-we-dream-of-put-children-at-the-heart-of-the-new-development-goals/

20. http://post2015.org/2013/01/08/ending-poverty-in-our-generation-save-the-childrens-vision-for-a-post-2015-framework/ *and* http://www.savethechildren.org.uk/sites/default/files/images/Ending_Poverty_in_Our_Generation_Africa.pdf

21. http://www.theguardian.com/global-development/2013/sep/25/new-development-goals-un-general-assembly
22. http://www.unicef.org/post2015/files/Post_2015_OWG_review_CR_FINAL.pdf
23. UNICEF, 2012. Humanitarian Action for Children 2011, p. 2.
24. UNICEF, 2012. Humanitarian Action for Children 2011, p. 2.
25. World Health Organization, http://www.who.int/nutrition/topics/idd/en/
26. Erica Kochi, Co-Lead, UNICEF Innovation, Interview, February 28, 2014 (Maya Ajmera and Clare Dreyfus, interviewers).
27. http://www.usaid.gov/usaidforward
28. http://www.usaid.gov/who-we-are/mission-vision-values
29. http://www.usaid.gov/who-we-are/mission-vision-values
30. http://usaid.gov/what-we-do
31. http://www.usaid.gov/results-data/success-stories/helping-child-soldiers-reintegrate
32. http://www.usaid.gov/results-and-data
33. PEPFAR, Working Together for an AIDS-free Generation: Latest PEPFAR Results. www.pepfar.gov
34. http://www.savethechildren.org/site/c.8rKLIXMGIpI4E/b.6151613/k.C6C4/Emergency_Response.htm
35. http://www.savethechildren.org/site/c.8rKLIXMGIpI4E/b.6153021/k.51E5/Health_and_Nutrition.htm
36. http://www.gavialliance.org/about/mission/what/
37. http://www.gavialliance.org/support/nvs/pentavalent/
38. http://www.unicef.org/supply/index_55207.html
39. UNICEF, 2010. Progress for Children Achieving the MDGs with Equity, pp.14–17.
40. http://www.unicef.org/education/bege_61657.html
41. UNICEF, 2010. Progress for Children Achieving the MDGs with Equity, p.18.
42. UNICEF, 2010. Progress for Children Achieving the MDGs with Equity, p.18.
43. UNICEF, 2009. The State of the World's Children Celebrating 20 Years of the Convention on the Rights of the Child, p. 17.
44. UNICEF, 2009. The State of the World's Children, p. 16.
45. UNICEF, 2009. The State of the World's Children, p. 16.
46. UNICEF, 2013. *Committing to Child Survival: A Promise Renewed Progress Report 2013*, p. 3.
47. UNICEF, 2013. *Committing to Child Survival: A Promise Renewed Progress Report 2013*, p. 4.
48. UN Inter-agency Group for Child Mortality Estimation, 2013. Levels and Trends in Child Mortality Report 2013, UNICEF, p. 1

49. UNICEF, 2013. *Committing to Child Survival: A Promise Renewed Progress Report 2013*, p. 4–5.
50. UNICEF, 2009. The State of the World's Children, p. 16.
51. UN Interagency Group for Child Mortality Estimation, 2013. Levels and Trends in Child Mortality Report 2013, UNICEF, p. 1
52. https://www.unfpa.org/webdav/site/global/shared/factsheets/media_fact_sheet_youngpeople.pdf
53. http://www.who.int/hiv/topics/paediatric/en/
54. http://www.unaids.org/en/media/unaids/contentassets/documents/factsheet/2012/20120417_FS_adolescentsyoungpeoplehiv_en.pdf
55. http://www.who.int/malaria/media/world_malaria_report_2013/en/
56. UNICEF, 2010. Progress for Children Achieving the MDGs with Equity, p. 40.
57. UNICEF, 2010. Progress for Children Achieving the MDGs with Equity, p.42.
58. UNICEF, 2010. Progress for Children Achieving the MDGs with Equity, p.42.
59. UNICEF, 2009. The State of the World's Children, p. 18.
60. http://www.ft.com/cms/s/0/d321500c-2e27-11e4-b760-00144fe-abdc0.html#axzz3Yze6dz6H
61. http://www.economist.com/news/leaders/21647286-proposed-sustainable-development-goals-would-be-worse-useless-169-commandments
62. https://sustainabledevelopment.un.org/post2015/transformingourworld
63. https://sustainabledevelopment.un.org/post2015/transformingourworld
64. UNICEF, 2009. The State of the World's Children, p. 9.
65. UNICEF, 2009. The State of the World's Children, p.10.
66. UNICEF, 2012. Humanitarian Action for Children 2011, p. 2–3. www.unicef.org/hac2012
67. UNICEF, 2012. Humanitarian Action for Children 2011, p. 6. www.unicef.org/hac2012
68. UNICEF, 2012. Humanitarian Action for Children 2011, p. 6. www.unicef.org/hac2012
69. UNICEF, 2012. Humanitarian Action for Children 2011, p. 9. www.unicef.org/hac2012
70. UN Interagency Group for Child Mortality Estimation, 2013. Levels and Trends in Child Mortality Report 2013, UNICEF, p. 5.
71. Rajesh Panjabi, Co-Founder and CEO, Last Mile Health, Interview, January 14, 2014, transcript p. 9 (Maya Ajmera and Julia Wallin, interviewers).
72. http://www.marshallfoundation.org/TheMarshallPlan.htm
73. http://www.marshallfoundation.org/TheMarshallPlan.htm
74. Nicolaus Mills, *Winning the Peace: The Marshall Plan and America's coming of Age as a Superpower,* Hoboken: John Wiley and Sons Press, 2008.

75. Daubon, R. (2002). *Inter-American Foundation*. Retrieved November 11, 2013, from A Grassroots View of Development Assistance: http://www.iaf.gov/index.aspx?page=914.
76. Daubon, R. (2002). *Inter-American Foundation*.
77. US Government. 2011. "A United States Government Interagency Approach to Assisting the World's Most Vulnerable Children." http://www.childreninadversity.gov/docs/default-source/annual-reports/hvc_ar5.pdf?sfvrsn=2
78. Analysis commissioned by authors and conducted by Madeleine Gleave, an independent consultant and former coder for AidData, using project-level data provided by AidData.org. The text of US aid project descriptions was analyzed to flag keywords, including "child," "youth," and sector or purpose-specific terms. Compiled in unpublished memorandum report: Madeleine Gleave, "Is US Foreign Assistance Reaching Children at the Grassroots Level?", May 27, 2014, p.2.
79. Unpublished memorandum report: Madeleine Gleave, "Is US Foreign Assistance Reaching Children at the Grassroots Level?", May 27, 2014, p.2.
80. http://www.usaid.gov/usaidforward
81. Ron Nixon, "In Switch, Development Agency Welcomes Business and Technology to Poverty Fight," *New York Times*, April 7, 2014.
82. Ron Nixon, "In Switch, Development Agency Welcomes Business and Technology to Poverty Fight."
83. http://www.americanprogress.org/issues/security/report/2013/11/04/78693/is-local-spending-better/
84. Breslin, P. (2004). *Thinking Outside of Newton's Box*. Retrieved November 11, 2013, from Inter-American Foundation: http://www.iaf.gov/index.aspx?page=817
85. White, S.C. (1996). Depoliticising development: the uses and abuses of participation. *Development in Practice, 6* (1).
86. Unpublished memorandum report: Madeleine Gleave, "Is US Foreign Assistance Reaching Children at the Grassroots Level?", May 27, 2014, p.5.
87. Unpublished memorandum report: Madeleine Gleave, "Is US Foreign Assistance Reaching Children at the Grassroots Level?", May 27, 2014, p.6.
88. "Country Information: Malawi." 2014. Feed the Children, http://www.feedthechildren.org/site/PageServer?pagename=International%20Plan/malawi
89. Unpublished memorandum report: Madeleine Gleave, "Is US Foreign Assistance Reaching Children at the Grassroots Level?", May 27, 2014, p.6.

90. http://www.cgdev.org/blog/foreignassistancegov-getting-bigger-heres-how-make-it-better?utm_source=140701&utm_medium=cgd_email&utm_content=alpha&utm_campaign=cgd_weekly&utm

91. Unpublished memorandum report: Madeleine Gleave, "Is US Foreign Assistance Reaching Children at the Grassroots Level?", May 27, 2014,, p.6.

92. William Easterly in *White Man's Burden* draws a distinction between *planners*, who regard development as a technical problem that can be overcome by well-financed centrally controlled campaigns, and *searchers*, who have neither predetermined ideas nor ambitious plans but develop programs through trial-and-error experiences in the field.

93. William Easterly, 'The White Man's Burden: Why the West's Efforts to Aid the Rest Have Done so Much Ill and so Little Good', The Penguin Press, New York, 2006. chapter 1.

94. William Easterly, 'The White Man's Burden, chapter 1.

95. http://www.usaid.gov/results-data/success-stories/karenni-youth-join-reform-process

96. Breslin, P. (2004). *Thinking Outside of Newton's Box*. Retrieved November 11, 2013, from Inter-American Foundation: http://www.iaf.gov/index.aspx?page=817

97. Collier, Paul. The Bottom Billion: Why the Poorest Countries are Failing and What can be Done About It. Oxford University Press: Oxford. April 15, 2007. Chapter 7.

98. William Easterly, 'The White Man's Burden, chapter 5.

99. Breslin, P., & Durbin, P. (2004). *Local Development: An Interview with David Valenzuela*. Retrieved November 10, 2013, from Inter-American Foundation: http://www.iaf.gov/index.aspx?page=866

100. Daubon, R. (2002). *Inter-American Foundation*. Retrieved November 11, 2013, from A Grassroots View of Development Assistance: http://www.iaf.gov/index.aspx?page=914.

101. Daubon, R. (2002). *Inter-American Foundation*.

102. Daubon, R. (2002). *Inter-American Foundation*.

103. Moyo, Dambisa. Dead Aid: Why Aid is Not Working and How There is a Better Way for Africa. Penguin Books: UK. February 2010. Chapter 4.

104. Breslin, P. (2004). *Thinking Outside of Newton's Box*. Retrieved November 11, 2013, from Inter-American Foundation: http://www.iaf.gov/index.aspx?page=817

105. Moyo, Dambisa. Dead Aid, Chapter 3.

106. Moyo, Dambisa. Dead Aid, Chapter 4.

107. http://news.bbc.co.uk/2/hi/africa/2265387.stm

108. Ezra Sihite, "Corruption Costs Indonesia $238 m in 2011," *Jakarta Globe,* January 30, 2012; http://www.thejakartaglobe.com/archive/corruption-costs-indonesia-238m-in-2011/494558/
109. http://www.transparency.org/files/content/feature/2014_CorruptionSouthAsia_factsheet_Bangladesh.pdf
110. http://www.transparency.org/files/content/feature/2014_CorruptionSouthAsia_factsheet_SriLanka.pdf
111. http://cpi.transparency.org/cpi2013/results/
112. Collier, Paul. The Bottom Billion: Why the Poorest Countries are Failing and What can be Done About It. Oxford University Press: Oxford. April 15, 2007. Chapter 3.
113. Collier, Paul. The Bottom Billion, Chapter 16.
114. Josh Kron, "In Uganda, an AIDS Success Story Comes Undone," *New York Times,* 2012-08-02.
115. Rod Nordland, "Despite Education Advances, a Host of Afghan School Woes," *New York Times,* 2013-07-20.
116. Vijaya Ramachandran and Julie Walz, "Haiti: Where Has All the Money Gone?" CGD Policy Paper 004, Center for Global Development, p. 17–18, 20.
117. http://www.usip.org/events/haiti-republic-ngos
118. http://www.usip.org/events/haiti-republic-ngos
119. National Public Radio, *In Search of the Red Cross' $500 Million in Haiti Relief,* Laura Sullivan reporting, June 15, 2015.
120. http://georgia.usembassy.gov/usaid2/programs/bil_dollar_pledge.html
121. Eric Rosenthal, Founder and Executive Director, Disability Rights International, Interview, July 25, 2013, p. 5–8 (Maya Ajmera and Clare Dreyfus, interviewers) and Eric Rosenthal, Founder and Executive Director, Disability Rights International, email message to Clare Dreyfus, July 8, 2014.
122. Unpublished memorandum report: Madeleine Gleave, "Is US Foreign Assistance Reaching Children at the Grassroots Level?", May 27, 2014, p.4
123. Because each project may have multiple target populations, the total is not a direct sum of the individual categories
124. Unpublished memorandum report: Madeleine Gleave, "Is US Foreign Assistance Reaching Children at the Grassroots Level?", May 27, 2014, p.6

CHAPTER 5

Boxed in by Good Intentions—Working in Silos

The global development community—consisting of nongovernmental organizations (NGOs) engaged in development or assistance projects, multilateral funders, government and public sector-based aid programs, and the academics and analysts who support this work—tends to draw hard lines around issues that are at their root complex and interconnected. The result is a siloing that oversimplifies the very problems that are being addressed and, in so doing, limits the capacity to find effective, sustainable solutions.

Almost all foreign assistance efforts, whether launched in the public sector or through NGOs, begin with a single purpose, a concept of a problem that needs attention and an idea of what that attention should be. Both funding and the programs funded most often stem from a single focus.

We can cite numbers, for example, of street-connected children, asserting that more than 100 million young people survive on their own outside the home. We devise programs to identify and reach this demographic, developing methods to get them off the streets and into safe living environments. We silo these children around this single issue. But in truth, many of these children are also migrants, refugees, or internally displaced. They may be orphans, have disabilities, be engaged in hazardous labor to survive, or have escaped violence or trafficking. Each of these conditions has its own silo, its own data, and its own best practices for addressing the issue at hand.

© The Editor(s) (if applicable) and The Author(s) 2016
M. Ajmera, G.A. Fields, *Invisible Children*,
DOI 10.1057/978-1-137-57838-9_5

Social conditions impacting vulnerable children are not so easily categorized, yet the exigencies of program development, funding avenues, and output measurement compel the development community to build these silos so that issues can be well sorted, cataloged, and advanced for support. Siloing ignores the overlap that invariably affects the most marginalized.

WORKING IN SILOS

With limited resources and focused attention, organizations tend to work in silos, conscripted by their specific issues. Consortia work around single themes. NGOs may work effectively in a defined geographic area, but success seldom informs public policy or goes to scale. Donors choose to work within certain issue areas—health, education, the environment, and so on—but find it difficult in their operating environment to reach across sectors for deeper, more holistic solutions. While the specialization of these efforts has a certain logic—like some measurable results and definable benefits—the end result is a fragmented development landscape. Efforts are seldom synergistic. Actors find impediments in sharing with and learning from one another and policies are not informed by a reflective practice. Sectors compete with each other for limited resources.

Separate Schools of Thought

We are taught to look at the world's problems in clean, logical boxes. In leading Western universities, there is a paucity of formal study involving children and young people as part of the international development equation. At most major international relations and public policy programs, children's issues in international development do not stand alone. They are most often subsumed into broader topics spanning multiple demographics. The state of marginalized young people comes up in health and education courses, embedded in political courses, or as part of larger issues such as refugees, humanitarian assistance, HIV/AIDS, or civil conflict, but it is rarely addressed comprehensively.

At Johns Hopkins University School of Advanced International Studies, the course "Social Innovations in Poverty Alleviation for Children and Youth" is its first ever child-issue focused academic offering.[1] At Harvard, children's courses are cross-listed within the law, public health, and education schools. Siloed issues receive some attention, and courses dealing with trafficking, maternal and child health, labor, and violence are commonly offered, but each of these courses can only evaluate one aspect of the multilayered influences on vulnerable children. The same could be said for upper-level and graduate courses throughout the US academic system. In reviewing course offerings at the most highly regarded international programs, it is stunning to see what is not there.[2]

Universities in the UK do a somewhat better job at bringing these issues together comprehensively. Brunel University in London offers a graduate degree in Children, Youth, and International Development within its School of Health Sciences,[3] and Oxford University offers a Children, Youth, and Development emphasis within its MPhil in Development Studies. As previously discussed, Oxford's Jo Boyden has directed the international children's research project, *Young Lives*, out of Oxford since 2005.[4]

But the major academicians and researchers continue to be largely isolated within their disciplines. Those working on trafficking do not recognize those working in issues of violence, and those delving into educational access often do not know those working across the way in economic development. Moreover, studies tend to be US-centric rather than global, emphasizing issues from a US perspective instead of regarding the voices and thoughts of those at the grassroots level.

And then, as referenced in earlier, marginalized children can be double- or triple-counted by an insistence to categorize them when in fact conditions overlap and children are impacted by several negative influences. Each issue looks at the children impacted as its own, and cooperation between issue-focused efforts can become thin when in fact they might be dealing with the same children.

A failure to coordinate, or to look at the plight of children holistically, can have unintended negative consequences. For example, a number of NGOs seek to provide support for poor rural families by providing gifts of livestock, especially cattle and pigs. But if the recipients do not know and are not taught proper hygiene with their new animals, they may become prone to illnesses and even death. Taeniasis is an intestinal infection caused by the ingestion of tapeworms found in undercooked pork, or in pork which comes from pigs that have themselves ingested this parasite by eating fecal matter.[5] The tapeworm larvae can migrate to the brain, and form larval cysts, the pressure from which can cause epilepsy. The disease can be prevented quite simply by segregating the animals from human waste and improved animal husbandry,[6] but the gifts of livestock rarely come with operating instructions. There is almost no integration of basic knowledge between the veterinary and development components impacting the lives of children and their families in these programs.

Vertical Programming

The fragmentation of issues also prohibits maximum impact for even the most well-intentioned programs. In sub-Saharan Africa, much attention, and much funding, has been directed to the eradication of HIV/AIDS. As a result, efforts to combat other diseases in the region, such as malaria and tuberculosis, have had to struggle for their own funding as resources from major funders and multilateral organizations have been redirected to HIV/AIDS. Little coordination exists in disease amelioration efforts, despite the reality that these diseases often overlap.

Recent developments with the US President's Emergency Plan for AIDS Relief (PEPFAR) underscore the challenges of vertical approaches to disease. In May 2009, shortly after taking office, President Obama announced the Global Health Initiative (GHI), a six-year $63-billion initiative that would develop the first comprehensive US global health strategy. The GHI was conceived to act as an umbrella over all existing US global health programs, including PEPFAR.[7] As President Obama said at the time, "We cannot simply confront individual preventable illnesses in isolation. The world is interconnected, and that demands an integrated approach to global health."[8]

GHI's launch became part of a broader discussion concerning the efficacy of vertical programs. With PEPFAR the most prominent example, development experts both within and outside government circles questioned whether siloed health programs with a singular focus could be wasteful and ultimately fail to achieve optimal health outcomes for people in low-income countries who face more than one disease threat or health challenge.[9]

A quick look at statistics related to PEPFAR's work deepens the discussion. In the nine countries where PEPFAR focuses, adult mortality from the disease has decreased. Working with implementing agencies including the Office of the Global AIDS Coordinator and the Peace Corps, PEPFAR was responsible for increasing the number of Africans receiving antiretroviral treatments from 50,000 in 2004 to more than 1.2 million in 2008,[10] the year PEPFAR appropriations were increased by another $5.4 billion.[11] Their orphans and vulnerable children (OVC) initiative makes small grants to innovative local projects providing care for these children and their households.[12] In fact, OVCs as a target group has come into common usage, thanks in large part to PEPFAR.

But in 2008, the mean assistance per person with HIV in focus countries was $171, a figure more than 2.5 times as high as the $77 per person figure in non-PEPFAR countries.[13] Perhaps more significantly, though, HIV is not the primary health concern in low-income countries, whether measured by overall mortality or disability-adjusted life-years (DALYs).[14] Respiratory diseases, especially pneumonia, and diarrhea cause significantly more deaths and DALYs lost than HIV/AIDS. Malaria's impact remains more pronounced as well, leading to over 50% more deaths than HIV/AIDS. Even so, US government funding for malaria prevention is just 10% that of HIV/AIDS.[15]

While PEPFAR has in fact saved lives, its vertical orientation raises the question of its total effect. PEPFAR, by almost any measure, is not cost-effective. We are left to speculate whether more lives could be saved by directing some resources to other diseases, including respiratory diseases, diarrhea, malaria, and congenital syphilis, in an integrated community-based context.

Judith-Ann Walker, a well-known founder of the Nigerian NGO *development Research and Projects Center* (dRPC) who worked with international NGOs (INGOs) for 22 years, explains, "What I saw was sort of vertical programming from the top to the bottom without building capacity at the grassroots levels. And... external entities were brought in... ranging from consultants who were paid $500, $600, $700 a day, the total income of someone for a month or a year... Paid in one day. Or nonprofits who speak the language of helping the poor, but the way they're structured and framed, they are not addressing the problems."[16]

Numerous studies from expert groups such as the National Institutes of Health, UNICEF, the World Food Program, and the World Health Organization have shown a clear relationship between a child's nutritional intake and his or her capacity to learn. Quite simply, hungry children cannot absorb new information as readily as children who are adequately fed. Schools in low-income areas show better results when a nutritional component for undernourished children is made part of their daily schedules. In 2012, the World Food Program provided school meals to more than 24 million children in 60 countries, including millions of take-home rations for the very poor. In most countries, both nutritional intake and school attendance rates increased because parents were incentivized to educate their hungry children.[17] Feeding children a simple breakfast or a protein-based lunch makes them better students and, more importantly, healthier individuals.[18]

Many funders, though, from private foundations to multilateral organizations, routinely fund schools in marginal areas without provisions for health or nutrition. A brief survey of private foundations with a funding emphasis on education finds that most do not have guidelines incorporating funding for nutritional or health-based programs. According to the Foundation Center database, only slightly more than a third of foundations with an international focus on education will also support health initiatives, and less than 10% have guidelines that incorporate nutrition.[19] The intersection between these needs remains blurred for funders with legitimate intentions but narrow approaches. Consequently, programs that receive funding may only be able to achieve truncated results if the other elements necessary for success are not present.

The picture is further complicated by evidence from India that shows a causal relationship between malnutrition and poor sanitation. The development community has long wondered why India, with its booming economy, has a higher percentage of stunted children than many lower-income countries in Africa. The reason may fall outside the sphere of nutrition and within the arena of hygiene. India's poor sanitation systems and common practice of open defecation may well be a critical factor. Dean Spears, an economist at the Delhi School of Economics, explains that "the difference in average height between Indian and African children can be explained entirely by differing concentrations of open defecation."[20] Thanks to this research, UNICEF now believes that poor sanitation could be responsible for more than half of all stunting globally. Exposure to bacteria and disease from feces compromises immunity and leaves many children unable to reach a healthy body weight even if they are getting enough calories and proper nutrients.[21]

A siloed focus on food alone, then, will not completely address child malnutrition or learning capacity, yet just two years ago, UNICEF, the World Health Organization, and the World Bank released a major child nutrition report that focused entirely on increasing food intake as the solution. There was no mention of sanitation anywhere in the report.[22] The division between nutrition experts and sanitation experts, who routinely work in separate organizations or separate departments within large agencies, has obscured the complex relationship between these two issues and left many malnourished and stunted children without the comprehensive integrated interventions they need.

Similarly, programs run by large INGOs that provide shelter, clothing, and nutrition for abandoned or street-connected children without provisions for educational or social development address only a portion of the problem. Young people require more than the simple necessities of life: they also require some sense of a future, an aspiration that they can attain something better than what they have. Yet many organizations working with street-connected children do not provide, or have not partnered with organizations that do provide, wraparound services like education or vocational training. In the end, these children will be better off physically than they would be on the streets but will not benefit from efforts to reintegrate them as productive, hopeful members of their communities. Lacking alternatives or aspirations, many ultimately return to the streets.[23]

In situations where multiple players each take only a portion of the total range of work, gaps necessarily ensue. Programs that only offer one piece of a complex puzzle provide only a portion of a total solution, and in such cases work is duplicated, or, more significantly, holes in services can exist. Moreover, the duplication of organizational infrastructures by multiple groups working in the same region on singular issues wastes resources.

Funding, though, can blind us all, and it becomes easy and natural to follow the pathways to greater resources, even when those resources cause an organization to overlap the work of others or step outside its own area of expertise. INGOs have become very good and extremely professional in going after grants. But chasing money without adherence to strategy opens the door to waste.

Refugee camps provide a clear illustration of this piecemeal approach. Organizations such as the American Refugee Committee and the International Rescue Committee provide truly outstanding service in creating safe havens for those displaced by civil violence. These groups, working with support from the United Nations High Commissioner for Refugees and the US Department of State, establish and maintain camps for thousands at a time.

But services in these camps—food, health, water and sanitation, and so on—are usually offered by separate groups subcontracted for these specific purposes. Few refugee camps offer little more than subsistence services and education; training or recreational programs for young people in these camps are rare. While some camps provide support for reintegrating refugees into their host societies, resources directed to displaced persons focus overwhelmingly on basic survival and maintenance, and too seldom feed programs of development. As a result, children in these camps are virtually stranded, with no homes to which to return and few options to rebuild productive lives in their current locations. They can remain in these camps, left in limbo, for two decades or more. It is no surprise then that many young people, such as those in camps along the border between Rwanda and the Democratic Republic of Congo (DRC), ultimately leave their camps to return to their homelands, joining the fighting they originally fled.[24]

Where the Lines Blur

We see where the siloing of the issues affecting vulnerable children begins. Each silo—each specific issue—has its own terminology, its own databases, and its own theories concerning alleviating the causes of the issue and its impact on the children involved. Each silo has its own best practices. But we see that the real world does not function within clearly drawn lines. Vulnerable children are subject to a variety of factors and influences. As a result, their lives assume a complexity that tightly drawn models cannot address.

Single-issue programs, then, can be effective only in part. While interventions focused on a particular set of circumstances that impact one aspect of a child's underdevelopment may ameliorate that issue—for example, a new school might allow a child access to education where none existed previously—these programs cannot address the interconnected complexities that define that child's situation. For example, a program that offers health and nutritional support for children under five but cuts off service when that child turns six, or begins school, or becomes too healthy, provides little in the way of long-term development. Services such as this become a tease, and while life in that particular silo might be better than it was before, it becomes only a matter of time before the child must step outside that silo into a reality that is too little changed.

Similarly, a program offering vaccinations and medications in remote settings where health care is poor and diseases are rampant will provide cures for the body. But without new circumstances to change the social metrics that created the impoverishment that first spawned these diseases and kept effective health care distant, such a program is little more than a band-aid that covers the wound.

A community's development, and its subsequent health, is the product of multiple factors, including education, safety, access to food and clean water, a clean environment, economic vitality, and other components that define a healthy society. An emphasis on any one of these components may, and in most cases certainly does, provide some benefit in that arena. But single-issue applications by their very nature cannot author comprehensive development.

Whenever children are siloed, whether by issue or age or location, they are done a disservice as any effort to ameliorate their traumas will be incomplete. Consider the role of gender in this siloing. As Chief Economist at the World Bank, Dr. Lawrence Summers wrote, "Investment in girls' education may well be the highest return investment in low-income countries."[25] Increasing educational access for girls and young women has been shown to have demonstrable benefits in low-income societies, including lower infant, child, and maternal mortality rates, decreased HIV/AIDS infection, and improved participation in the labor force, with a corresponding boost to local economies.[26] Elevating the societal role of girls and women makes overwhelming sense from all vantage points—economic, social, and ethical—and investments to that end are both necessary and welcome.

But in making these investments and carrying forward this emphasis, we ignore the plight of boys at our own risk. Boys in many low-income countries are buffeted by family disintegration, war, disease, and violence. They share with girls a high risk for prostitution, drug and alcohol abuse, criminal activity, poor health, malnutrition, exploitation, and premature death. Boys are the majority of those young people living on the streets. Such life circumstances make boys and young men prime fodder for violent activities, entering into the repressive cycles working against young girls and women.

The increased focus on girls' issues is an unqualified positive in the field of sustainable development and the struggle to alleviate the plight of the most vulnerable. More needs to be done. But in advancing this focus, we cannot pit the needs of girls and young women against the needs of boys and young men. There should be no competition here. To be sure, gender factors must be considered for any intervention to be effective. It makes sense to target girls and boys differently, depending on how a particular issue might apply to their demographic. But too often, those directing programs with a girls' focus do not even talk to those working on the same issue with a boys' focus, and vice versa. Many times they do not even know who their counterparts might be.

When resources are parsed according to gender, the entire process of developing global society's poorest sectors becomes weakened. Part of the picture will inevitably be obscured. Sarah Thomas de Benitez, who leads the Consortium for Street Children, addressed the tension between gender emphases: "To me it's not either … it's a 'both.' But I get worried when donors say, 'I want to support a project which is working with girls on the street.' I say, 'Well, that's fine, but you do understand that [girls are] a smaller proportion in many places… This is a problem where boys are very much in a central role."[27]

Even within the girls' movement, there are divisions. Some education programs focus on adolescent girls, excluding early childhood education and younger girls. Other programs focus on infant and maternal health with no consideration for those just entering puberty who may benefit from health counsel that incorporates family planning. The notion of working through a child's entire life cycle too often does not apply, and the walls drawn around programs for girls at various stages of their lives are another form of siloing.

Best practices, too, often attend to a single issue without regard for the corollary impact of those practices. For example, programs addressing hazardous child labor conditions may focus on removing young people from situations that imperil their safety and keep them socially underdeveloped. Yet, unless the child is unpaid, each of these work situations generates some level of much-needed income for the child and his or her family. Removing the child from dangerous or forced labor will also usually result in income loss for the family, which in turn can exacerbate the family's poor economic station while removing a potential avenue for financial improvement. Joseph, the young Ghanaian boy forced into indenture twice before he turned 14, is not unique. Many children become chattel for sale to the highest bidding employer simply because their families are desperate. Removal from these circumstances, while well intentioned, can unleash other issues that a program with a single focus cannot address.

Why Children Fall through the Gaps

With almost any single-issue program there will be children who are unreachable, those who fall outside the systems and places where such programs are implemented. They are the most invisible of all this world's invisible millions. They struggle to survive outside the range of programs that rely on traditional methods of identification, support, and aid dispersal. The Afghan children who froze to death embody these lost, unseen young people.

For single-issue organizations, or for "top-down" organizations that import their models, the availability of resources is often not the major issue. The Afghan children were surrounded by billions of dollars of resources, a good deal of it specifically targeted for safe shelter, warm clothing, and necessary medicines. Distribution systems failed them, as they also fail the millions of children outside standard dispersal infrastructures. While we might argue whether there are ever sufficient resources to provide adequately for all those who need these essential services, there is ample evidence that the resources that do exist and are committed to humanitarian or development concerns do not filter to all needy sectors.

This is not to say that these failures are the result of neglect, disregard, or incompetence. The integrity of the mission and intention of such programs is beyond dispute, and almost all relief and development organizations are motivated by the sharpest humanitarian instincts. But we cannot help who we do not see, and the children and young people entrenched in lives that lie beyond normal distribution and aid systems remain at peril.

Groups arising from within the fabric of their communities have a far better chance to reach these lost children than organizations that import their programs from outside models. Indigenous groups know better where these children are and what they need. Moreover, single-issue interventions tend to service only those young people within the demographics identified for support. A new school, for example, will seek to educate those children who are currently without educational access or alternatives. Children suppressed in labor situations, or those living on the streets without a fixed or stable home, are less likely to be connected to these types of programs.

Programs that focus on singular issues to the exclusion of other elements pursuant to the social vulnerability they are seeking to address necessarily provide incomplete responses. Funders who believe that their investments must target specific initiatives or interventions, frequently without consideration of the affiliated influences on those initiatives, reduce the impact of their funding, and create the need for other funders to step in against those corollary problems. And while the individual issues may be profound—we have seen earlier that the numbers associated with particular issues are staggering—the creation of issue-based silos focused on individual issues prevents the development of more cost-effective, multilayered approaches that can better address the multilayered problems impacting vulnerable young people.

Many may well question whether children in themselves constitute one of these silos and argue that the analysis put forward in these pages incorporates the same segmentation by identifying children as a separate demographic. But the plight of children and young people, as our collective legacy, our sustainability and our hope for a better society, creates an ethical basis that differentiates their issues and compels to be viewed holistically.

When coupled with the practical considerations attending these issues—the economic cost of inaction, the social costs of lost potential and opportunity, the immense resources being directed at problems which are abating too slowly, all of which can be quantified—these arguments make a compelling case for the need to break down these silos rather than define them further. Children have little voice themselves, and that which they do have is often under heard. Children warrant special considerations and their own advocacy independent of public funding.

Short Attention Spans

Donors can be fickle. When issues or events explode, the responding generosity can be truly inspiring. The earthquake in Haiti in 2010 spurred more than $500 million in private donations within the first two weeks,[28] while tens of billions of dollars have been directed to fighting the HIV/ AIDS pandemic in sub-Saharan Africa.[29] Attention spurs compassion, which in turn can impel stirring responses encompassing huge sums of donations and armies of human resources.

But the solutions to complex and intertwined social issues do not reside in the short term. Unpeeling the causal layers that contribute to childhood poverty, lack of educational access, violence, abandonment, and a host of other problems requires more than episodic bursts of funding and programs. They require commitments that span years, that adapt to ongoing socioeconomic changes, and that respond with flexibility to cultural and social demands on the ground.

"Hot Button" issues that rose quickly over the past two decades struggle to find space in the public imagination today. Yet even though the public eye looks elsewhere, there are still child soldiers fighting distant wars in the DRC and South Sudan. Despite the fall of apartheid, South Africa remains a cauldron of desperate, dehumanizing social issues, including one of the highest murder rates in the world, along with the world's second highest rate of sexual violence. One in four young girls in South

Africa faces the prospect of being raped before the age of 16.[30] Clearly, the burst of enthusiasm that greeted the emergence of South Africa into the world's community has not necessarily resulted in happier lives for that country's young people. Even so, most donors who supported racial reconciliation during the height of the apartheid struggle have cut back their funding for that country and moved on to the next big campaign.[31]

Donors with good intentions can also be manipulated by entrepreneurial approaches that play upon high-interest issues in exploitive ways. For example, the plight of orphans in Cambodia caught the public's eye periodically over the past several years. The Khmer Rouge purges left tens of thousands of orphans more than three decades ago, but attention has not diminished over time. Young people regularly enter Cambodia to volunteer to work in orphanages, and high-profile adoptions, such as Angelina Jolie's, have kept the issue fresh. Seeing an opportunity to capitalize on these sentiments, orphanages have opened in Cambodia that solicit donations under false pretenses, claiming to house orphans who in fact have been sent by their families to these institutions by the lure of the chance for a better education and more regular care. As a result, the number of orphanages in Cambodia has risen while the number of orphans has decreased. [32]

When natural disasters strike, donors are quick to respond. Much of that response is emotional, based on horrific images of loss and destruction, and the expectation is that funds given will alleviate suffering brought about by forces beyond man's control. But in most instances, natural disasters carry with them more than immediate heartbreak. They often usher in new social conditions that prey especially upon children and young people. Donors, focused on the event, too easily overlook the long-term impacts in favor of short-term relief.

When the South Asian tsunami struck in December 2004, entire communities in India, Sri Lanka, Indonesia, and the island nations were completely uprooted or, in some instances, destroyed. Donors rushed to provide shelter, medicine, food, and clothing. Almost as soon as the waves receded, child traffickers descended on the afflicted areas and sought the children whose families had been dispersed or lost altogether. Children and young people were compelled into forced or hazardous labor situations, and many without family or community support were left to a life on whatever streets remained. Others headed for the major cities, with all the attendant enticements that easily transform children from rural dreamers into desperate urbanites scavenging for survival.

Donors, whether they are private citizens, public foundations, or multilateral organizations such as the World Bank, are confronted with needs that far outstrip their giving capacities. And while a certain amount of shifting between issues is certainly necessary to provide new funding avenues for emerging problems and conditions, any hope of solving longstanding, complex, multilayered issues resides in extended support, even after the news cameras stop rolling and the public has moved on to the next crisis.

TOP-DOWN VERSUS BOTTOM-UP

Top-down approaches authored by those outside the recipient community can only go so far. It is community-based programs, reflective of the distinctive characteristics of the demographics they seek to serve, that tend to be more creative. Such programs have helped author some of the most innovative and impactful interventions to alleviate the conditions affecting marginalized young people. Not all of them work, and a fair number of these initiatives flame out in a short time. Still, the successes outweigh the failures, especially in their ability to develop sustainable programs embedded in the community and embraced by the targeted demographic.

Yet in the eyes of major funders, most of these programs are as invisible as the children they attempt to reach. With no track record and modest financial means, they have great difficulty in appealing to funders who are most comfortable with predictable outputs. Owing to several factors, including the remote location of their work and a more comprehensive programmatic approach that might entail multiple activities, these groups do not fit the more traditional criteria for funding. When funders focus on pure numbers—cost per beneficiary, indirect costs, and so on—it becomes easy to lose sight of these small efforts working in the most challenging conditions. These organizations are not "safe" investments, but they may provide the best opportunity to overturn social patterns that have resisted the best efforts of billions of dollars of traditional risk-averse aid.

Foreign assistance that imports programs and implements them in low-income societies as fully formed, prepackaged entities faces long odds for either success or sustainability. Because they frequently do not incorporate the social, political, or cultural fabric of the communities they serve, such programs can be viewed by the very people they attempt to help as outside efforts, imports that, because they did not arise within the communities themselves, fail to achieve acceptance, and can even engender resentment.

By contrast, community-based programs which have been devised and implemented by local leaders, familiar with the local nuances of their issue, and most significantly, the people impacted by that issue, are emanations of the community itself. Beyond the immediate impact of such programs, these efforts more readily gain acceptance because the players are recognizable, their methods are reflective of the communities in which they are embedded, and their efforts are organic, derived from their own culture and society. Most community-based programs tend to be small, especially at their inception. But where top-down interventions might carry with them greater resources, organizations ingrained in their communities may well exert greater influence over time due to their acceptance, their focus reflective of an innate understanding of their communities, and their sustainability, which can allow these initially small efforts to last long after larger efforts are gone.

Further compounding the issue of sustainability is the cultural nuance in which these programs are implemented. Each country, each region, each community, and sometimes each clan can have a distinctive interpretation of their culture and the values that fuel it. What works in one country—what works in one village—may not be applicable once a border is crossed. Even within borders, people from the city can be considered outsiders in rural areas, and vice versa.

Large-scale programs, often driven by formal and inflexible protocols developed by professionals an ocean away, may be accepted over the short term but, if not ingrained in a cultural ethos, can vanish. For example, polio immunization programs face stiff resistance in some parts of South Asia because of religious and political objections, even though the disease remains endemic. In Tanzania, tetanus injections were halted when religious figures, relying on local beliefs, objected.[33] We have seen in parts of Africa a cultural resistance to efforts to end female genital mutilation (FGM), so that even the most logical programs are met with hostility by local leaders who see FGM as part of their cultural identity.

Sustainability is best achieved when local actors have a sense of ownership of their efforts. In many cases, local people may be hired by major agencies or governmental programs to provide immunizations, distribute supplies, run water and sanitation plants, or, in general, fuel the processes of the initiatives at work. But if those initiatives come from sources outside their communities, their countries and their social or cultural comfort zones, then the chances for ownership of these projects and programs becomes remote. They are participants, not partners. The locus of power remains external.

The demographics attending children at risk remain intimidating. Enormous sums have been directed to children's issues, but, as in the tragic Afghanistan case noted earlier, the distribution of these resources remains a problem. In the best sense, the gains of the past generation provide a platform upon which future efforts can be based. It remains clear, though, that old approaches have a limited capacity for success. New approaches are needed, incorporating realistic strategies for overcoming innate political, cultural, and implementation obstacles, especially as the immense numbers of marginalized young people continues to grow, and the demographic of young people born into low-income societies becomes larger and larger.

CHILDREN OF THE LAST MILE

Large-scale programs are structured to infuse significant sums of money for targeted purposes in the relief of conditions that place children and young people at risk. Smaller community-based initiatives find ways to address those conditions for those within their reach. But no program, or set of programs, has ever covered all the ground there is to cover or has ever followed the road of vulnerability and despair to its completion. There remain children beyond reach. These are the *children of the last mile*.

The numbers cited to document the depth of the issues confronting vulnerable young people do not include those who cannot be reckoned through any census or head count. Many of these numbers, in fact, are inexact, and vary from source to source because children fade in and out of situations where they might be counted. A child scavenging the garbage dumps for subsistence is difficult to see, and if he or she retreats to a back alley hovel at the end of the day, then it is unlikely that any census will find that child.

Many children fall beyond the reach of even the best crafted programs. Trafficked children are swept away in an underground economy, hidden from sight by their traffickers. Street-connected children live in shadows and dark corners. Children caught in the violence of warfare or civil conflict live lives in motion, running either away from or toward the next fight. Abused, addicted, brutalized children often do not come forward because of shame or fear. A thousand reasons exist in complex societies that relegate vulnerable young people to the background, out of sight and out of our awareness. The *children of the last mile* are those on the outer-most fringes, socially and economically beyond the reach of mainstream services and support.

If these children continue to exist in their uncountable numbers, despite a proliferation of well-intentioned and well-structured programs to reach them, then new approaches must be created that better identify these children and bring them into societal positions where they can be reached by effective interventions. Large-scale efforts, with controlled and prescribed methods to distribute their services, have less chance to find the children in the corners. Better odds lie with those programs that are closer to the ground, embedded in their communities and so more likely to know the hidden pockets of underserved young people within their areas. Accordingly, the best hope for the *children of the last mile* resides with community-based groups focused on multilayered approaches to ameliorating the conditions of those on society's outer margins.

Consequently, the parameters of international development and assistance to marginalized populations have changed. Any previous conception of people in poverty as monolithic, concentrated in the same area and beset by the same problems has been displaced. The Millennium Development Goals (MDGs) and subsequent Sustainable Development Goals (SDGs) were developed in part by this concept that people in poverty are all within reach, and that, because they are within reach, our best efforts can impel positive change across all demographics. But clearly that is not the case. Development and assistance efforts must find new ways to reach the billion people in poverty that are beyond the reach of traditional interventions. As long as these unreachables, including the hundreds of millions of *children of the last mile*, remain vulnerable, all development efforts will be incomplete, no matter how the general indicators of world poverty might improve.[34]

The 22 children who froze to death in the Afghan winter of 2012, and those who died in similar circumstances a year later, are graphic examples of the failure of current methods that rely on systems rather than organic, community groups with knowledge of and appreciation for the societies in which they work. Relief cannot merely be put forward with the expectation that the right people, the neediest people, will avail themselves of it. The best intentions did not save those Afghan children from a cold death in a predictable winter.

It is not enough to create the mechanisms of relief. We must find ways to make that relief increasingly proactive, to find ways to uncover at the local level those who require most the services that make life possible, and worth living. It is not enough to direct huge amounts of resources to solve intractable problems. We must use those resources strategically in the development of comprehensive programs of support and redemption, locally driven, to ultimately bring the *children of the last mile* into full participation.

THE CURRENT FRAMEWORK FOR CHILDREN'S DEVELOPMENT INITIATIVES

We have seen the impact of foreign assistance programs and measured the tendency of large international development organizations to view the world in silos. We will evaluate the impact of community-based efforts fueled by visionary leaders seeking to redraw the lines of their societies for the holistic benefit of those children on its edges. We shall look further at the role to be played by national governments and multilateral institutions in bringing about sustainable change for the millions of children we do not see.

Among these efforts, what exists now is a framework of unequal values and unequal resources. At the top, we see a lack of leadership—there is no one singular advocate for marginalized children and young people, nor is there a consolidated movement on their behalf. In the middle, the current distribution system for assistance and development support from all public and private sources constitutes the status quo, which, as has been shown, misses millions. At the bottom tier are community-based organizations (CBOs), which have impact, promise sustainability, and promote systems change, but lack resources and visibility.

It is this framework that defines the current identification and delivery of resources, services, and public issue awareness. This dynamic has evolved over time and continues now because it has been institutionalized in the structures of the entities at all three levels. Governments and multilaterals do not consolidate their approach, NGOs struggle for prominent roles within their territorial issues, and CBOs do the best they can with what little they have.

In the end, this dynamic informs the current status, helps clarify how children and young people can fall outside the reach of any assistance, and forms the basis for analysis of what must be done better. This is where we are. It is not where we need to be.

NOTES

1. Author Maya Ajmera developed and teaches this course.
2. Based on 2013 review of course lists, professor biographies, majors and concentrations, and syllabi available on websites of all top-ranked public and private International Studies and Public Policy schools in the United States, as well as affiliated schools of Law, Education, Public Health, and Social Work, conducted by research coordinator Clare Dreyfus on behalf of the authors.
3. http://www.brunel.ac.uk/courses/postgraduate/children-youth-international-development-ma
4. www.ox.ac.uk;   cf.   http://www.younglives.org.uk/who-we-are/young-lives-people-individual-biographies/jo-boyden
5. **World Health Organization, "Taeniasis/cysticercosis," http://www.who.int/mediacentre/factsheets/fs376/en/**
6. Cate Dewey, "Pigs, Poverty, and Epilepsy," in *Sick! Curious Tales of Pests and Parasites We Share with Animals,* Elizabeth Arnold Stone, editor, Ontario Veterinary College, 2014, pp. 95–99; and Cate Dewey, email message to Maya Ajmera and Clare Dreyfus, July 14, 2014.
7. Kates J, Michaud J., "The US Global Health Initiative: What is the Status?" *Lancet.,* 2012.
8. White House. Statement by the President on the Global Health Initiative. May 5, 2009.
9. Frank J. "Reinventing Primary Health Care: The Need for Systems Integration," *Lancet* 2009; 374: 170–173. And World Health Organization Maximizing Positive Synergies Collaborative Group. An Assessment of Interactions Between Global Health Initiatives and Country Health Systems. *Lancet* 2009; 373: 2137–69. Cf Kates J, Michaud J., "The US Global Health Initiative: What is the Status?" *Lancet.,* 2012.
10. Sheryl Gay Stolberg, "In Global Battle on AIDS, Bush Creates Legacy," *New York Times,* January 5, 2008.
11. Joe DeCapua. "President Bush Requests $5.4 Billion for PEPFAR in 2008." Voice of America, December 24, 2008.
12. http://www.pepfar.gov/documents/organization/137495.pdf, p. 163.
13. E. Emanuel E, "PEPFAR and Maximizing the Effects of Global Health Assistance," *JAMA* May 16, 2012—Vol 307(19).
14. *Disability-adjusted life-year (DALY)* is a measure of disease burden, expressed as the number of years lost due to ill-health, disability, or early death as a way to compare impact of different diseases and conditions. The measure was developed by Harvard University for the World Bank in 1990 and subsequently adopted by the World Health Organization in 1996.

15. The top 10 causes of death: fact sheet No. 310. World Health Organization.http://www.who.int/mediacentre/factsheets/fs310/en/index.html. Accessed April 26, 2012. And Standard DALYs, WHO regions by income. World Health Organization Global Health Observatory Data Repository. http://apps.who.int/ghodata/?vid=140001. Accessed April 26, 2012. Cited in Emanuel E (2012). PEPFAR and Maximizing the Effects of Global Health Assistance. *JAMA* May 16, 2012—Vol 307(19).
16. Judith-Ann Walker, Director, development Research and Projects Center, Interview, transcript pp. 3–4 (Maya Ajmera and Julia Wallin, interviewers).
17. World Food Programme, "School Meals," http://documents.wfp.org/stellent/groups/public/documents/communications/wfp249632.pdf
18. World Food Programme, "School Meals."
19. Foundation Center Online, fconline.foundationcenter.org. Review performed October 7, 2013.
20. http://www.nytimes.com/2014/07/15/world/asia/poor-sanitation-in-india-may-afflict-well-fed-children-with-malnutrition.html
21. http://www.nytimes.com/2014/07/15/world/asia/poor-sanitation-in-india-may-afflict-well-fed-children-with-malnutrition.html
22. http://www.nytimes.com/2014/07/15/world/asia/poor-sanitation-in-india-may-afflict-well-fed-children-with-malnutrition.html
23. http://streetchildren.org/about/street-children/
24. Tony Kozlowski, former CEO, American Refugee Committee, Interview, February 28, 2014 (Gregory Fields, interviewer).
25. World Bank, "Investing in All People," 1994, p. 1, http://www-wds.worldbank.org/external/default/WDSContentServer/WDSP/IB/1994/04/01/000009265_3970128112330/Rendered/PDF/multi_page.pdf
26. http://www.hks.harvard.edu/m-rcbg/CSRI/publications/report_40_investing_in_girls.pdf, pp. 4–5.
27. Sarah Thomas de Benitez, Interview, December 13, 2013, transcript p. 7–8 (Maya Ajmera and Clare Dreyfus, interviewers).
28. http://philanthropy.com/article/Donations-to-Aid-Haiti-Exce/63756/
29. http://www.avert.org/hiv-and-aids-africa.htm
30. http://news.bbc.co.uk/2/hi/africa/1909220.stm
31. http://fconline.foundationcenter.org/prof_search.php
32. Thomas Fuller, "Cambodian Activist's Fall Exposes Broad Deception," *New York Times*, June 14, 2014.
33. http://www.historyofvaccines.org/content/articles/cultural-perspectives-vaccination
34. Paul Collier, *The Bottom Billion*, Chapter 11.

PART II

Lights Breaking in Darkness

CHAPTER 6

Meeting Children Where They Are

In a world driven by a reliance on top-down solutions, and assuming more often than not that bigger is better, community-based organizations (CBOs) can be viewed as small, sometimes quirky responses that can do some good at the local level but offer little to the larger issues that confound global development experts and thought leaders. If billions of dollars cannot ensure universal educational access, then what can local groups on shoestring budgets truly accomplish?

A close examination, though, of the precepts that compel locally based interventions will yield lessons that would be well absorbed by global thinkers. CBOs function under different guidelines than traditional international development systems. Their work most often stems from direct observation, and sometimes direct experience, and the responses they derive emanate from a knowledge usually outside the grasp of most outside development experts.

We do well, then, to look at the unique characteristics of CBOs—their stories that show how they work, their motivations, their understanding of the social issues they seek to address, and where they fit in the broader development framework. Born from the forceful need to change the lives of children others cannot reach, and knowing that each of their stories carries with it something of distinctive value, CBOs can instruct the very architecture of international children's development.

Josefa Condori Quispe was a domestic servant in a home in Lima, Peru. At the age of nine, Josefa's father died, so she came to the city from her

© The Editor(s) (if applicable) and The Author(s) 2016
M. Ajmera, G.A. Fields, *Invisible Children*,
DOI 10.1057/978-1-137-57838-9_6

rural village to find work. This was a logical move for an impoverished family from a region with a 90% illiteracy rate, with a daughter who was willing and able to leave home. A wealthy family took advantage of Josefa, falsely promising her schooling and clothing if she worked as a maid and nanny to their children.

Conditions were hard. She was separated from her family and customs, could not read or write, and spoke Quechua, not Spanish, making communication difficult in the city. Her life was also segregated from the family she served. She took her meals alone, even forbidden from using the same dishware as the family. She did not attend school, nor receive any leisure time. At night she would make her bed beneath the stairs, a fairly open place, to make it more difficult for the son of the family, often drunk, to abuse her sexually.[1]

Josefa worked seven days a week in these conditions. After years of being neglected, abused, and dehumanized, she finally escaped this dead-end life. Armed with nothing beyond her strength of character and a determination to help other domestic servants, she, along with several other women she met along the way, founded Centro Yanapanakusun in Cusco, Peru, to work specifically with domestic servants whose harsh experience paralleled her own.[2]

But how to reach them? Most of these girls had no freedom of movement, and it would be almost impossible to try to talk to them where they worked about their stories and experiences.

Josefa knew that many were allowed out of their homes only to remove trash, and that this would be her opportunity to speak with them. She knew that if she could talk with them freely, most would be receptive to finding a way out of their situations. So she stationed representatives of her organization near the municipal trash bins to reach out to the girls and talk to them about getting out of their conditions.[3]

Founded in 2001, Yanapanakusun provides shelter, education, health care, and legal identification for girls caught in the trap of domestic servitude. The organization also attempts to reestablish contact with the girls' families and villages. Josefa, free at last to make her own decisions, created a sustainable community mechanism to change the lives of hundreds of others caught in her same web.[4]

Yanapanakusun provides a range of support that cannot be categorized into any single issue. Working with laborers, the Center offers services encompassing the wide range of needs for girls sprung from servitude without a stable social foundation. Although their work does target a single demographic—domestic workers—their approach is holistic, and does not fit into any single box or silo, nor does one initiative rank higher than the others. Programs overlap, centered on the individual who benefits from them. Josefa Condori Quispe has gone on to be internationally recognized as an anti-slavery advocate, a recipient of the Frederick Douglass Award.[5]

The same despair that Josefa encountered in Peru transcends location and takes different forms in different places. Train platforms in most major Indian cities are rife with crowds and chaos, fed by travelers in a hurry, vendors hawking a huge range of wares from food to clothing, taxi and pedicab drivers looking for fares, and a myriad of other agendas. The platform in Bhubaneswar, a city of more than one million in the country's eastern province of Orissa, is no different. One day Inderjit Khurana, a teacher passing through, noticed the children who scurried about the platforms, seemingly with nothing to do other than amuse themselves in simple ways or work for coins. None attended school. When she returned to the platform the next day, she brought with her "a box of magic"— paper, pencils, colors, and other things to attract the children's interest. They gathered around her, and when they did so, she began to teach. What the children quickly saw was that the magic she brought, the magic of education, was something different than the contents of the box that had first attracted them.[6]

The lessons at first were simple—letters, sounds, numbers, counting, and so on—but quickly grew into lessons about the world around them. The children came every day, and sat in circles near the platform's edges as travelers walked by and took notice of the odd sight of the singing, chanting, laughing children.

The teacher came to know that the children so eager to learn all lived, played, and foraged near the platform. They were living in extreme poverty, existing outside society's margins. Khurana and another teacher she recruited provided them education, food, and clothing. For slightly more than $400 in 1992[7] (about $700 today),[8] they were able to educate and care for 40 children, each of whom faced long odds for an education, ambition, or hope. In due course, educational programs were developed for children through the age of 14 with the goal of reintegrating them into formal government schools.[9]

A nonformal education was not the only thing these children took away from the train platforms. In time, the realization that these young people needed more than literacy began to take hold. In the early days, the teachers who joined this work offered nutritious meals, health care when a doctor could be recruited to tend to the children, and, eventually, safe shelter for those whose day-to-day lives had become intolerable. And each child, regardless of circumstances, took away self-esteem and a newfound wonder at a world that had previously offered little more than hardship.[10]

The train platform schools in Bhubaneswar grew into a formal social service organization that Ms. Khurana named Ruchika, meaning "beautiful" or "lovely" in Hindi. In bringing the school to the children, Ms. Khurana was able to integrate a nonformal educational process into the fabric of their daily lives where before no such possibility existed. Over the years, the program expanded, more teachers were hired, and Ruchika formalized other initiatives to bring meaning to the lives of Bhubaneswar's most destitute young people, including a residential shelter, nutritional programs, vocational skills, and public policy advocacy. Thousands of young people have been served by Ruchika since its inception in 1985. Ruchika is now the largest social service agency in Bhubaneswar and has drawn global praise, including a feature in a PBS documentary.[11]

Harsh conditions span from the crowded cities of India to the seemingly pristine lakes of Africa. In Ghana's Lake Volta district, as presented in Chap. 1, children as young as six work in the fishing trades. Others work in the coastal farms. Almost all of them are bound by labor agreements compelling the children to work for compensation that they and their families rarely see.[12] Joseph, the young boy sold into servitude twice before his fourteenth birthday, found his way back into full society through Challenging Heights, an organization founded by James Kofi Annan after his own seven years of bonded service on the lake. Challenging Heights had no preset model to implement nor was it motivated by a sophisticated strategic plan[13]; Annan sought only to reach out to others that shared his circumstances and provide whatever assistance was practical to redirect their lives.

Illiterate until the age of 13, James Kofi Annan managed to earn a university degree, something unimaginable during his younger years pulling fishing nets. His academic test scores set records, and upon receiving his degree, he took a job with Barclays. While still employed by the bank, James started Challenging Heights in 2003 with two children. Each year the program slowly grew, funded by James' salary as he continued his work at Barclays and used more than half of his salary to underwrite most of the early expenses himself. After Challenging Heights' first grant, James left his job at Barclays and devoted himself full time to the program. Two children quickly grew to 30 and then to 50. Today more than 1000 children a year are supported by Challenging Heights.

From its beginnings focused on the (primarily) young boys bonded to the fishing trades, Challenging Heights subsequently developed new initiatives addressing the root causes of poverty and desperation that led to such bondage. Its original emphasis on labor and trafficking has expanded into a women's empowerment program supplemented by a microlending initiative to help generate localized economic stability. They have incorporated a full range of activities for those they serve, including sports and recreation, and they have also allowed those in their programs to assume decision-making roles.[14] What began as direct outreach to pull young people out of hazardous labor situations has evolved into a comprehensive set of programs touching upon self-esteem, leadership development, economic growth, and healthy living, all of it coming about because perceived need dictated appropriate response.

When traffickers began to retaliate against Challenging Heights' pressure by threatening the safety of James, his family, and his staff—extending more than 30 death threats a day—James sought a way to make them his allies rather than his adversaries. Former traffickers are now part of Challenging Height's front line of advocacy, reaching out to other fishermen to help them see there is a way to fish without child labor in a voice of experienced authority with which the fishermen can relate.

In reflecting on his success, Annan had come to recognize that rescuing these young people from their servitude was only part of the solution. Once outside their bondage, they needed direction so that they could come to the same realizations he had learned, and so the organization grew to focus on education as a path to self-awareness, economic development as a means of building healthy communities, and human rights education to instill an ongoing sense of dignity and self-worth.[15]

Educational opportunities can be limited by exploitation, as Annan found in Ghana, or they can be curtailed by official governmental policy. During the ascendancy of the Taliban in Afghanistan in the 1990s, schools were prohibited from educating girls upon the strictest of penalties, including death.[16] One woman, though, Dr. Sakena Yacoobi, would not accept this ban. Dr. Yacoobi began her effort for education and health services in Afghan refugee camps in Peshawar, Pakistan, during the Taliban regime. As a child, she had witnessed the health problems among women in her Afghan community firsthand. Traveling to the United States to study public health, she developed a successful career as a public health consultant and science teacher, although her heart remained in Afghanistan. When the Russian invasion of Afghanistan pushed more than seven million Afghans across the border into Peshawar refugee camps, Yacoobi quit her job and traveled to Peshawar.

Walking around the refugee camps, Yacoobi witnessed families broken apart and destroyed from the war, women "more miserable than they were in Afghanistan," and thousands of lives sitting idle. Determined to help her sisters, as she describes them, Yacoobi decided education was the key to helping these women change their lives and their family's lives. Her idea to support schools wasn't readily accepted; more than 70% of the population was uneducated and many opposed education, believing schools would continue to destroy and threaten their community.

Yacoobi realized establishing schools required learning how to communicate in a way that the community could accept, working within the culture and traditions to introduce the idea. She began traveling through the camps, talking to community elders and families, attempting to convince them to send their daughters to school. Eventually convincing an elderly mullah, about 80 years old, that he could teach, Yacoobi set up a tent and established her first school inside the mullah's compound in Kohat Camp in Pakistan. The mullah, with training from Yacoobi, held classes and within a year attendance grew from 30 to 300 students. The mullah asked for his wife and daughters to be trained as teachers to meet the demand, establishing the first teacher cohort. Surrounding camps, trusting the mullah and respecting his authority, began to approach Yacoobi and request the same opportunity for their communities.

In one year, Yacoobi and her teaching cohort had about 15,000 students in school from first to twelfth grade. Word began to travel back to Taliban-controlled Afghanistan. "People from inside Afghanistan ... came and said they wanted this program to come to them," so Yacoobi trained a group of women who opened up a series of underground schools in Afghanistan. Meeting in unidentifiable houses, the women risked execution if they were to be discovered, but they believed it was worth the risk. By 2001, the last year of secret home schools, 80 teachers had been trained and 3000 girls were in the secret schools. Mobile libraries transported books between schools in Herat and Jalalabad. Seeking also to serve the unaddressed health needs of women and girls, underground health education programs were also introduced and a clinic was opened in Peshawar.

When the Taliban fell after the 9/11 attacks, the schools came out of the shadows, and the organization that shielded them, the Afghan Institute of

Learning (AIL), aggressively moved to meet the other needs of an emerging society. The Taliban's departure meant the program's activities could become visible and expansion would become easier. It also meant that the Afghan government could begin to open schools and address the needs of female education themselves. Accordingly, the organization grew, added staff, and developed new resources, always remaining keenly focused on the communities that spawned it. In fact, AIL only enters a community upon the request of the community itself. AIL's work has expanded to include health care, including reproductive health, women's rights, leadership, and peace. Dr. Yacoobi also wanted to educate boys and young men, recognizing that they, too, required better learning opportunities. Its educational work provides quality instruction from pre-school through university admission. In its communities it establishes health clinics and schools and trains workers in those communities to provide the essential services themselves.

Dr. Yacoobi has gone on to global acclaim for both her bravery and innovation. From its quiet, secretive beginnings, AIL has become a major actor in providing educational opportunities and health care, now serving more than 450,000 women and children annually throughout Afghanistan.[17]

Small ideas can grow organically if they remain rooted in the communities they serve. AIL's basic initiative, the one that launched its work, was an *ad hoc* response to educational and social repression of children and women, but from it grew an awareness, on the part of both the organization and the girls and women it was able to reach, that more needed to be done. Its growth stemmed from the critical need to address that repression across a region beset by political and social turmoil. Demand for the type of services it could develop was high, and AIL was able to meet that demand through careful growth that relied upon community support rather than outside models.

On the other side of Asia, in Cambodia, thousands of adults and children survive by scavenging the waste dumps of the capital, Phnom Penh. Of those involved in this basic survival strategy, more than half are children, and while many claim to have attended school at least for a time, literacy rates in this group fall far below Cambodia's national averages.[18] Despite foraging for eight to ten hours a day, more than nine out of ten people get by on less than $1.25 a day, well below the country's established poverty level.[19] More than half have no access to electricity, and less than 1 in 20 has access to safe water. With no education, no steady employment, and no income, hope becomes a precious commodity for the most marginalized.

One group, though, the Community Sanitation and Recycling Organization (CSARO), has gone into the communities where the municipal dumps attract hoards of scavengers, reaching out to them to develop healthier ways of living. [20] Founded by a former waste picker, Heng Yon Kora, who lost his entire family during the murderous purges of the Khmer Rouge, CSARO embraces the nature of the community it serves.

The group has taught waste pickers to organize themselves so that they might have a voice concerning the municipal development projects that impact them directly. They train communities in waste recycling and composting for improved health and provide skills development courses so that waste pickers might find regular employment elsewhere. And using a mobile outreach education program, the organization has brought curb-side learning to children throughout the lower-income districts of Phnom Penh.

At 14 points in the city, the group provides regular, substantive non-formal education to almost 200 waste-picker children.[21] Curbside lessons include literacy and basic mathematics, personal hygiene, food hygiene, and human rights. By establishing "beach heads" at these locations around the city, the outreach program creates a steady, predictable resource for young people who are otherwise outside any formal learning system. A number of children have moved on from the curbside schools to reenter Cambodia's formal educational system. When they do, the organization is there to provide them books, pens, pencils, and whatever tutoring they might need to succeed.[22]

Beyond education, the curbside schools provide opportunities for the children to take field trips outside of the city, build friendships with children from different low-income communities within the city, and bring first aid and health care. Wounds are cleaned and bandages are applied. Vitamins are distributed along with deworming medications. When more serious conditions become apparent, children are brought to clinics for treatment. Counselors help children with emotional issues, and women and girls receive training on family planning, reproductive health, and gender violence. CSARO does not seek to change where these children live, but strives to incorporate safe living into their daily existence. Children are taught how to safely handle dangerous medical and electronic waste. They are taught to wear gloves and, if they do not have them, CSARO provides the gloves they need.[23]

CSARO's method requires that those it benefits take active roles in the work itself. Waste pickers are trained regarding safety, health, hygiene, and recycling, and they are organized into councils that make decisions concerning community-wide issues. Moreover, CSARO's Mobile Outreach Education Program ventures aggressively into relevant communities to ensure that young people have at least the opportunity to learn.[24]

CSARO represents a community emanation that seeks to work with those living in squalid conditions to raise their quality of life and provide practical knowledge that mitigates their conditions. The organization does not attempt to relocate the people it serves nor does it seek to overturn their lifestyles. Rather, CSARO accepts the communities for what they are and is committed to broadening opportunities for young people within those communities while building safer, self-directed community structures.[25] While not beyond all possibility, it would be highly unlikely that an outside organization would adopt this type of approach to subsistence living based in and around garbage dumps. Certainly, no outside group would be able to understand the community ethos as well as an indigenous organization founded by a man who grew up as a waste picker himself.

On the other side of the world, in the municipality of Nebaj about 300 km outside the capital of Guatemala, indigenous children are singing and dancing in their classroom. To an outsider, and even to the average Guatemalan, it may look like chaos, but to Benito Terraza Cedillo, director of *Asociación para el Desarrollo Integral y Multidisciplinario* (APPEDIBIMI), it looks like learning.

Founded in 1996 and reconstituted in 2007 as APPEDIBIMI, the organization works throughout the Ixil region to provide bilingual early childhood education to children through the age of six years old in Ixil (Mayan) and Spanish languages to help them prepare to enter the formal, Spanish-based, school system. Using a program methodology focused on play, family participation, and community participation, APPEDIBIMI engages the entire ecosystem of indigenous children to encourage the longevity of their studies.[26]

Indigenous children are particularly vulnerable in Guatemala, and their families in poverty lack the money to enroll their children in school, and the average length of study is only four years.[27] Families are often forced to prioritize a single child's education while their siblings must enter the work force. These problems are especially pronounced when there is a language barrier between a child's native tongue and the official Spanish of the formal school system.[28]

For the Ixil community, these challenges are especially pressing. The Ixil have been the targets of minority repression and violence by elements of Guatemalan society that want to extinguish Mayan culture and heritage. The Guatemalan Civil War, which raged until 1996, took a heavy toll on Ixil communities and violently pushed them to the outermost margins of society, neglected, reviled, and underserved.[29]

APPEDIBIMI's methodology works: the school retention rate of its participants is higher than their regional averages, and many students have gone on to graduate from university, well past the four-year educational average of their community. As a result, the Guatemalan Ministry of Education is working with the organization to train teachers in the participatory method.[30]

As we have noted, the marginalization of children is not reserved solely for low-income countries. Young men growing up in Washington, DC, in unstable homes, often without fathers or a strong male presence, face a multitude of risks. Violence, substance abuse, and crime are rampant in Wards 7 and 8, home to many of the city's lowest-income communities, and young men are often left on their own. High school graduation rates in these wards are 33%, less than half the national average.[31] Corresponding statistics concerning violent crime indicate that these same wards contain the city's most dangerous areas. Income levels are low, and young men with no jobs and no belief in their prospects act out their despair in destructive ways.[32]

Life Pieces to Masterpieces (LPTM) was founded in 1996 by Mary and Larry Quick. As a young man from Ward 7 who had gone to the Corcoran School of Art in Washington, DC. Seeing the need for creative outlets, he returned to his part of the city to use his art as a tool to give young men direction and structure. LPTM works with young African–American males aged 3–25 through a range of programs providing art instruction, recreation, tutoring, affirmative reinforcement, leadership development, and college/career preparation. Their work is based on principles of self-expression, self-awareness, and positive decision-making. Young men receive what they need including counseling, the space to make friends without judgment, field trips out of their neighborhoods, and leadership training. LPTM uses art as a therapeutic outlet, based on the simple premise that anyone can create art and that the art they create should reflect their experiences, their challenges, their sadness, and their sense of hope. The works are drawn directly from the young men's lives, in all their forms. The art, usually collage paintings created in small groups, are sold publicly, with the resulting impact that young men who previously found little in the way of self-worth can now see something they create valued and paid for.[33]

LPTM works with more than 150 young men annually through their after school, weekend, and summer programs. Those who have graduated from LPTM are encouraged to return as mentors, and many do, so that the core of LPTM's values is carried forth on a peer-to-peer basis. LPTM's model has had a demonstrable impact on those who take part: 100% of all those who have graduated from LPTM have completed high school and gone on to higher learning.[34] Under LPTM's guidance, these young men are encouraged to stay connected to their home communities so that they can help make real change in the lives of those left behind.[35]

Community-based change is authored in various ways. Some CBOs enlist the ideas and energies of the very children they assist to galvanize the momentum for change or reform of systems that come up short. Prayasam was founded in Kolkata in 1996 by Amlan Ganguly to assist the city's most marginalized children, especially children in the migrant brickfield communities. Children in the brickfields are deprived of government health, education, and sanitation services and the brickfield owners frequently exploit them in various ways. Fatal but easily preventable diseases such as diarrhea and malaria plague the community, and a major part of already scant incomes are spent on ineffective folk remedies. Prayasam encourages the children themselves to become change agents through their mission of "each one, teach one." While they maintain a host of programs touching upon education, environmental awareness, and alternatives to child labor, much of their work emphasizes the health of the communities in which these young people live. Peer-to-peer teaching and mentoring permeates all of their programs.[36]

Prayasam's main project equips children to conduct household surveys to assess the health needs and financial activities of their community. Designated as "Area Health Minders," the children meet with Prayasam staff to map goals for their community and to develop year-long plans to introduce new habits, knowledge, and understanding through their families to the community at large. Plans are derived from the surveys, and they then leverage special religious and social occasions as knowledge building and sharing events. With this plan in hand, young people spend time three days a week and most of the day Sunday in the community, gathering data, performing skits and engaging their peers and families with knowledge of good health practices. If the children decide they need to approach the municipality on an issue, an adult from the community will accompany them to backstop their efforts. At every level of interaction, children are the primary changemakers, empowered and educated by an organization that sees them as resources rather than victims.[37]

One group of young people at Prayasam has been named *Nirmaan Dakabuko*, or the daredevils.[38] These are adolescents who enter their communities for various purposes, including mapping, researching, motivating, communicating positive messages, and serving as peer educators. One of their projects is neighborhood mapping that transcends physical geography. Using smartphones donated by Google, Prayasam's daredevils track the health of every household in their targeted neighborhood, including vaccinations, or lack thereof, access to clean water, sanitation, disease, and general health issues. In teams usually of four, daredevils march through neighborhoods shouting "Listen," imploring parents to bring their children for polio immunizations, or distributing malaria information, or teaching proper hand washing techniques.[39]

Through the efforts of their daredevils, Prayasam has been able to map a comprehensive health profile of four of Kolkata's worst slums in the South Dum Dum Municipality and Bidhannagar Municipality, areas that have been all but ignored by established healthcare agencies.[40] The slums have seen dramatic improvements in the first ten years of the daredevils' work. A soccer field has arisen from a former trash dump, city officials have been pressed for electricity and clean drinking water, and diarrhea and malaria rates have dropped. Polio vaccination rates now top 80%, double their previous level.[41]

Prayasam's entry into the world of mobile technology takes various forms. The organization has established community youth relief stations in dispossessed areas. Here young people can come together to discuss their problems and share their aspirations. They can also register for job information and skills training, passing through the windows that simple telecommunications technology have opened for them.[42]

Significantly, Prayasam's influence has transcended its communities. Inspired by *The Revolutionary Optimists*, a PBS documentary highlighting Prayasam's emphasis on child participation, Bay Area Video Coalition's Producers Institute for New Technologies has developed *Map Your World*, a multiplatform application using Google maps, android phones, and global positioning to allow similar mapping in low-income communities anywhere in the world.[43]

Structural change impelled by CBOs can influence all social sectors. In Nepal, for example, support systems for children living with their mothers in prison have undergone a significant evolution spurred by a single organization. Recognizing the overcrowding in Nepal's prisons and seeing its impact on the children of those housed in these prisons, Indira Ramanagar established Prisoners Assistance Nepal (PA Nepal) in 2000. Nepal's government has struggled to meet the needs of those within its prisons, and it has no systems of care for the children left behind. PA Nepal has taken these children under its wing. The organization has established three children's homes which house collectively about 200 children who would otherwise be living on the streets or with their mothers in prison, subject to the potential abuses and deprivations of that setting. The homes provide the children a safe, nonjudgmental environment, and they receive food, health care, and loving attention. They also provide educational support for an additional 200 children. All 400 children attend government schools and regularly visit their incarcerated parents.[44]

PA Nepal also provides a host of services for the women in prison, including education and skills development. The organization seeks to reintegrate women into their home communities upon release through economic programs that give them the skills to provide for their children without social stigmatization. In effect, PA Nepal has created a separate mechanism of support for a distinctive group of children who would otherwise fall outside all systems of care.[45]

The young people these groups are able to reach capture a number of truths reflective of the condition of marginalized children globally. As hard as we might try to categorize their circumstances, the complexities they face on a daily basis defy easy definitions.

Each of these children could be included in various data surveys. Josefa in Peru, for example, started as a child laborer, but she had also migrated to the city from the countryside with her mother looking for work. Neither was she enrolled in any formal educational system. How, then, do we count her? Was Josefa a laborer, a migrant, or one of the millions lacking access to education? Similarly, the children living near the train platforms—are they laborers, street-connected children, migrants, educationally excluded, or all of the above? There are children in all these previously referenced programs that have some form of physical disability or emotional trauma. Others still have been impacted by domestic violence.

And so what we see is the wisdom of CBOs in approaching these young people as individuals rather than issues. Each child carries with him or her a range of needs that transcend easy or simple categorization. Organizations with their roots in the communities that spawn children like Josefa are better able to understand the comprehensive nature of the circumstances attending her life. Locally based social entrepreneurs do not consider whether a child is a day laborer or a runaway, whether she has been sexually abused or is malnourished. What matters is that there are children in need, and that the most effective, sustainable, and proper response to these children is to nurture the whole character rather than the separate parts classified by statistical studies or demographic assessments. Top-down programs funded on the basis of single issue interventions cannot do this. This, in the end, is one of the strongest attributes of CBOs: the ability to recognize the whole child as an individual trapped in particular circumstances and not a statistic reflective of a single programmatic emphasis.

The groups profiled above reflect the organic approach of CBOs to the interconnected complexities of development issues. They are by no means unique. Each of these groups reflects aspects of local intervention and development that permeate this growing sector and provides lessons in cost-effective, scalable programmatic implementation.

These CBOs have the unique ability to find children that other types of organizations cannot see, and in most cases to bring their work to these invisible young people. Most vulnerable children—those working in hazardous situations, those indentured for exploitive purposes, those who have run away or been stolen, and so on—have neither the capacity nor the will to seek out help. They are consigned to lives of despair unless an intervention comes to them. CBOs, wherever they take root, seek out the dark places where these children struggle, and they come to where they are, whether a train platform, a garbage dump, an impoverished slum, a mine or a mill, to change the trajectories of these young lives.

Across low-income countries, hundreds of thousands of young people's lives have been redirected by the efforts of CBOs arising to address serious social issues embedded where they live. These organizations, often small in budget and staff but fueled by a relentless passion to right the wrongs afflicting children and young people, are proliferating in all corners of the globe, with incredible impact.

Examples abound: In Vietnam, Friends for Street Children operates schools for runaways and orphans in and around Ho Chi Minh City, providing shelter, stability, education, and guidance for abandoned young people who would otherwise be targeted by traffickers, all for roughly $35 per child per year.[46] In Beirut, *Association du Foyer de l'Enfant Libanais* works with potentially delinquent youth, mostly young boys, to provide alternative activities, education, and hope in a safe shelter away from the abusive conditions that push them to the edges of crime.[47] Pazapa provides health care and education to children in Haiti who are home-bound because of disabilities or diseases such as epilepsy or cerebral palsy.[48]

Even the most developed countries rely on the localized interventions of CBOs. In the United States, in Minneapolis, the Bridge for Youth provides safe haven and transitional services for hundreds of runaway or unaccompanied young people.[49] In Milwaukee, Kids Matter provides counseling and support, including legal advocacy, for children in the child welfare system.[50] The list could go on almost indefinitely.

These organizations sprout from their communities, driven by the vision and commitment of entrepreneurial leaders who see first-hand the problems obstructing the health, happiness, and futures of the marginalized young. They reflect the best of the human instinct: creativity, survival, and protection.

These organizations sometimes exist as quietly and as sheltered from notice as the children they seek to reach. But CBOs are there, in great and growing numbers, and they contain within themselves the potential to alter the disturbing statistics that dominate discussions of global poverty and underdevelopment. Without them, the sad figures quoted earlier in this book would be even higher. CBOs can be a critical ingredient in drawing down the heartbreak. We cannot afford to look past their work.

NOTES

1. https://www.globalfundforchildren.org/from-child-slave-to-grassroots-leader-josefas-story/
2. Free the Slaves. (2013, June). *Video Profile of Frederick Douglass Award Winner Josefa Condori Quispe*. Retrieved March 26, 2014, from Free the Slaves: http://vimeo.com/69032314
3. Vittoria Savio, Yanapanakusun, Interview, May 2, 2012 (Saudamini Dabak, interviewer).
4. https://www.globalfundforchildren.org/from-child-slave-to-grassroots-leader-josefas-story/
5. https://www.freetheslaves.net/SSLPage.aspx?pid=667
6. Benudhar Senapati, Program Manager, Ruchika, Interview, January 4, 2012 (Saudamini Dabak, interviewer); and Indirjiit Khurana, Founder, Ruchika, Conversations with Maya Ajmera.

7. Benudhar Senapati, Program Manager, Ruchika, Interview, January 4, 2012 (Saudamini Dabak, interviewer); and Indirjiit Khurana, Founder, Ruchika, Conversations with Maya Ajmera.
8. PBS. (n.d.). *The Train Platform Schools of India*. Retrieved March 26, 2014, from http://www.ruchika.org/video/video.htm
9. Benudhar Senapati, Program Manager, Ruchika, Interview, January 4, 2012 (Saudamini Dabak, interviewer); and Indirjiit Khurana, Founder, Ruchika, Conversations with Maya Ajmera.
10. Indirjiit Khurana, Founder, Ruchika, Conversations with Maya Ajmera.
11. PBS. (n.d.). *The Train Platform Schools of India*. Retrieved March 26, 2014, from http://www.ruchika.org/video/video.htm
12. FAO. (2010, April). *Child Labour in Fisheries and Aquaculture, a Ghananian Perspective*, p. 2–6. Retrieved March 26, 2014, from Food and Agriculture Organization of the United Nations: http://www.fao-ilo.org/fileadmin/user_upload/fao_ilo/pdf/WorkshopFisheries2010/WFPapers/DAfenyaduChild_LabourGhana.pdf
13. James Kofi Annan, Founder, Challenging Heights, Interview, April 16, 2012 (Saudamini Dabak, interviewer).
14. Challenging Heights. (2014). *Core Projects*. Retrieved March 26, 2014, from Challenging Heights: http://challengingheights.org/what-we-do/core-projects
15. James Kofi Annan, Founder, Challenging Heights, Interview, April 16, 2012 (Saudamini Dabak, interviewer).
16. Berkley Center for Religion Peace and World Affairs, Georgetown University. (2013). *A Discussion with Sakena Yacoobi Founder of the Afghan Institute of Learning (AIL)*. Retrieved March 26, 2014, from Interviews: http://berkleycenter.georgetown.edu/interviews/a-discussion-with-sakena-yacoobi-founder-of-the-afghan-institute-of-learning-ail
17. Sakena Yacoobi, President and Executive Director, Afghan Institute of Learning, Interview, May 7, 2012 (Saudamini Dabak, interviewer); and Sakena Yacoobi, President and Executive Director, Afghan Institute of Learning, email message to Clare Dreyfus and Maya Ajmera, June 23, 2014.
18. Heng Yon Kora, Executive Director, CSARO, email message to Clare Dreyfus, June 17, 2014; and http://www.csaro.org/page.php?mainid=21&sub1=27
19. Heng Yon Kora, Executive Director, CSARO, email message to Clare Dreyfus, June 17, 2014; and http://www.csaro.org/page.php?mainid=21&sub1=27
20. Heng Yon Kora, Executive Director, CSARO, email message to Clare Dreyfus, June 17, 2014; and CSARO. (n.d.). *Community Sanitation and Recycling Organization*. Retrieved March 26, 2014, from CSARO: http://www.csaro.org/

21. http://www.csaro.org/page.php?mainid=21&sub1=27
22. Heng Yon Kora, Executive Director, CSARO, email message to Clare Dreyfus, June .17, 2014; and http://www.csaro.org/page.php?mainid=21&sub1=27
23. Heng Yon Kora, Executive Director, CSARO, email message to Clare Dreyfus, June 17, 2014; and http://www.csaro.org/page.php?mainid=21&sub1=27
24. Heng Yon Kora, Executive Director, CSARO, email message to Clare Dreyfus, June 17, 2014; and http://www.csaro.org/page.php?mainid=21&sub1=27
25. Heng Yon Kora, Executive Director, CSARO, email message to Clare Dreyfus, June 17, 2014; and http://www.csaro.org/page.php?mainid=21&sub1=27
26. Benito Terraza Cedillo, Director, APPEDIBIMI, Interview, June 22, 2012 (Saudamini Dabak, interviewer) and Benito Terraza Cedillo, Director, APPEDIBIMI, email message to Clare Dreyfus, June 25, 2014.
27. USAID. (2014). *Guatemala: Education.* Retrieved March 16, 2014, from USAID: http://www.usaid.gov/guatemala/education
28. Benito Terraza Cedillo, Director, APPEDIBIMI, Interview, June 22, 2012 (Saudamini Dabak, interviewer) and Benito Terraza Cedillo, Director, APPEDIBIMI, email message to Clare Dreyfus, June 25, 2014.
29. Benito Terraza Cedillo, Director, APPEDIBIMI, email message to Clare Dreyfus, June 25, 2014.
30. Benito Terraza Cedillo, Director, APPEDIBIMI, Interview, June 22, 2012 (Saudamini Dabak, interviewer) and Benito Terraza Cedillo, Director, APPEDIBIMI, email message to Clare Dreyfus, June 25, 2014.
31. http://www.justicepolicy.org/uploads/justicepolicy/documents/education_of_dc_-_final.pdf, p.4.
32. http://www.justicepolicy.org/uploads/justicepolicy/documents/education_of_dc_-_final.pdf, p.6.
33. Mary Brown, Co-Founder, Life Pieces to Masterpieces, Interview, April 12, 2012 (Saudamini Dabak, interviewer); and Joseph Donovan, Communications and Development Coordinator, Life Pieces to Masterpieces, email message to Clare Dreyfus, June 12, 2014.
34. www.lifepieces.org/making-case;andhttp://www.npr.org/2013/04/18/177608823/in-d-c-art-program-turns-boys-lives-into-masterpieces
35. Mary Brown, Co-Founder, Life Pieces to Masterpieces, Interview, April 12, 2012 (Saudamini Dabak, interviewer); Joseph Donovan, Communications and Development Coordinator for Life Pieces to Masterpieces, email message to Clare Dreyfus, June 12, 2014.
36. Amlan Ganguly, Founder, Prayasam, Questionnaire Response sent to the Global Fund for Children, 2012; and Amlan Ganguly, Founder, Prayasam, email message to Clare Dreyfus, June 15, 2014.

37. Amlan Ganguly, Founder, Prayasam, Questionnaire Response sent to the Global Fund for Children, 2012; and Amlan Ganguly, Founder, Prayasam, email message to Clare Dreyfus, June 15, 2014.
38. Patra, S. (2012, September 12). *Vaccine Heroes*. Retrieved March 26, 2014, from Impatient Optimists: Bill and Melinda Gates Foundation: http://www.impatientoptimists.org/Posts/2012/09/Vaccine-Hero-Sikha-Patra
39. Diana Coulter, "India: Children Spread Awareness Through Slum Maps," *One World South Asia*, April 29, 2011; http://southasia.oneworld.net/features/india-children-spread-awareness-through-slum-maps#.U4NAVtJDvyo
40. http://www.prayasam.org/endeavour.asp
41. http://www.unicef.org/immunization/index_68585.html
42. http://www.prayasam.org/endeavour.asp
43. http://revolutionaryoptimists.org/map-your-world; cf. http://medethicsfilms.stanford.edu/films/MapYourWorld.html
44. Prisoners Assistance Nepal, http://www.panepal.org/Default.aspx?PageId=4&ContentId=9; cf. http://worldschildrensprize.org/indiraranamagar; and Indira Ranamagar, email message to Clare Dreyfus, July 8, 2014.
45. Prisoners Assistance Nepal, http://www.panepal.org/Default.aspx?PageId=4&ContentId=9; cf. http://worldschildrensprize.org/indiraranamagar; and Indira Ranamagar, email message to Clare Dreyfus, July 8, 2014.
46. Friends For Street Children. (2012). *About Us*. Retrieved March 26, 2014, from Friends for Street Children.
47. CRIN. (2013). *Association du Foyer de L'enfant Libanais*. Retrieved March 26, 2014, from the Child Rights International Network: http://www.crin.org/en/library/organisations/association-du-foyer-de-lenfant-libanais
48. Orla Ryan, "Stigma Holds Back the Disabled in Haiti," *Financial Times*, December 28, 2012; and Marika MacRae, Executive Director, Pazapa, Interview, May 3, 2012 (Saudamini Dabak, interviewer).
49. http://www.bridgeforyouth.org/
50. http://www.kidsmatterinc.org/about-us/

CHAPTER 7

Community-Based Organizations—
Organic Seeds of Change

Communities are organic. They come into being with their own momentum, good or bad, forged by common people in common circumstances. Each evolves from settlement through challenges to some level of identity, yet each is different in its own right, defined by culture, character, and composition. Each has its own leaders, drawn from their ranks and elevated through accomplishment, talent, or influence, and each has its own economy, whether strong or ill.

Communities live together, work together, and, when things go sour, suffer together. And as with any organism, when wounds appear, the tissue congeals to heal itself. The best healing comes from within.

As long as there have been communities, there have been collective efforts to meet the needs of those on the outskirts. History notes that in every civilization individuals have stepped forward to feed the hungry and house those without shelter. And we have seen earlier that a collective ethic to provide for and nurture the most vulnerable permeates virtually all cultures, religions, and philosophies.

While applications of locally based aid have become more sophisticated as the issues this aid addresses have become more complex, the motivation has remained essentially the same—to comfort the broken segments of the immediate society in the places and circumstances shared with the broader community. In most cases, they do so without extensive resources, modern infrastructure, or an initial long-term strategy. Most arise as *ad hoc* organizations directed by committed leadership from the communities

© The Editor(s) (if applicable) and The Author(s) 2016
M. Ajmera, G.A. Fields, *Invisible Children*,
DOI 10.1057/978-1-137-57838-9_7

themselves; individuals deeply aware of the nuances of culture, economy, society, religion, and politics that dictate how well any social initiative will be received and whether that initiative has a chance at sustainability.

COMMUNITY-BASED ORGANIZATIONS— WHAT PRECISELY ARE THEY?

Nongovernmental organizations (NGOs) themselves are amorphous, often nebulous and ill-defined. NGOs comprise a broad community with few external boundaries or delineations. It is often easier to define NGOs by what they are not than by what they are.[1]

Marc Nerfin provided an early attempt at defining the sector as he outlined the three systems of power—the Prince (government), the Merchant (economic and commercial entities), and the Citizen, which acts as a balance and a conscience. The Citizen sector "is most concerned with the articulation and actualization of particular social visions…; it represents the interest of the minority… and operates in the realm of civil society."[2] This third sector stems from the "demands by citizens for accountability from the prince and the merchant."[3]

Norman Uphoff expanded this definition by identifying the third sector's reliance on voluntaristic mechanisms, discussion, and persuasion, given that its existence is not predicated on either state authority or the lure of profit. He sees the sector as emanating from the public and private sectors, existing alongside them, rather than as a counterpoint.[4]

Within this context, community-based organizations (CBOs) are loosely defined. Generally, CBOs are distinguished from international, national, or regional organizations, but that definition points more toward what CBOs are not rather than what they are. Clearly CBOs are not homogenous. They run a wide gamut of structures, inputs, and purposes. In high-income countries, associations as diverse as churches, labor organizations, self-help groups, and ethnic affinity organizations could be classified as CBOs. In low-income countries, with their panoply of problems, issues, and initiatives, the definition can be even more inclusive[5]

It is crucial to note that CBOs are a subset of NGOs. Not all NGOs are CBOs, but most certainly all CBOs are NGOs, even if they lack legal status. Some CBOs grow and evolve to the point where their mandate encompasses more than their immediate community, thereby becoming NGOs rather than purely community-based. But CBOs must be regarded as those special entities which draw their purpose from the communities in which they are located.

Uphoff delineates ten separate levels at which development activity can be implemented, beginning with the international, then siphoning down through national, regional, district, subdistrict, and locality levels. Below these more general strata comes involvement at the community level, the group level, the household, and the individual. He explains, "The basic characteristic of what is 'local' from a socioeconomic perspective is that most people within a locality, community or group have face-to-face relationships and are likely to have multi-stranded connections—as members of a common church, as buyers at the same market, as relatives through extended families, and so on. This provides a better basis for collective action than found above or outside these levels."[6]

CBOs, then, function intimately, on the basis of personal familiarity with the communities at hand and the members of those communities. They are embodiments of some aspect of a community ethos, and the community's aspirations, including schools for their children, immunizations that keep them healthy, protection from the perils of a workplace, or security from exploitation. Accordingly, CBOs can take multiple forms and show varying structures. They can function voluntarily or on a budget, and that budget can be large (rarely) or tiny (common).

What CBOs provide, exclusive of any other type of development organization, is a community conscience. Because they are rooted where they work, because leadership has an intimate view of the issues to be addressed, and has often been embroiled personally in those issues, and because they function as an emanation of the community itself, CBOs occupy a distinctive and effective perch from which sustainable systemic change has a better opportunity to take flight.

There are, though, areas in which CBOs will have no chance to author sustainable change. Ungoverned territories, where even the most basic civil authority does not exist, defy even the most well put-together community effort, simply because there is no community. Such work cannot take root in anarchy, nor can an organization function when it is uprooted by limitless, brutal violence.

The NGO sector in general has a distinctive social and economic function. The sector arises from within, responding to societal conflict or tension, specific crises that break down traditional social structures, and the realization that neither the government nor the private sector has either the means or the will to address ongoing social problems.[7] NGOs are by nature strategic institutions interacting at some level with both the public and private sectors within their host countries. CBOs fill this role at the most intimate level.

Within the NGO sector, CBOs are proliferating. They put the lie to the notion that NGOs exist simply to channel aid from outside sources. As they continue to grow, CBOs form networks, consolidate resources and strategies, and, based on the necessities of their communities, develop different areas of expertise. Rarely do successful, high-impact CBOs confine themselves to single, set-in-stone approaches that do not adapt to changing conditions or the discovery of deeper needs within their home communities. As such, the best CBOs embed themselves more centrally into their communities and assume the role of providing sustainable social interventions for the most unfortunate.[8]

Certainly not all CBOs have within themselves the capacity to effect lasting change. Because communities are organic, each one is different. As a result, political, economic, and cultural influences can impair a CBOs ability and willingness to change the system in which they operate. Many, if not most, remain in survival mode and do not wish to risk upsetting whatever stability they might have, especially if that stability comes from kind and cooperative authorities that allow them to function as long as they don't upset the order of things. Many are just doing day-to-day work to help children survive.

For these groups, the good they accomplish is quite real, but it cannot rewrite the social systems that make their work necessary.

There are, though, innumerable CBOs that work boldly and bravely to overturn the conditions that lead to marginalization. It is these organizations, and their entrepreneurial leaders, that merit our focus here. They are not the majority, but they may well be the prototype.

Community-Based Development

Gaining increasing traction within the realm of international development and poverty alleviation is the notion that cultural context has a heavy bearing on the impact of social programs. The theory of endogenous growth—growth sparked not by external forces but by the human capital, knowledge, and entrepreneurship within social and cultural contexts— came into focus in the mid-1980s as a concept for economic more so than social development.[9]

Similarly, endogenous development comes from within communities, initiated by leadership within these locales that mobilizes available resources, both human and financial capital, and galvanizes these resources around innovative programs of action. These programs are conceived, led, and evaluated by local people within their specific cultural and social contexts. This type of development stems not from outside models or abstract social engineering but from direct experience and observation of the conditions to be addressed.[10]

The flexible, amorphous quality of endogenous development dictates that no two programs, even with similar goals, will be exactly alike if the conditions in which they spawn have cultural, social, or religious differences. Self-determination sits at the heart of endogenous efforts, which can only be supported, not directed, by outsiders.

Any community experiencing economic or social marginalization will tend to develop endogenous approaches to these problems. It could be argued that such efforts are already present and active in any area with the slightest resources to put toward these conditions. Even small efforts such as garbage collection or the cultivation of community gardens are examples of endogenous development.

Accordingly, there are no set methodologies for this type of approach. Each program, each effort, and each thought is crafted and implemented solely as local realities demand. The potential tension, then, between programs imported by outside NGOs becomes clear within this framework. Goals, although well intentioned, may not be confluent with the genuine needs identified by the communities themselves.[11]

This tension between outside programs with relatively extensive resources and locally based development efforts has ebbed and flowed through the past several years. Further exacerbating this tension is the tendency for outside initiatives to base success on measurable infusions of financial resources rather than systemic changes that reflect alterations in how societies function and combat the root causes of the problems themselves. Inputs and outputs are measured more easily than outcomes, so impact measurements become simplified. An outside program charged with providing HIV/AIDS awareness information, for example, will measure its success on the basis of how many people attended their information sessions, regardless of whether infection rates went up or down during the term of the program. But local initiatives have no choice but to focus on the outcomes, on what they are able to accomplish in the amelioration of the circumstances marginalizing their most vulnerable.

The best community-based initiatives do not, then, emphasize singular or siloed problems. They do not seek only to educate a child if that child is hungry, nor do they want merely to rescue a child from servitude if that child has no place else to go. Community-based solutions tend to be multilayered, confronting the various interrelated assaults on a child's well-being. Because they are intimately connected with their beneficiaries, community-based initiatives acknowledge that development is incomplete if the whole person is not made well.[12]

Urie Bronfenbrenner underscored this need for comprehensive protection and nurturing of a child as he or she grows. He advanced an ecological theory of child development, arguing that a child's growth and well-being is influenced by complex environmental factors at numerous entry points in his life. These include family, culture, education, and social contributors such as friends, teachers, and community figures. These influences begin at the most intimate level—home, neighborhood, and school—then grow outward through broader strata, such as regional or national, political and cultural movements, violence, and loss. All of these influences are accentuated over time so that the compendium of a child's development is a function of various environmental inputs experienced over the course of his or her early and middle years.[13]

This theory has been buttressed in recent years by the recognition that negative childhood experiences impact severely a child's health, functionality, emotional stability, and social development. The Adverse Childhood Experiences (ACE) study, a ten-year review commissioned by the Centers for Disease Control and Prevention and Kaiser Permanente under the direction of Dr. Robert Anda, concluded that children exposed to multiple traumatic events, including abuse, neglect, violence, abandonment, or crime were several times more likely to develop cognitive, emotional, behavioral, and social issues than those without such exposures.[14]

Bronfenbrenner's theory and Anda's supporting research confirm that children in marginalized or vulnerable circumstances run abnormally high risks for abnormal development, which in turn impacts the community around them. In the face of such stakes, it is clearly in the interest of the communities themselves to find effective and lasting solutions to the adverse impacts that compromise their children's futures.

CBOs' trade is social capital, which is defined as the collective benefits derived from individuals acting together as community. Robert Putnam, one of the first to evaluate this concept in the 1990s, has argued that social capital is a stronger measure of a society's sustainable well-being than any economic indicator.[15] Putnam has stated that, by facilitating cooperation and mutually supportive relationships, social capital has strong intrinsic value in combating social disorders.[16] Because they are based on a collective civic engagement, CBOs hold greater promise for sustainable change than any outside influences.

Putnam further draws a distinction between "bonding social capital," which fosters cooperation among a homogeneous set of people, and "bridging social capital," which spans heterogeneous groups. For example, a group whose inclusion is based on ethnic or political identity would constitute bonding social capital, while an open nonformal school would define bridging social capital. Putnam has argued that bridging capital creates immense benefits to societies in general by maximizing inclusion, talent, energy, and insight.[17]

CBOs, then, have the potential to bridge outward through the different social strata of their communities. They possess the capacity to unite around issues with practical solutions rather than ethnic, political, gender, or economic status. We have seen in the examples cited earlier how social capital which builds these bridges can in fact generate social actions that transcend their immediate communities. When done well, these actions create a basis for widespread community embrace and thus sustainability.

NGOs have proliferated like wildflowers over the past two decades, especially in high- and middle-income countries. France, for example, has seen at least 50,000 new NGOs registered each year over the past decade, up from a rate of 10,000 per year in the late 1960s. More than 220,000 NGOs are on record in Brazil, and half of all NGOs in Italy came into being within the last 15 years.[18] In India, which now has more NGOs than any other country, an estimated 3.3 million groups are on file, or roughly one NGO for every 400 people.[19]

These are just the organizations that are visible enough for legal recognition. Operating outside official view are innumerable groups that follow, often unintentionally, the patterns of endogenous development. These small groups, locally focused, exist precariously, and most will have short tenures. Others, though, will find their footing, carry forward work based on innovative models that exhibit both efficiency and impact, and, in so doing, burrow deeply into their community fabric.

CBOs provide strong evidence for the efficacy of endogenous development. Characteristically overlooked by traditional models of international assistance, CBOs have grown organically within the social and cultural contexts that launch them. Even so, most face immense challenges to their survival.

Capital Starved

While billions of dollars have been directed toward extensive foreign assistance programs by various governments and multilaterals, comparatively little of these resources make their way to CBOs. Most of these resources underwrite programs drawn by social engineers far outside the communities they seek to serve. They allow the importation of initiatives that fit well into logic models, draw all the proper lines between implementers and beneficiaries, yet have not reached those at the far edges of vulnerability. Their impact on certain segments of low-income societies has been well documented.[20] Especially in areas of disease mitigation, nutrition, and educational access, these programs, and the resources behind them, have had a positive impact on millions of people living in desperate circumstances.

But we have also seen that the most marginalized have not shared equally in these gains, and that millions more continue to struggle for survival despite the best efforts of well-funded top-down programs brought in from abroad. The development framework that places decision-making at the top does not work. The struggles of the most marginalized can most often only be addressed by what is at hand in the communities in which those struggles play out.

Most CBOs are undercapitalized. Many grow out of responses by leadership within suffering communities to conditions directly observed and often directly experienced. In the absence of adequate funding, certainly at the beginning of their efforts, their work is carried forward by a variety of nonfinancial factors, including voluntary labor, community donations, and gifts in kind. In the best scenarios, these groups come to develop administrative structures that create program goals and oversee consistent implementation. If their work gains sufficient foothold to expand outward, they may look to develop a fund-raising capacity to encourage contributions, growing from the general community into increasingly wider circles. In recent years, many local CBOs have aspired to establish fund-raising footholds in Western Europe and the United States.

This type of outward expansion is fueled by the desire to do more work, to do it better, and to do it more broadly, all of which must be fueled by funds to provide services, and to pay those who provide those services. The entrepreneurs establishing such organizations have often shown themselves to be as creative financially and administratively as they are programmatically. A deeper look at an organization that fits this pattern illustrates the curve of this evolution.

In Mumbai, SUPPORT (Society Undertaking Poor People's Onus for Rehabilitation) seeks to eliminate substance use and abuse among street-connected children and homeless youth. As one of the first, and only, CBOs offering a residential rehabilitation program for drug-using children, SUPPORT is serving a population that is among the most invisible of those already consigned to society's dark corners.

SUPPORT's program of detoxification, rehabilitation, and mainstreaming begins with a series of day care centers run near railway stations, places where street-connected children and homeless children congregate. The centers are safe places where children and youth can access facilities for personal hygiene, medical checkups, and recreation.

If a child wants to detox, SUPPORT will take them to their residential center, providing detoxification services that range from 15 days to 1 month. Upon graduating from detox, the children are then put into SUPPORT's residential rehabilitation homes. Operating under the organization's philosophy of FLUTE—Freedom, Listening, Understanding, Transformation, and Enjoyment—the homes seek to offer discipline and structure while also helping children reintegrate into society through municipal schooling or vocational training.

SUPPORT follows an elegant and necessary concept, but one that has trouble drawing sufficient resources to do the work. The organization's director, Sujata Ganega, describes the program as a "behavior transformation program" that helps the children change from within. Ganega points out that working with adult addicts is a shorter intervention—1–2 years maximum—but when intervening in the life of a child, "you have to keep the child for ten, eleven years," and the intervention needs to be comprehensive by providing nutrition, education, housing, and counseling.[21] More than 200 children annually enter their residential centers, ranging in age from 6 to 18 years old. Upon entering, each child begins a unique process and relationship that lasts the span of their young lives.[22]

This process, which Ganega believes is necessarily holistic, requires a residential approach, which inherently requires considerable resources for each participant. It is extremely expensive to detox children on society's edges. Residential costs amount to $100 per month per resident, or $1200 annually.[23] This cost-per-beneficiary ratio is relatively high if viewed on a single issue basis rather than the multitude of services provided to each child. Moreover, as Ms. Ganega indicates, the concept of drug addicted children flies in the faces of most people's concept of who and what children are. [24] In a competitive fund-raising environment, this can be a challenge, even though the work offered is distinctive, no comparable alternative exists, and comprehensive services that defy siloing are being offered.

Often perceptions of foreign assistance are clouded by notions of vast sums of money underwriting programs of questionable efficiency, frequently diluted through corruption or waste. While we might argue the accuracy of this stereotype, the circumstances of CBO financing make this viewpoint moot. Owing to their very nature, CBOs do not have the benefit of large pockets of financing at their inception. In due course, if their work is of high quality and their programmatic model effective, they may attract funders from outside their immediate circle.

Most CBOs operate on annual budgets of skeletal proportions. Few have reserve funds, and most live hand to mouth. Yet the cost-benefit of investments in these organizations can be striking. For example, it takes no more than $5000 to maintain a school for 125 students in Vietnam for an entire academic year.[25] Train platform schools can educate hundreds of children for about $700 a year.[26] A mobile dental clinic that moves through low-income neighborhoods in Bogotá, Colombia, can provide a child's first ever dental care for less than a dollar a visit.[27]

Taken together, the efficiencies of CBOs can bend the cost curve for development projects focused on the poorest of the poor. Because the hardest to reach children require extra expenditures from outside agencies to cover difficult logistics, long-range delivery and a compendium of services, the work of localized CBOs is far more cost-effective. That in itself is a compelling answer to the challenges of reaching 100% of those in need, a challenge abrogated by the MDGs. This is not to criticize those efforts. But new approaches that originate within these remote and underserved communities have the potential to alter long-standing cost-curve analyses that have dictated much of the world's response.

When it comes time to assess the value-added of all programs providing life-altering services to marginalized children and young people, it is the CBOs that carry the most impressive cost-per-beneficiary ratios. While these ratios are necessarily flawed as evaluation tools regarding a program's effectiveness—development programs that dig deeply into the lowest-income communities rather than spread broadly tend to have fewer beneficiaries and greater delivery costs—they nonetheless hint that CBOs are able to accomplish more with less compared to the handsomely funded top-down programs imported from abroad.

A Lack of Appreciation

We have seen that well-run, well-conceived CBOs can accomplish what other larger organizations cannot. These small locally focused groups can find the most vulnerable children, author interventions that speak to the complexities of their circumstances, and create sustainable solutions that elevate the lifeblood of children at risk, their families, and the community itself. By definition, these efforts begin small in scope and small in scale, rooted in a confined geographic area, and targeting specific conditions endemic to time, place, and demography.

Because they are small in scope, they do not usually produce high numbers of beneficiaries. A CBO operating, for example, a nonformal school for rural children in Kenya might have 75 students, some of whom do not or cannot regularly attend. At first blush, it would be easy to dismiss this type of work as inconsequential, especially in contrast to a school established by a large international NGO (INGO) that accommodates up to 1200 students. But the rural school may in fact present a more dramatic alternative for its students. CBOs are able to engage young people on the periphery, and it would be reasonable to assume that the small CBO-run school is educating children that have no other avenues to basic skills. These are the *children of the last mile*, the ones no one else can reach despite the size of their programs or their investments.

CBO programs with the capacity to dig deeply into the social fabric of the communities in which they work have impacts that surpass the number of their beneficiaries. We have seen that many such groups create a ripple effect through their basic programs. The 75 students in the example above represent strategic entry points to wider, more comprehensive community engagement, and the social development that goes with it. Small groups with limited resources but far-reaching vision can change their communities more sustainably than the largest imported program.

Any indices that base programmatic impact solely on the numbers served will undervalue the role of CBOs. Taken together, these smaller local organizations create a critical mass of beneficiaries. But more significantly, the ones they reach can be reached by no others.

Multilateral organizations, governments, and the larger NGOs have slowly come to recognize the place of indigenous organizations in the development spectrum. USAID has set aside growing amounts of its funding pool for smaller, locally driven efforts in support of its target issues, although as indicated by the analysis of AidData's information in Chap. 4, the flow of USAID funding to the community-level lacks transparency. USAID has stated directly that two of its main goals are now to "promote sustainable development through ...local solutions," and to "identify and scale up innovative, breakthrough solutions to intractable development challenges."[28] The World Bank is directing resources to programs emphasizing local development and local control of development processes.[29] Large-scale groups are also finding ways to complement their core programs by relying on local direction. World Vision, for example, is shifting their hiring focus to a "local plus" model which employs local citizens to work in their home countries, [30] Save the Children is emphasizing response to local priorities,[31] and Mercy Corps employs a Local Partnerships Guide for its field teams.[32]

Still, this is only a beginning. The definition of "local" to most major agencies, from USAID and the World Bank through most major INGOs, means only an affiliation with the country in which funding will be disbursed, and are typically large organizations based in the capital or other large cities and not the community level. This also implies neither direction nor ownership. Rather, assistance is funneled through local partners, even though programs and initiatives are authored outside the country. These efforts continue to maintain a top-down emphasis, and if local people are engaged, they are brought on as workers and not leaders.

Invisibility

We cannot know with any confidence precisely how many CBOs are operating, where they are working, and what their total impact might be. While we can identify the growing number that are rising to levels of recognition because they have grown in size, expanded programmatic work, developed innovative models that are replicated by other organizations, or have developed sophisticated infrastructures that boost both their work and their external profiles, there are countless more that we cannot see.

Groups that labor outside the public eye place themselves at a notable disadvantage in the philanthropic marketplace. Most CBOs that fall by the wayside fail because of a lack of resources, even though they usually require very little to sustain their work. Small localized organizations have few avenues to secure those resources and fewer still when they lack either the infrastructure or the sophistication to push their work forward. A CBO providing necessary services to children in a remote corner of Zambia will be hard-pressed to capture the attention of a foundation funder in the

UK or the United States, nor is it likely to be identified by a multinational looking for local implementation partners for an issue-focused initiative.

Imagination

Some of the most innovative programs to address complex social conditions arise not from planners[33] or social engineers but from people who find themselves in circumstances that demand a humanistic response. Because they are free from outside direction, and because they function on the periphery of established social delivery systems, CBOs tend to see things differently. Without being locked into programmatic guidelines or timetables, these groups can be flexible in their approaches, and their leaders can explore solutions based on conclusions derived from direct experience. They can be experimental, they can be daring in what they do, and they can be entrepreneurial.

Many ideas begin not from an elaborate formula for social change, but from an immediate desire to fix what's wrong. By fixing what's at hand, systems can change, and problems can be addressed at their root. Entrepreneurship, in many cases, begins from the simplest local initiatives building a base of impact that changes the lives of vulnerable children and informs a wider society of where its problems lay and how they might be mitigated.

Examples of distinctive interventions authored by creative and committed leaders directing effective community organizations can go on and on. And while their individual interventions might be good reading, what becomes clear is the quality of experimentation and creativity that permeates the culture of CBOs.

CBOs develop approaches that no one from the outside will readily see, and the work of these groups often redefines the issues themselves. These organizations have the room to try things no one else can try and to implement ideas which anyone who lives apart from the communities themselves is not likely to have. There is tremendous freedom in this, since the marginalized of these communities are generally outside the reach of any intervention whatsoever. CBOs can find what works. They can develop programs drawing from the local ethos and maximizing local resources. They can experiment, retool, and revise until they come up with their own product, and they need not care if they are providing proper return on investment. Their investment is homegrown, and their returns are self-defining.

Sustainability

Most CBOs have had to struggle for survival since their inception. The best CBOs have sustainability embedded in their DNA. By scrambling for resources and navigating new programs in underdeveloped locations, those that survive have found what works, and they will most likely continue to survive as entrenched community assets. The same resourcefulness that launched these groups will sustain them as their work continues.

This is not always the case when outside efforts with predetermined agendas enter low-income communities. Computer labs in rural schools built by outside groups with the best intentions but with no capacity to ensure a steady flow of electricity or to train children how to use these wondrous machines well run the risk of falling into disuse. Mosquito nets distributed to combat malaria are used as fishing nets, because the urge to eat surpasses the urge to stay healthy, and because many are treated with insecticides, water supplies become fouled and hazardous.[34] By aligning resources with purpose that is borne at the community level, and by burrowing that purpose into the fabric of their host communities, CBOs increase the odds for sustainability of work that is not only essential but understood and welcomed by those they serve.

LEADERSHIP

Leadership is, on the scale of things, difficult to define. Especially at the community level, effective program leadership becomes an essential characteristic in creating and implementing creative, sustainable interventions in the lives of vulnerable young people. And, as with the programs themselves, what produces great results in one arena may prove to be ineffective in another. Leadership in the particular is often not replicable, although the qualities of leadership provide lessons that can, and should, inform any community-based effort.

Leadership at the community level for an organization that has most likely begun on the basis of an ideal rather than a sophisticated business plan is distinctive from traditional, for-profit leadership models. With a paucity of resources and a fluid clientele that lacks a social gravitas, most CBOs face an unsteady birth. The qualities that can nurture an effort through such fragile beginnings, grow it, and keep it focused on the purposes of its work are not learned in business schools or captured in management theory courses. They stem from distinctive, highly motivated, creative, flexible, and adaptable instincts that emphasize the welfare of those at risk.

But what constitutes effective grassroots leadership, and who are the people who emerge as innovators at the community level and compel consolidated local action to change the lives of the most marginalized? How do they do it, and what can we learn from them?

Social Entrepreneurs

To embark on projects or programs designed to alter the trajectories of the lives of those on society's periphery is to engage in entrepreneurship. At its simplest, social entrepreneurship entails the pursuit of innovative solutions to complex social issues, and this certainly applies to the efforts of CBOs focused on one or more aspects of child and youth development. At its most expansive, social entrepreneurship speaks to systems change to altering the dynamics that make children vulnerable and curtail their futures.

Social entrepreneurs do more than change lives. They change the way people think, how they regard the issues that impact the marginalized, and how formal institutions, such as courts, legislatures, and enforcement agencies, respond to those issues. Systems change cannot come about through a single initiative, so entrepreneurs will seek to grow their programs through replication where appropriate or by serving as a prototype that can be reproduced by other problem solvers in other places.[35] Leadership at the community level is the work of social entrepreneurs, many of whom are driven almost obsessively to find ways to overcome the debilitation they see so clearly.

Amlan Ganguly had a promising career as a lawyer, apprenticed to one of Kolkata's most renowned attorneys. Yet his work was unsatisfying, and he saw a legal system that had no regard for people in poverty. In 1996, he changed his career to work with Lutheran World Service (LWS). He came to notice that children irregularly attended his organization's educational and cultural programs, and when he visited their homes to find out why, he saw that many suffered from serious but preventable ailments such as diarrhea or malaria. He quit LWS and founded Prayasam, profiled in Chap. 6, determined to improve community health and make the children themselves partners in bringing about these changes.

Ganguly had to be creative to start this new organization. Initial funding came through sales from a clothing boutique that Ganguly set up with LWS's help. He told Prayasam's early stories in every radio and television interview he could grab, and, over time, developed partnerships with UNDP, UNICEF, DFID, and others to manage events in Kolkata. Until Prayasam found its funding legs, Ganguly translated his programmatic creativity to the fund-raising arena. But through it all there could be no acceptance, no possibility, of failure. No one else could pursue his model, and so he had to make it work.[36]

Organizations have arisen that recognize the unique character of social entrepreneurship and fund their efforts. Ashoka, founded in 1980 by Bill Drayton, provides financing, professional support and networking opportunities for social entrepreneurs around the world. Nearly 3000 individuals in 70 countries are Ashoka Fellows, each directing community-based efforts aimed at embedded localized problems.[37] The Echoing Green foundation is the only funder at the seed stage, funding nearly 600 social entrepreneurs with investments surpassing $35 million. Many of the leaders profiled in these pages have been recognized by these and other organizations as innovative social entrepreneurs.

Almost all CBOs begin from the observation of and reaction to a specific social problem. Yet even with the simplest aspirations, social change is in play. Issues recur unless the systems creating those issues are somehow altered. Leadership at the community level is by its nature entrepreneurial, a quality that given the proper environment, adequate resources, a logical and sound business model, and compelling articulation can move entire countries.

Local Communities—Localized Solutions

Leadership that emerges from local roots by definition cannot help but view the situations at hand through local perspectives. This allows the cultivation of solutions that are "organic," reflective of the ethos of those being served. As well, this creates a programmatic advantage that cannot be duplicated by outside agencies imposing preconceived, formulaic notions of development. Such programs can in fact become embedded within their service communities, but the odds are longer and the steps needed to gain community trust are much more demanding than those programs that are rooted locally.

Guayaquil, Ecuador, is a city of nearly three million, including more than 200 street gangs with nearly 60,000 members.[38] Most get by through petty theft or the sale of drugs; violence is a daily occurrence. In one of Guayaquil's most notorious barrios, Nelsa Curbelo, a former nun and schoolteacher from the barrio, sensed that gang members acted out violently from a desperate need to be heard, to be acknowledged, and to be validated. She began to spend nights in the barrio talking with any gang member who would speak with her, trying to understand what motivated them and where their aspirations lay.[39]

In 1999, she founded Ser Paz, whose mission is to facilitate nonviolence on the streets of the barrio while offering gang members, mostly adolescent boys, alternative possibilities.[40] Drawing from her conversations, Curbelo and Ser Paz do not dismiss gangs as inherently and comprehensively negative. The organization stresses the positive byproducts of gang affiliation, including teamwork, loyalty, and communication. Ser Paz insists that violence be abandoned as a way of life. The organization offers small business loans to gang members seeking to establish legitimate income, and recipients have started food stores, print shops, and service centers, all of which contribute to the economic viability of the barrio. But recipients of these loans must pledge to renounce violence and crime, and each enterprise must include members from a rival gang. The results have been impressive: within the barrio, now nicknamed El Barrio de Paz ("peace town"), the monthly murder rate has dropped from 100 in 2005 to 10 in 2012. At one point, gang members assembled their weapons, piled them in the street, and ran them over with a steamroller.[41]

The identity of Nelsa Curbelo as a member of this violent neighborhood was the critical factor in creating this transformative program. Her ability to listen to young people otherwise cast as delinquent and beyond hope, her comfort in negotiating the violent streets of the barrio, and the trust she was able to establish among initially suspicious young men and women stem from her role as a member of the community.

Local leadership has the innate ability to see and to understand localized social problems with a clarity outsiders often cannot grasp. Emanating from the communities that they know intimately are programs whose focus reflects key elements of the social, economic, and cultural environment in which they must function to be both effective and sustainable. A critical factor in CBO leadership is this local genesis.

Leaders Who Walked the Walk

Surviving the traumas associated with violence, poverty, or exploitation is challenge enough. Emerging intact with minimal intellectual, physical, emotional, or spiritual scars is a victory. Making the conscious decision to reenter the arenas of trauma in service to other young people is inspirational.

Rwanda's genocide in 1994 left everyone in the country with a story. No one was removed from the violence, and each family to this day retains shreds of the genocide as either victim or perpetrator. The challenge remains more than two decades later to repair the devastated social fabric and bring the quality of life in a rebuilding country back to a peaceful normality.

Betty Gahima lived through her country's genocide as a refugee in Uganda. Returning to Rwanda in 1994 as a teacher, she saw its impact in the creation of countless orphans and widows, many of whom she knew personally. She co-founded Benishyaka Association with 17 other women immediately afterward to provide some level of support for these people and the devastated society that needed to be rebuilt. Benishyaka's approach is multilayered, incorporating economic empowerment and microlending for women, a community health center, and a thriving scholarship program for orphans to continue their educations.[42] The lasting support for the victims of the genocide who still struggle with its aftereffects comes in large measure from organizations such as Benishyaka, those that will be operating for as long as need is apparent. And the most personal of these efforts will be led by those whose own lives were irrevocably altered by the tragic events of war, violence, and ethnic hatred.

In the country next door, Kakenya Ntaiya was destined for a typical life of a typical girl in impoverished rural Kenya. She was engaged at the age of five to another boy in her village Enoosaen, and her future seemed sure to be rooted in the traditional role played by a young woman. Kakenya loved school, though, and she developed a rebellious streak. When she was scheduled for ritualistic female genital mutilation (FGM) at the age of 12, she did the unthinkable: she bargained with her father. If he would allow her to finish high school, she would submit to FGM. Once he agreed, she approached the village elders and continued her negotiations: if they would allow her to go to college in the United States, she would return to Enoosaen and use her education to benefit the village.

She became the first Maasai woman from her region to go to college, and she remained true to her promise. Committed to girls' education, she established the Kakenya Center for Excellence, a boarding school for girls in her village. From its inception in 2009, the school has grown to accommodate more than 190 young girls who otherwise would have faced the same dynamic that Kakenya was able to overcome. The social dynamics of

Enoosaen have changed as well. FGM is no longer expected, child marriages are on the wane, and girls and young women have found a stronger voice in contributing to village affairs.[43]

Earlier the work of James Kofi Annan, who escaped the fishing boats of Lake Volta in Ghana to establish Challenging Heights, and Josefa Condori Quispe, whose experience as a domestic servant led to the creation of Centro Yanapanakusun in Peru, referenced singular programs rooted in the direct experiences of its leadership. CBO leaders that have an intimate understanding of the issues confronting the most marginalized carry with them motivations that can break down walls which would stop a less driven individual.

Examples of "walking the walk" are not the sole province of the developing world. CBO leadership in any context can be drawn from shared experience. Rachel Lloyd grew up in England with her mother and an abusive stepfather. She left school at the age of 13 and supported herself, eventually through nude modeling, which led to commercial sexual exploitation. She survived rape and a murder attempt by her pimp.[44]

In 1997, Lloyd moved to New York to work with incarcerated women. She founded Girls Education and Mentoring Services (GEMS) to support girls and young women who have been victimized by the commercial sex trades or trafficked for sexual purposes. It is now the largest service provider of its kind in the nation,[45] and provides a range of services, including direct intervention on behalf of women caught in the trades, legal assistance where needed, transitional housing, and counseling. GEMS also has an aggressive advocacy and public policy program seeking to prevent young women from becoming trapped. In all, the organization seeks to reinstill a sense of self-worth in young women who have been severely abused, exploited, and traumatized.[46] Their programs stem from Rachel Lloyd's direct experience and escape from the conditions that diminished her, attempting to create support systems that the overwhelming majority of exploited and trafficked girls in both low- and high-income societies lack.

Experience is often the harshest teacher. Leaders who have learned the lessons of their hard times have the unique capacity to share those lessons through organizational structures made wise by their suffering. Their resiliency—the strength and flexibility that enabled them to survive their own situations—compels action on behalf of others who share those situations. Resiliency entails regeneration, sensing emerging risks, responding creatively to disruptions, and, ultimately, learning from those disruptions and translating that wisdom into protections against further risk.[47] It is a tragic irony that the very conditions that marginalize millions of children globally also spawn the leaders that can ultimately release them from their traumas.

Many CBO leaders are themselves products of the abuses they seek to address. Drawing from the knowledge and insights of their experiences, leaders are able to formulate effective responses from perspectives of genuine understanding and empathy. If one of the failings of outside organizations in confronting indigenous issues impacting children and young people is a reliance on formulas, which can be impersonal and detached, then one of the strengths of CBOs is their proximity to the problems they attack. The closest proximity comes from those who have lived through it.

Sharing the Success—Giving Back to Communities Left Behind

Those who are able to escape conditions of poverty or despair often forge new lives without ever looking back. There are no expectations when one is able to recreate a life in positive new forms, and coming from situations of stress where opportunities are limited at best or nonexistent at worst is reason enough for gratification.

But there are those who cannot entirely leave what it is they left behind. Many CBO leaders have in fact forged successful niches for themselves elsewhere, but have felt compelled to return to their communities to give something back.

Abul Hasanat Mohammed Rezwan grew up in Bangladesh near the rural provinces that were accessible only by river. With some familial advantages, he was able to complete his education as an architect, and he was asked to design for the rich. Yet the images of the river villages stayed with him. Recognizing that he had the rare privilege of an education in his country, he started working as a social entrepreneur and formed Shidhulai Swanirvar Sangstha, an organization whose purpose was to bring education to the young people upriver.

The children in these villages had little educational access, and that which did exist was reserved for boys. In response, Rezwan invented floating schools that would dock at set places during set times and provide basic primary education to the village's girls. The program expanded steadily as the impact on the quality of life in these villages became apparent. Shidhulai currently operates a fleet of 56 floating schools, libraries, health clinics, and training centers that ply the waterways in rural Bangladesh, educating boys now as well as girls year round. Using solar power, many are equipped with computer technology and wireless Internet access. At the same time, Shidhulai promotes environmental awareness and climate adaptation, including sustainable farming and solar energy.[48]

Rezwan had no motivation to abandon a lucrative professional career other than a realization that others left behind would have no such opportunities. In his own words, "Why can't an architect design exciting things to help the poor in their own communities? As an architect the school-boat was something very important for me to do. It was really my dream."[49]

Enjoying academic success similar to Rezwan's, Twesigye "Jackson" Kaguri grew up in Nyakagyezi, a village in rural Uganda and was diligent enough to win a scholarship to the national university. From there, he went abroad to study at Columbia University in the United States. He had married and was anticipating a lucrative career.[50]

Then the HIV/AIDS epidemic sliced through his dreams and called him back to his village. His older brother, the family's firstborn, married and with three children, died of AIDS. The next year, his sister also died of AIDS.

Both his brother and sister left behind young children who needed to go to school and needed support to get through their studies. So Jackson went back to Uganda to visit his orphaned nieces and nephews. In the village, Jackson saw the hundreds of other children who had lost their parents to HIV/AIDS and needed a pencil or school fees to stay in school but didn't have an uncle like him to provide it. From there, an idea was sparked: Jackson would build a school for his village. In 2003, he opened the Nyaka School for AIDS orphans.[51]

In the ensuing decade, Nyaka was able to open a second school. At each, children receive a free education through high school, two meals each day, and access to an onsite health clinic. As well, in realization that the death of parents from the disease most often placed huge burdens on the grandmothers to whom care for orphaned children fell, Nyaka organized an economic support program so that caretakers could learn a trade, open a business, or otherwise better provide for themselves and their grandchildren. "You see the grandmothers over and over whose own children have died and left them ... Some of them have up to 14 [grandchildren] to raise in their homes," Kaguri said.[52] In addition to the thousands of children that Nyaka has educated, thousands of grandparents have benefited from Nyaka's support programs.[53]

The call of service to dispossessed children and young people transcends social and economic status. Those who have found a perch outside the conditions of trauma or stress they have observed behind in their homelands often cannot stay away. While they may not have been among the marginalized, they had eyes enough to see them, and so helped devise and implement effective interventions, led by their empathy, their compassion, and personal commitment that would not let them rest.

Social Disruption

Leaders possess more than vision and compassion. Each of the CBO leaders referenced above, and the thousands of others who devote their lives to similar pursuits, carry with them a willingness to disrupt the social order. If their cause merits, they are willing to overturn the social structures, principles, and practices that define their culture. The niceties of procedure (those same procedures that often contribute to the diminution of those in poverty) and the respect for institutions (those same institutions that can cement the marginal status of those on society's outskirts) take secondary priority to the exigencies of systems change. Although many would not characterize it as such, and others would be appalled at the designation, the leaders of entrepreneurial CBOs are rebels. To be effective, they must be willing to embrace the social disruption and rearrangement their actions engender.

From Sakena Yacoobi's undermining of the rigid exclusion of girls from education to Kakenya Ntaiya's negotiations to disrupt the traditional patterns of child marriage and FGM to Nelsa Curbelo's conviction that gang members in the most economically stressed barrios could become positive contributors to their communities, the most effective CBO leaders challenge existing thought. They seek to overturn conventions and practices that lock in poverty, abuse, or exploitation.

It requires a special conviction and courage to be disruptive. Each of these leaders in his or her own way faced personal dangers ranging from self-imposed poverty to violent death. Yet each sees the value in rewriting societal rules, or, more precisely, unbending those rules so that societal practices can be more inclusive.

CBO leaders share a special fearlessness that allows the disruption of existing structures to accelerate our collective social evolution. Their work is based in change, which is inherently intimidating. But more intimidating to these leaders is the possibility that the lives of countless children and young people will continue to be compromised by conditions which their work can affect.

INCREASED GLOBAL RECOGNITION FOR TINY RIPPLES OF HOPE

The innovative work of CBOs, fueled by creative leadership, often works in low profile, less noticeable than broad-brush, resource-heavy programs launched by organizations with high name recognition. At times, it seems as if these groups can be as invisible as the children they seek to reach. When viewed in terms of sheer numbers, a program educating 150 children in poverty in rural Uganda is less spectacular than a multimillion dollar effort to build schools across several countries.

Yet smaller efforts rooted in their communities and sustainable through organically derived models reflective of the community ethos tend to survive. As prototypes, they can educate others to the necessities of successful implementation and spawn correlated efforts. New forms of intervention, new approaches, can change the way the complex, siloed field of international child and youth development regards itself, and how it might work. Small efforts done well create lasting ripples of ever broader scope.

The world has begun to take notice. Shidhulai's floating schools have won numerous awards, including the Bill and Melinda Gates Foundation Access to Learning Award in 2005 and the World Innovation Summit for Education Award in 2012. With each award, leaders participate in global conferences and roundtable discussions to profile the project and the thinking behind it. Thousands of thought leaders have been exposed to the concept of the boat schools, and many are finding ways to adapt some of its principles to their own cultural situations.

Sakena Yacoobi's direction of the Afghan Institute of Learning has come to be recognized by both practitioners and academics worldwide, including the Afghan Ministry of Education, the Skoll Foundation, and Harvard University. She has also been nominated for the Nobel Peace Prize.

A single physician working alone to bring neonatal care to infants in one of Karachi, Pakistan's worst slums, Dr. Anita Zaidi, has won a $1 million prize to further her work. The initial Caplow Children's Prize in 2013 was awarded to Dr. Zaidi for her work in tending to children in such extreme poverty that 11% die before the age of five and most of those within the first month after birth. Embracing the necessary concept of social disruption, Dr. Zaidi will use her award to build a broader effort by training midwives and setting up a transportation network to local hospitals. She will also work to overturn societal prejudices against hospitals, vitamins, and vaccinations.[54] No one else has found the courage to undertake this work on behalf of the forgotten children in Karachi's slums, and her work is just beginning.

Many of the leaders who began with small efforts have gained sufficient recognition to be profiled in major national and international media. Jackson Kaguri and Kakenya Ntaiya have been featured on CNN Heroes, and almost every other CBO leader referenced above has been the focus of media attention at some level. Every story confirms their approach and imparts lessons for other budding entrepreneurs, social thinkers, and potential partners.

The World Children's Prize is awarded annually to global champions of children's rights, but beyond this it seeks "to catalyze the growth and development of a more human global community through an integrated global educational program."[55] Juried by 15 children from across the world, the Prize provides a forum for press events, ceremonies, seminars, and networking to highlight the plight of children and young people. The child jurors themselves have survived their own trauma, including time spent in servitude, on the street, as child soldiers, or as refugees. Three nominees are honored, and awarded prize money to further their work, and typically each nominee has a community-based focus. Past winners include many of those profiled in these pages, like Sakena Yacoobi, James Kofi Annan, Inderjit Khurana, and Indira Ranamagar. Patrons of the World Children's Prize include some of the most prominent human rights and children's advocates in the world, including Desmond Tutu, Graca Michel, Aung San Suu Kyi, and José Ramos-Horta.[56]

The International Youth Foundation has instituted the IYF Youth Action Awards to recognize youth-led ventures around the world. Annually 20 young founders of social change projects, some as young as 18, are named Laureate Global Fellows. In addition to the prize money that goes with this designation, Fellows receive personal coaching and counsel from experts in their fields and are networked with other past recipients to strengthen their work. Young people have devised creative solutions to economic and social challenges, such as using a mobile phone service to help job seekers in the most marginalized communities access immediate information about employment opportunities, or producing solar lamps to avoid dangerous emissions from kerosene lamps, then directing the proceeds to scholarship opportunities for children in poverty.[57]

The success of any program is contingent in huge measure on the quality and motivations of its leadership. The best leaders blend idealism with practicality and pursue their work on behalf of society's most vulnerable with an almost obsessive passion. And although their individual efforts might be smaller in scope than programs with higher recognition, broader mandates, and seemingly bottomless resources, their work is shifting the parameters of child and youth development.

Over the past several years, the number of CBOs has expanded, and their work has become more comprehensive. Leaders are employing modern communication tools to become more visible, and the developed world is taking increasing notice of what is germinating at the ground level. The sector is gradually emerging from obscurity, providing us all a real moment of opportunity to seize this evolution and drive it forward.

CBOs, with their innate capacity to identify and reach those beyond the recognition and scope of these larger interventions, provide the best hope for children at society's farthest edges. These small and localized efforts, drop by drop, can rewrite traditional international development approaches.

In a landmark speech at Cape Town University in South Africa in 1966, at the height of apartheid's most brutal repressions, Robert Kennedy said, "Each time a man stands up for an ideal, or acts to improve the lot of others, or strikes out against injustice, he sends forth a tiny ripple of hope, and crossing each other from a million different centers of energy and daring, those ripples build a current which can sweep down the mightiest walls of oppression...."[58]

It is the leadership of community-based efforts that change the trajectories of children's lives that author countless ripples of hope. They must be heeded.

NOTES

1. This discussion has been aided by Leslie R. Crutchfield and Heather McLeod Grant, *Forces for Good: The Six Practices of High-Impact Nonprofits* (Jossey-Bass, 2007).
2. M. Nerfin, "Neither Prince nor Merchant: Citizen—an Introduction to the Third System." In K. Ahooja-Patel, A.G. Drabek, and M. Nerfin (eds.),

World Economy in Transition. (Oxford, England: Pergamon Press, 1986) as cited in Adil Najam, "Understanding the Third Sector: Revisiting the Prince, the Merchant, and the Citizen," *Nonprofit Management & Leadership* (Jossey-Bass Publishers) 7, no. 2 (Winter 1996): 218.

3. Guy Hunter, *Modernizing Peasant Societies* (New York: Oxford University Press, 1969) as cited by Norman Uphoff, "Grassroots Organizations and NGOs in Rural Development: Opportunities with Diminishing States and Expanding Markets," *World Development* (Pergamon Press, Ltd) 21, no. 4 (1993): 610.

4. Norman Uphoff, "Grassroots Organizations and NGOs in Rural Development: Opportunities with Diminishing States and Expanding Markets," *World Development* (Pergamon Press, Ltd) 21, no. 4 (1993): 609.

5. Sheldon Annis, "Can Small-scale Development be a Large-scale Policy? The Case of Latin America." *World Development* (Pergamon Journals, Ltd.) 15, Supplement (1987): 130.

6. Norman Uphoff, "Grassroots Organizations and NGOs in Rural Development: 609.

7. E. Garilao, "Indigenous NGOs as Strategic Institutions: Managing the Relationship with Government and Resource Agencies," *World Development*, 1987, *15*, 114.

8. E. Garilao, "Indigenous NGOs as Strategic Institutions", 116.

9. *Strengthening Endogenous Development in Africa: A Methodological Guide.* (2010, July). Retrieved November 12, 2013, from Ground Swell International: http://www.groundswellinternational.org/wp-content/uploads/Strengthening-Endogenous-Development-in-Africa-1-July-2010.pdf

10. *Strengthening Endogenous Development in Africa: A Methodological Guide.* (2010, July).

11. *Strengthening Endogenous Development in Africa: A Methodological Guide.* (2010, July).

12. *Strengthening Endogenous Development in Africa: A Methodological Guide.* (2010, July).

13. Urie Bronfenbrenner, *The Ecology of Human Development: Experiments by Nature and Design.* Cambridge, MA: Harvard University Press, (1979).

14. Robert Anda, "The Health and Social Impact of Growing Up with Adverse Childhood Experiences," http://www.acestudy.org/files/Review_of_ACE_Study_with_references_summary_table_2_.pdf.

15. Robert D. Putnam, *Bowling Alone: America's Declining Social Capital"*, New York, NY: Simon and Schuster, (1995), pp. 65–78.

16. Robert D. Putnam, *Bowling Alone,* pp. 65–78.

17. Robert D. Putnam, *Bowling Alone,* pp. 65–78.

18. Lester Salamon, "The Third Sector in Global Perspectives," Inter-American Foundation, http://www.iaf.gov/index.aspx?page=915
19. http://www.indianexpress.com/news/first-official-estimate-an-ngo-for-every-400-people-in-india/643302/
20. Cf. Chapter 3, "A Glass Half Full; A Glass Half-Empty" for references of impactful programs.
21. Sujata Ganega, Executive Director, SUPPORT, Interview, January 10, 2012 (Saudamini Dabak, interviewer).
22. Sujata Ganega, Executive Director, SUPPORT, Interview, January 10, 2012 (Saudamini Dabak, interviewer).
23. 2009 financial profile on SUPPORT summary at www.guidestarindia.com.
24. Sujata Ganega, Executive Director, SUPPORT, Interview, January 10, 2012 (Saudamini Dabak, interviewer).
25. Trip report, Gregory Fields, Global Fund for Children, September 2003; and Friends for Street Children http://ffscvn.org/index.php?lang=en
26. PBS. (n.d.). *The Train Platform Schools of India.* Retrieved March 26, 2014, from http://www.ruchika.org/video/video.htm
27. Trip report, Michael Gale, Global Fund for Children, November 2011; and GFC: *Annual Report: 2006–2007,* p. 35. Retrieved March 27, 2014 from The Global Fund for Children: https://www.globalfundforchildren.org/wp-content/uploads/2012/01/It-All-Starts-With-A-Spark.pdf
28. http://www.usaid.gov/usaidforward/
29. http://web.worldbank.org/WBSITE/EXTERNAL/TOPICS/EXTURBANDEVELOPMENT/EXTLED/0,,menuPK:341145~pagePK:149018~piPK:149093~theSitePK:341139,00.html
30. Rogers, K. (2013, November 7). *Another Way of 'Going Local': Engaging the Diaspora.* Retrieved November 8, 2013, from Devex: https://www.devex.com/en/news/another-way-of-going-local-engaging-the-diaspora/82253
31. http://www.savethechildren.org/site/c.8rKLIXMGIpI4E/b.6151901/k.A29A/Aid_Effectiveness.htm
32. http://www.mercycorps.org/research-resources/local-partnerships-guide
33. William Easterly, 'The White Man's Burden: Why the West's Efforts to Aid the Rest Have Done so Much Ill and so Little Good', The Penguin Press, New York, 2006. chapter 1.
34. Jeffrey Gettleman, "Meant to Keep Malaria Out, Fishing Nets are Used to Haul Fish In," *The New York Times,* January 24.2015.
35. https://www.ashoka.org/knowinghistory
36. https://www.ashoka.org/fellow/amlan-ganguly; cf. http://prayasam.org/history.asp
37. https://www.ashoka.org/about

38. www.huffingtonpost.com/2008/06/24/nelsa-curtado-former-nun_n_108869.html

39. www.huffingtonpost.com/2008/06/24/nelsa-curtado-former-nun_n_108869.html

40. Johnston, Vanessa. (Jan 29, 2009). *In Ecuador, gang members trade guns for scissors and nail polish.* Retrieved March 27 from Christian Science Monitor: *http://www.csmonitor.com/World/Americas/2009/0122/p01s03-woam.html; and Learn about Ser Paz in Ecuador.* Video. Retrieved March 27, 2014 from Huffington Post: http://videos.huffingtonpost.com/entertainment/learn-about-ser-paz-in-ecuador-511847015; *and* Gale, Michael. (November 14, 2013). *Peace Comes to the Streets of Guayaquil.* Retrieved March 27, 2014 from Global Fund for Children: *https://www.globalfundforchildren.org/peace-comes-to-the-streets-of-guayaquil/; and* Global Fund for Children. (Jan 5, 2012). *Partners: Ser Paz.* Retrieved March 27, 2014 from Global Fund for Children: https://www.globalfundforchildren.org/partners/ser-paz/

41. www.huffingtonpost.com/2008/06/24/nelsa-curtado-former-nun_n_108869.html

42. GFC. (January 5, 2012). *Partners: Benishyaka Association.* Retrieved March 26, 2014 from Global Fund for Children: https://www.globalfundforchildren.org/partners/benishyaka-association/; and Betty Gahima, email message to Clare Dreyfus, June 25, 2014.

43. www.kakenyasdream.org/about-us/kakenyas-story/; and CNN. (2014). *CNN Heroes: 2013 Heroes—Kakenya Ntaiya, Community Crusader.* Retrieved March 27, 2014 from CNN Living: http://www.cnn.com/SPECIALS/cnn.heroes/2013.heroes/kakenya.ntaiya.html; *and* Kakenya Ntaiya Mugoh, Founder and Director, 'Interview, June 19, 2012 (Saudamini Dabak, interviewer).

44. Connelly, Phoebe. (March 8, 2010). *Advocating for Women: Girls Educational & Mentoring Services.* Retrieved March 26, 2014 from The American Prospect: http://prospect.org/article/advocating-women-girls-educational-mentoring-services; and http://www.gems-girls.org; and GFC. *Annual Report: 2004–2005,* p. 20. Retrieved March 27, 2014 from The Global Fund for Children; and GFC: *Annual Report: 2006–2007,* p. 100. Retrieved March 27, 2014 from The Global Fund for Children; *and* Julie Laurence, Chief Program Officer, GEMS, email messages to Clare Dreyfus, July 13, 2014 and July 15, 2014.

45. Connelly, Phoebe. (March 8, 2010). *Advocating for Women: Girls Educational & Mentoring Services;* and http://www.gems-girls.org; and GFC. *Annual Report: 2004–2005,* p. 20; and GFC: *Annual Report: 2006–2007,* p. 100; and Twanna Toliver, Executive Assistant to Rachel Lloyd, email message to Clare Dreyfus, July 10, 2014.

46. Connelly, Phoebe. (March 8, 2010). *Advocating for Women: Girls Educational & Mentoring Services;* and http://www.gems-girls.org; and GFC. *Annual Report: 2004–2005,* p. 20; and GFC: *Annual Report: 2006–2007,* p. 100.

47. http://andrewzolli.com/the-verbs-of-resilience/

48. Shidhulai.org/aboutshidhulai.html; and Ashden Awards. (2009). *Case Study Summary: Shidhulai Swanirvar Sangstha.* Retrieved March 26, 2014 from Ashden Awards: http://www.ashden.org/files/Shidhulai%20 case%20study%20full.pdf; and Yee, Amy. (June 30, 2013). *"Floating Schools" Bring Classrooms to Stranded Students. The New York Times.*

49. Gregory Fields, Global Fund for Children, trip report, November 2003; and Abul Hasanat Mohammed Rezwan, email message to Clare Dreyfus, July 4, 2014.

50. Jackson Kaguri, Founder, Nyaka, Interview, February 24, 2012 (Saudamini. Dabak, interviewer) and Allie Togan (June 22, 2012). *Cashing in the American dream to help AIDS orphans, those who raise them.* CNN. Retrieved March 26, 2014 from CNN: http://www.cnn.com/2012/06/21/ world/africa/cnnheroes-kaguri-uganda; and Torrealba, Alexandra. (June 28, 2012). *Our Partners- CNN Heroes,* Retrieved March 27, 2014 from Global Fund for Children: https://www.globalfundforchildren.org/ our-partners-cnn-heroes/

51. http://www.huffingtonpost.com/2012/06/28/jackson-kaguri-founder-of_n_1628704.html

52. http://www.huffingtonpost.com/2012/06/28/jackson-kaguri-founder-of_n_1628704.html

53. http://www.huffingtonpost.com/2012/06/28/jackson-kaguri-founder-of_n_1628704.html

54. Zaidi, Anita. (December 30, 2013). *$1 Million Prize for Pakistani Pediatrician. New York Times.*

55. www.worldschildrensprize.org

56. www.worldschildrensprize.org

57. http://www.youthactionnet.org/fellows

58. www.americanrhetoric.com/speeches/rfkcapetown.htm

CHAPTER 8

Going to Scale

In the face of the immense statistics and stories defining the plight of the world's invisible young people, small projects showing lasting, sustainable impact and changing the trajectories of marginalized lives shine forth like beacons in a dark night sky. And when we see these lights, we have a natural tendency to want to see them shine more broadly, to extend the influence of these beacons into more communities, into more lives.

Bill Clinton said, "Nearly every problem has been solved by someone, somewhere. The challenge of the twenty-first century is to scale it up."[1] In the examples provided of community-based organization's (CBO's) approaches to the issues plaguing children in poverty, solutions are apparent. But these solutions are, for the most part, particular to time, place, and culture. The issue of scaling is clearly not as easy as simply taking the components of one successful program and transplanting them to other areas where they are needed. The objective of effective scaling should not necessarily be the replication of a program piece by piece, but the reproduction of a program's success based on the factors that created that success. Such factors often require adaptation and adjustment to their new circumstances, a step that is often overlooked in the process of seeking to grow effective programs.

If scaling is dependent upon demonstrable evidence, then that evidence needs to be clear. Scaling poor or ineffective programs is a waste of both financial and human resources. Any organization that seeks to scale its work must be certain of its effect. Its theory of social change

© The Editor(s) (if applicable) and The Author(s) 2016
M. Ajmera, G.A. Fields, *Invisible Children*,
DOI 10.1057/978-1-137-57838-9_8

must be clear, and its outcomes both measurable and positive. Scaling a program merely for the sake of expansion is at best questionable and at worst a squandering of a community's very finite capacity for program implementation.[2]

Many groups with good ideas that could inform or propel other work lack the resources to go to scale in any form. This is especially true of CBOs that often must struggle for their own survival and cannot direct financial or human resources to scaling their programs or expanding their work elsewhere. Scaling can only be effective when it is the logical emanation of carefully constructed strategy backed by adequate resources to implement scaling without debilitating either the new effort or the original program.

The issue of resources permeates all aspects of the work of CBOs, including the potential to scale that work. CBOs are most often too small to penetrate the radar of major funders. Much of their support is localized, and, if they are fortunate and sophisticated enough to attract contributions from outside their immediate region, most of their funds will go toward existing programs. Quite simply, CBOs are often too small to be noticed by the big funders, but they need that financial support to grow, to spawn their good ideas for broader application.

Still, when ideas are put into action and show results against previously intractable social problems, lessons can be learned that might inform the work of others and make that work more effective. The best work seeks broader implementation so that more lives can be changed. Effective scaling can bring about greater efficiency throughout the sector by developing new best practices. Scaling can attract greater resources through increased visibility, which in turn can bestow greater credibility in the eyes of funders. It can consolidate capital and make that capital more impactful because its disbursement is based on proven models with proven results. If a world with finite financial and human reserves is to tackle the immense scope of the issues affecting vulnerable young people, it must do so at least in part by scaling what works.

SMALL IS BEAUTIFUL

Our society tends to believe that bigger is better. We aspire to be the strongest, the fastest, the richest, and our collective values gravitate toward those ends. We expect that something good is made better by securing more of it, and that we can never have enough of what we want. And we tend to assume that what works for us should work for everyone. More is better.

Such a view ignores the power of persistence, and the integrity of small efforts that remain true to their purpose. CBOs carve their own places, their own niches, and in those niches they work effectively to the full limits of their resources. Some of the most significant, dynamic, and essential movements have begun with small and simple steps. The American Red Cross started with one woman's effort—Clara Barton—to provide medical supplies for wounded soldiers in the US Civil War. One man's efforts—Muhammad Yunus—to lend women in poverty small amounts of money in rural Bangladesh led to a Nobel Peace Prize and an innovative new method of financing economic and social development.

Small groups carry an innate power to burrow into their communities, digging deeply into the lives of the people affected by issues of marginalization and attaining sustainable results. The CBOs profiled earlier are examples of the hundreds of thousands of such groups, often invisible to the broader world but pursuing vital, innovative programs that hold valuable lessons for their sectors.

In his book *Small Giants*, Bo Burlingham takes a look at several privately held for-profit companies that have chosen to focus not on growth and higher revenues but on being the very best at what they do. They have remained small, yet they are industry leaders in terms of quality, with far-reaching reputations for excellence in both product and management. The growth they have enjoyed has been driven by need for what they do within the parameters of how they do it. They have changed nothing in their approach, and their excellence remains intact.[3]

There are lessons here for the social sector. An adherence to quality provides the foundation for any expansion. Without that adherence, scaling is meaningless. The capacity of CBOs to identify approaches that are holistic and locally focused has great value in reaching children that are beyond the range of larger, better funded programs. As a result, the sector would be remiss in not evaluating ways in which these small "industry leaders" might go to scale.

What Does Scale Really Mean?

Simply put, going to scale is generally accepted to mean bringing more programmatic benefits to more people in more places. Immersed in our collective notion that "bigger is better," scale is seen as desirable and the mark of a successful product. In most corners of the commercial sector, management's goal is to expand markets, to maximize visibility and, in so doing, to sell more product to more people. If, then, a social program works well for a certain group of people, would it not be better if that program were ramped up to reach more markets?

Most viable programs addressing the needs of marginalized young people carry forward this sentiment at some level. Their good work can change lives for the better, and, if so, then logic demands that more lives be reached. There is always one more child to be fed, one more girl to be educated, one more boy to be reclaimed from a lost childhood.

But the approaches to scaling a social program are necessarily different than expanding the market for a tangible product. It is, in the end, a much clearer process to design a campaign to sell more smartphones than it is to bring an effective educational program across regional lines. Where product expansion can be planned in accordance with income studies, demographic models, and market saturation analysis, supplemented by creative and compelling marketing campaigns, the expansion of social programs relies on measuring less quantifiable factors. Each issue is impacted by culture, family structures, economic opportunities, and a myriad of other social factors that are not easily captured and are certainly not controllable.

Scale is also contingent upon the aspirations of an organization's leadership. Some groups do not, or cannot, look beyond their immediate arena. The challenges of maintaining their work in place might dampen any notions of going broader, or they may lack the conceptual and human resources needed to grow their programs beyond their current status. The inherent and ongoing challenge of financing community-based efforts often limits any ambitions to expand. And any type of expansion carries with it the need to ensure programmatic integrity, recruit and retain effective staff to implement this new work, and build credibility in new places and with new constituencies. Sometimes it just seems simpler to stay in place and do well the work at hand.

Even programs that are seemingly simple in concept can face insurmountable challenges if brought out of their cultural, social, political, or religious context. A highly successful program providing shelter and education for AIDS orphans in Zambia—taking them off the streets of the capital and relocating them to the countryside where they were organized into quasi-family units to care for one another—failed in its expansion into Mozambique because social interpretations of family in that country precluded the organizational component that was at the heart of the program's effectiveness in Zambia.[4] Even something as rudimentary as providing polio vaccines can be subject to violence in places such as Nigeria and Pakistan because of political suspicions that did not haunt successful immunization efforts in Rwanda or Burundi.[5]

Taking a successful effort to scale requires that a CBO know with precision what it is about, what it wants to do, and what it can reasonably do within the subtle yet defining characteristics of culture, society, and place. Scaling is not merely a matter of doing more or going to new places.

Scaling occurs in three ways:

Going Wide—Bringing an existing program to more places to reach more people;

Going Deep—Expanding programs and interventions so that they burrow into a community's problems in multiple ways; and

Going Up—Using the knowledge and experience of a program to impact public awareness and public policy.

We will look at scaling through these three lenses.

Scaling—Going Wide

The most commonly accepted notion of going to scale is expanding a working program to new people or locations. Most CBOs originate at a single point, or possibly a few locations close together. As their programs develop, patterns of operation become less tentative, and the impact of what they do becomes clearer, some CBOs strive to expand outward, to go as wide as resources permit in bringing their work to more people.

There are three ways in which this can occur: *franchising*—offering an exact program model to a leader in another location; *replication*—spawning the same program elsewhere under original leadership; and *reproduction*—providing a prototype that others can develop within their own communities and within their own social contexts. CBOs have used each of these approaches in bringing their programs to other locations.

India accounts for the largest national share of global undernutrition, and that country's recent economic growth has not acceptably reduced the level of children without enough food.[6] "I see dramatic improvements in four-lane roads ... airports getting fancier, which helps people like me when I'm traveling," says Dr. S.V. Subramanian, a social epidemiologist at Harvard University and the senior author of a report on the correlation between economic development and malnutrition, published in *The Lancet*.[7] "However, for the majority of the population, I don't see improvements for the slums that I pass[ed] through every day where I lived."[8]

Near Kolkata, one man looked out his window one morning and saw a group of children fighting with street dogs for a few scraps of food. Realizing that temples had kitchens that were seldom used, he organized a group to cook food and take it to local government schools to feed the malnourished children who frequently went without a daily meal. Years later, the group he inspired, Akshaya Patra, started by feeding 1500 children in five schools. Today, through replication of its program, it reaches more than 1.39 million children a day, operating in 10,600 schools from 23 locations across nine Indian states.[9]

Akshaya Patra came into being to address the dual challenges of hunger and education in India by providing nutrition-rich midday meals to underprivileged children in India to increase school enrollment, reduce dropout rates, and improve academic performance. As its work expanded, the organization negotiated partnerships with India's ministries and the corporate sector. The state and federal governments of India provide up to 60% of meal costs through cash and grain subsidies. Another 30% of funding comes from corporate and individual donors in India. Fundraising branch offices in the United States and UK provide the remaining 10% of program funding. The predominance of local investment in Akshaya Patra's midday program has ensured the organization's unique sustainability.[10]

In one province where the organization now works, approximately one million children were out of school before the meal program was launched. But within a short time, that number had dropped to 70,000. Free meals attracted children to school, and parents in turn had fewer mouths to feed at home. Akshaya Patra's focus on impactful investment extends into their kitchens, and the midday meal law is written to guarantee that at least one cook in the kitchen is from the "untouchable class" and that all cooks must work equally. [11]

Akshaya Patra, along with countless other CBOs across the globe, have filled definable gaps in services that can reasonably be expected to issue from public sources. In the ideal, governments educate their children, feed them, and ensure their safety. When for whatever reason they cannot, CBOs step into the void out of necessity. When the efforts of these CBOs provide a complement to public programs, governments do well to enter partnerships that allow these services to be delivered to greater numbers efficiently and without undue stress on limited public budgets. In these configurations, governments become more effective, CBOs go to scale, and, most significantly, marginalized populations see benefits and opportunities that would otherwise be beyond their grasp.

Elsewhere in Asia, in one of the temporary camps in Mae Sot, Thailand, on the Thai–Myanmar border, Women's Education for Advancement and Empowerment (WEAVE) was founded to support indigenous and refugee women living in poverty by facilitating access to education, health care, and economic development. With the influx of refugees from Myanmar over the past 25 years, the organization shifted its focus to encompass displaced families fleeing Myanmar's longstanding conflict. From its single launch point and its original programming, WEAVE developed a program for early childhood development incorporating the specific needs and learning obstacles faced by refugee children that has been reproduced in other locations. Its work grew outward and now reaches the localities of Mae Sod, Mae Hong Son, Ratchaburi, and Kanchanaburi, as well as some villages in Myanmar. WEAVE has based projects in the refugee camps along the Thai–Myanmar border and expanded northward to the Chinese border as well. Its work within the refugee populations has expanded into microlending, with a corollary advocacy program stressing fair trade practices.[12] In all, WEAVE provides support for more than 10,000 preschool children in more than 50 locations along both sides of the Thai–Myanmar border.[13]

These programs, and thousands like them, all began with a concept based on direct intervention to counter the issues marginalizing young people and putting them at risk for further violence, subjugation, exploitation, or loss. Once that concept gained an operational foothold at its inception, these organizations sought to expand their work into new areas while maintaining the integrity and quality of the efforts they had launched on a smaller scale.

This approach is the customary interpretation of going to scale, and without question the impact of this scaling is essential in addressing problems that most commonly know no geographic bounds. In each case, expansion is neither automatic nor formulaic. Programmatic scaling can only come with a recognition of any program's compatibility with the ethos of those communities into which it seeks to move. The young people reached by the programs cited in these examples showed a commonality that allowed ready expansion and did not threaten cultural, social, or political identities. Accordingly, expansion could occur as the product of resources and intentions nuanced into appropriate cultural contexts.

Scaling—Going Deep

Often programs come into existence with a single or limited focal point, only to discover that single issues rarely stand alone. In such circumstances, organizations that concentrate on a single entry point of service confront the enormity of their task. An approach to any one of these issues, no matter how well constructed, will be incomplete. Organizations and their leadership must find ways to peel away the layers of a very complex onion.

Once engaged in addressing the inequalities of low-income communities, sound programs will recognize the further steps needed to come closer to implementing sustainable change. They find ways to expand their work according to what needs doing. Rather than scale outward, or going wide, these groups dig deeply into the complex, interconnected hearts of their communities. In so doing, they exert a greater impact on the lives of young people, their families, and their communities as a whole than if they had remained true to a single focus. This more subtle form of scaling carries inestimable value.

In Nairobi's Kibera slums, one million people, nearly half of Nairobi's total population, live in an area the size of New York's Central Park. Unrecognized by the Kenyan government, who contends that residents are illegally squatting and therefore does not provide sufficient services or infrastructure like toilets, roads, schools, or hospitals, Kibera is one of the most densely populated places on the planet. Life expectancy is approximated at 30 years. For women and girls, the most marginalized of the slum community, reality is even worse. Seven in ten girls in Kibera experience acts of violence and young women contract HIV at a rate five times that of their male counterparts. Only about 29% of girls in Kibera have the chance to attend primary school, compared to about 43% of boys.[14]

The oldest of eight children, Kennedy Odede ran away from his home in Kibera at the age of ten because his family could not afford to feed him. Kennedy left, choosing to become homeless, living on the streets, and eating from garbage while trying to raise money to put himself and his sisters through school by selling peanuts and collecting bottles. At the age of 17, Kennedy took a job at a factory, earning $1.50 daily for 10 hours of work. Encountering the stories of Nelson Mandela and Martin Luther King, Jr., Kennedy became inspired that change in his community was possible. He eventually saved enough money to purchase a secondhand soccer ball, using the game as a way to gather people to dream and talk about their issues.[15]

Kennedy started Shining Hope for Communities (SHOFCO) and expanded his organization in partnership with an American volunteer, Jessica Posner. With a mission of combating intergenerational cycles of poverty and gender inequality, SHOFCO links tuition-free school for girls to essential social services for the community, using a holistic, community-driven approach to reinforce the benefit of investing in women and cultivate a community ethos of female respect. Their flagship, the Kibera School for Girls, provides girls with an education as well as free health care, food, and psychosocial services. Built with the help of community members and staffed with women leaders to act as female role models to the students, the school is the first tuition-free school for girls in Kibera. [16]

The school offers Kibera a vibrant community center with a computer lab and library, as well as adult education and legal services. Monitoring the program's progress through a series of baseline and program-intensive surveys, SHOFCO has found their program participants were less likely to report domestic violence and abuse. The organization continues to see their young students emerge as community leaders, teaching family and neighbors to read, and organizing themselves to set up food drives and donations if a tragedy befalls their neighbors.

Community-based responses to social stresses are not limited to low-income societies. Examples of holistic, locally driven initiatives with demonstrable impact abound in the United States and Western Europe. When the crack cocaine epidemic of the 1980s and 1990s tore through New York City, a small truancy prevention program in Harlem saw the need to deepen its work to provide alternatives to young people likely to be swept up by that and other vices. They initiated the concept of turning public schools into community centers after hours and made recreational and educational programs accessible to all comers. They established a Peacemakers Program using adult volunteers to keep schools safe during the day. The group, originally called Rheedlen, transformed itself into the Harlem Children's Zone (HCZ).[17]

Under the leadership of founder Geoffrey Canada, HCZ did not try to be all things to all people. Instead, it focused its efforts on a single block of Harlem and sought within it to address the full range of social and economic problems faced by people in poverty, including housing, education, health, and nutrition. As its work progressed, HCZ monitored its impact and was one of the first organizations to rely on outcome measurements to determine programmatic strategy. Within seven years, HCZ expanded its scope to encompass a 24-block radius. Within that limited and clearly defined territory, HCZ monitored and supported the academic careers of young men and women in a particularly vulnerable demographic, working with them through college and their entry into the job market. Its mandate of breaking the generational cycles of poverty has compelled HCZ to launch a variety of initiatives, some more successful than others, but each evaluated and measured closely.[18]

This localized, focused "drilling-down" approach has proven attractive to funders seeking to undo the seemingly intractable problems of the most marginalized urban neighborhoods, and as a result HCZ has raised millions of dollars for its work. At the same time, Geoffrey Canada has been approached by other municipalities to replicate his program in their cities. He has always declined these offers, stating that he will not replicate HCZ, but that he will encourage its reproduction by other cities in accordance with their own needs. HCZ's own program has remained rooted in Harlem. HCZ's geographic focus has slowly crept outward but always remained within Harlem's most economically stressed blocks.[19]

Because they are close to the ground, CBOs have the unique capacity to expand or redirect their work to areas of greatest community need, and broadest positive impact. They are not bound by strict programmatic guidelines that control the direction of their resources in predetermined ways, nor are they confined by narrow missions that can exclude segments of a low-income society. Many CBOs will, in accordance with their available human and financial resources, seek to find ways to go beyond initial efforts or initiatives if it becomes apparent that those initiatives are part of a broader set of problems afflicting their target population.

This resolve leads to deep community engagement. By going below the surface of their focused efforts, these organizations are able to scale their work in ways that maximize their impact on local demographics. They may not go wide—seeking to bring in more and more beneficiaries—but they are able to make sustainable, lasting impacts on the lives of those within their sphere of work.

Scaling—Going Up

CBOs that work intensely in issues with broad policy implications can scale their efforts by spurring the public into awareness, discussion, and

response. By developing aggressive, targeted advocacy efforts to complement their work on the ground, CBOs can lend an authoritative voice
to considerations of any arena of public policy that impacts the lives of
vulnerable young people.

Many CBOs have determined that a critical aspect of their programs
of service is expanding their programs to address general societal issues.
Their work has led to wellsprings of knowledge that arise uniquely from
engagement at the community level. This knowledge comes in the form of
a distinctive awareness of the source of the issues jeopardizing the young,
the singular community resources that can be mobilized to address them,
the leadership at the community level that can be engaged in these efforts,
and the corresponding lessons that this leadership has learned and is willing to share in support of more enlightened public policy. Scaling up is
perhaps the best way for an effective program to have the widest possible
impact, superseding program replication.

In the red light district of Mumbai, Prerana runs a night care center
for children of prostitutes in Mumbai, providing hot meals, recreation,
nonformal education, health care, and a safe haven without stigma or
judgment. But Prerana's influence does not stop at its community's boundaries. The organization's founders, Pravin and Priti Patkar, have emerged
as leading voices regarding issues of trafficking, child involvement in the
sex industry, minimum standards of care and support services, and safety
standards for the victims of trafficking. After a dozen years of operation,
Prerana's work was referenced in 1998 by the Indian Ministry of Human
Resource Development's *National Plan of Action to Combat Trafficking
and Commercial Sexual Exploitation of Women and Children.* Four years
later, Pravin Patkar was appointed to Ministry of Health working groups
to develop five- and ten-year plans regarding the curbing of sexual exploitation. From these platforms, Prerana was able to influence Indian legisla-
tive efforts on the issue, and in fact Prerana's leadership helped draft nearly
four dozen pieces of relevant legislation over a three-year period.

By 2007, Prerana had become recognized as a major national resource
in efforts to combat trafficking and exploitation. That year Prerana was
charged with developing police training protocols dealing with these
issues. In 2011, Priti was invited to serve on an Indian Supreme Court
panel to discuss problems faced by women in the sex industry, with recommendations for the best pathways to rehabilitation.[20]

Prerana's work succeeded on many levels. At its most basic, the organization provides shelter and alternatives for children caught in the crossfire

of their mothers' work. But the willingness, indeed the insistence, of its founders to carry the discussion into broader public arenas has multiplied the impact of their model countless times over. By pushing their knowledge upward through the corridors of national and regional power, Prerana has become a respected, recognized advocate for the women and children caught in these destructive trades. While their direct programmatic work has touched thousands, their advocacy efforts have scaled the impact of that work to a point where it is increasingly embedded into the national fabric.

Halfway around the world from Prerana's innovative model, children living in poverty in Huachipa, Peru, on the outskirts of the capital Lima, gravitate to the brickmaking kilns that offer small pay for long hours of hot, dangerous work. Still, the tiny salaries can be critical for families struggling to survive. In the late 1990s, Alfredo Robles noted the plight of the young children in the kilns—"At the age of 14 most European children are at school. Here in Huachipa a child of 14 has already been working for a decade."[21] He helped establish Asociación de Defensa de la Vida (ADEVI) to provide these children nonformal education, preventive health awareness, and skills training so that they can redirect themselves out of the kilns. In time, ADEVI also developed a small microlending program to assist the older children in establishing their own businesses.[22]

By the middle of the next decade, ADEVI had grown sufficiently in resources and programmatic stability to send its messages upward. The organization had always maintained a delicate relationship with the kiln owners and had seen some success in compelling them to ease the conditions under which the children worked. In fact, ADEVI's model allows the children to work two days each week in the kilns and go to school three days.

With the experiences of the children in the kilns informing their efforts, ADEVI became assertive as an advocate for child workers at the local and national levels. Although still a relatively small group, ADEVI is a regular participant in a growing movement to safeguard Peru's child laborers, and ADEVI's leadership lobbies Peru's legislators strongly on this issue. The organization has adopted an aggressive advocacy initiative as part of its strategic planning and has come to embrace this responsibility as central to its mission.[23]

Advocacy work such as ADEVI's can develop organically as an organization's central focus. In 2001, Suparna Gupta quit her position with an advertising agency in Mumbai to utilize her degree in psychology for the benefit of young people consigned to India's state-run juvenile homes for delinquents, runaways, and abandoned children. Within a year, she had developed a program of psychological support, to provide the counseling these young people desperately needed, and convinced one juvenile home to grudgingly implement it on a trial basis. These institutions, run by ground-level government staff "not used to people coming in, not used to children being able to access outsiders to say 'look what's happening to us, we are getting beaten up here, we're being locked up, we're not being given food, we don't do anything the whole day, where are our parents?'" were naturally resistant.[24]

But a year later, her program had shown such strong results in raising self-esteem, steering children away from destructive behaviors and instilling positive values that the regional government granted permission for its implementation in all juvenile homes in Mumbai. Her small organization, Aangan Trust, became embedded in more than 100 juvenile homes and trained more than 600 staff in its programs.

Unlike other nongovernmental organizations (NGOs) and programs that witnessed abuses of the system and filed a case against the government, Aangan takes a different route. Gupta explains, "File a case and you know that you'll never be allowed in again." Aangan's strategy is to view the government as their best ally. "When you're trying to reach the most vulnerable child or when we're trying to reach the most hard to reach population then the government partnership gets very important."[25] The partnership Aangan has forged with the government as a result is providing the scale Aangan could never have achieved on its own, and it is also allowing them to influence the government's monitoring and evaluation of the juvenile homes in ways other NGOs have been unable to access.

"We don't want to just run a program. We want to build a model in such a way that it can get replicated and scale and become part of the mainstream. As an organization, we've taken a call that we need to strengthen the government systems," explains Gupta.[26]

Aangan began as a CBO, very focused in both its work and its community, is now one of India's premier NGOs, working across communities and throughout various regions. But it is Aangan's core program that has transformed India's juvenile justice system. Partnering with UNICEF, Aangan has developed a "Standards for Care Monitoring Tool" that incorporates the protocols of the 2000 Juvenile Justice Act into a monitoring tool that also promotes child-friendly institutions. This is required reading for local juvenile home administrators. As a result, juvenile homes that were never monitored before are being monitored, and the central government is beginning to understand the power of ground-level coaching.[27] For young people in the juvenile homes, it is a new world.

Eastern Europe is a major locus for human trafficking. Major cities such as Sofia and Belgrade are transit points for those coming from further east, and the region's splintered economy makes it a source for traffickers who can entice young people into their trades. Atina was founded in 2004 in Belgrade, Serbia, to reintegrate those who have been trafficked back into common society. The organization provides safe housing, medical and psychological support, and basic nonformal education for children as young as 12. Atina will also help victims file police reports, cover legal fees, and provide family mediation.[28]

Atina has also sought to transform the attitudes of officials working with trafficking victims while raising awareness of the extent of the problem throughout Serbia through workshops and training initiatives concerning issues pertaining to trafficking and sexual exploitation. The organization seeks to build the capacity of institutions and organizations to provide adequate, holistic support for trafficking victims. As well, they have provided a voice for the children they have served by emerging as a credible policy advocate within Serbia, enhancing their position through participation in field research and analysis with the University of Belgrade. They have taken a keen role in advocating reforms of Serbia's legal system to make it more responsive to those who have been trafficked and stricter with the traffickers themselves.[29]

In India, Pratham was founded in 1994 to expand educational access for impoverished children in Mumbai. It has since emerged as one of India's premier organizations, serving as many as 34 million children across the country. In 2005, it formed volunteer teams in all 600 Indian districts to survey children to see what they were actually learning in their schools. Their work created the Annual Survey of Education Report (ASER), which has become a valuable tool for the Indian government. Drawing from the poor results of their initial survey (only 35% between the ages of 7 and 14 could read a simple paragraph), Pratham developed volunteer-driven community-based interventions that supplemented formal educational programs. Working in partnership with other educational organizations throughout India, Pratham brought their methodologies to scale, with a graphic impact on literacy and mathematics levels in the regions where their program is in place.[30]

It is important to recognize that scaling up is only possible where governments are willing to embrace the issues brought before them. In situations where repressive governments limit public dialog, no amount of pressure will likely be able to amend governmental will or influence standing policies. The efforts we have seen would be impossible today in North Korea, Uzbekistan, or Somalia. Nor do these approaches work in fragile or failed states beset by civil violence or natural disasters, where governmental emphasis is directed toward reestablishing some level of control. And in those areas with no control, the ungoverned spaces mentioned earlier, it becomes nearly impossible for any civil society effort to take hold.

CBOs have an immense latent power to spread beyond the contours of their direct work. Through widening their reach with reproduction, replication, or franchising, through drilling deeply into the multiple layers of problems impacting vulnerable communities, or through public advocacy and issue awareness, CBOs can employ a multiplier effect that leverages their work and distributes its impact even further. Accordingly, each CBO that is well structured and maintaining programs of demonstrable impact has within it a capacity to make their work ripple in ever broader circles, encompassing greater numbers of the marginalized and the dispossessed.

Considering the Audience—When and How to Scale

While CBOs hold the capacity to scale their work in some form, the processes of scaling are as nuanced as the communities in which CBOs operate. There is no one formula or pattern that can be followed, no silver bullet that can automatically transform an effective local program into a regional, national, or international model. Each CBO must evaluate the nature of its work, the areas in which that work is being pursued, its financial and human resources, and its intellectual capital to determine how, and even whether, going to scale makes sense.

As noted earlier, the most common assumption is that going to scale entails replication of effective programs into new locations. But as shown by the examples presented, and confirmed by the tens of thousands of distinctive CBOs that have arisen in response to localized, deep-seated issues, the impetus of most such organizations is to find ways to provide wrap-around services, to unravel an issue to find the varied entry points that create the problems any program seeks to address.

In this way, CBOs actually create communities. When an organization builds a school in a low-income district, offers a school day meal to its students, and then provides classes on hygiene or parenting for mothers and fathers in the evenings, it galvanizes the best intentions of a community around a single entity. If it rescues young people from dangerous or exploitive situations and reintegrates them back into positive social roles through either education or skills training, it defuses a negative influence and creates a new infusion of energy, talent, and hope into a community's collective efforts.

CBOs can emphasize a community's potential, and in so doing, can deepen its self-esteem and refine its identity. This type of impact is by definition localized. While individual programs and initiatives might be scalable, communities are not. Each one is distinct, each one is reflective of its own circumstances of social, cultural, religious, and political factors, and each one is carried forth on the strength of its own leadership, citizenry, and vision. Although we have seen too many recent examples in which the factors of a community's identity can spiral into sectarian or ethnic violence, as in Rwanda, the Balkans, Sri Lanka, and Syria, if crafted in positive terms, identity defines a community's distinctive character, and why it is difficult to replicate.

It becomes important, then, in considering a program's potential to be able to separate the program from the community in which it works. As a result, replicability is a much more delicate alternative than it may seem. If a program works well within its host community, it may well be a product of the distinctive air of that community, a function of the localized ethos in which it grew, and unable to flourish outside its region.

The impediments to scaling effective programs are considerable. As entities spawned from the community fabric, CBOs carry a high level of trust within their home communities. They are localized, and the people they serve can recognize the leadership and the contexts of the service while sharing a common vision of what that service hopes to achieve. This trust is a precious commodity, and, as such, is not readily or automatically exported with a program seeking to scale. To a local community, any imported program, whether from the United States or Western Europe, or even from the next village over, must first be trusted in order to be effective.

Given its distinctive model, community legitimacy, and remarkable record of success, Prerana has often been approached by other urban communities in India struggling with their own problems of prostitution to replicate their work. At times the incentives have been attractive, but

Prerana remains rooted in its home communities in Mumbai. They have acknowledged that the work they do is not easily portable. Co-founder Priti Patkar explained that it has taken more than 20 years to build trust within a community beset by sexual exploitation and gender violence and influenced by the darker elements of the sex trade. Prerana is able to work so well because it has spent time demonstrating itself to those around it, both participants and observers. Why, then, would Prerana spread itself even thinner to begin that arduous and time-consuming process of trust building in a new city? Ms. Patkar suggested that the best course was for others to come and learn from Prerana's model, then adapt it to their own locations.[31] She stresses, as does Geoffrey Canada, reproduction rather than replication.

Whatever form scaling may take, the act itself is not immediate. Scaling involves trust, which is best built over time, nor can the expansion of new programs be coerced. Old systems and familiar ways of looking at things do not go away at once. They are changed through demonstration, through persuasion, and ultimately through the trust that new ways and new approaches are not threatening, but in the end provide advantages which would otherwise be out of reach.[32]

In the end, the size of an enterprise does not matter, nor does it matter whether a CBO is able to generate attention or recognition beyond its own community. What matters is the collective efforts that change the bleak landscapes in which they work, either by going wide, by burrowing deeply, or by influencing public thought and policy. President George H.W. Bush spoke "of a thousand points of light, of all the community organizations that are spread like stars throughout the Nation, doing good."[33] While President Bush was speaking of US efforts, his words echo in the global community. It is those points of light breaking through lingering darkness that constitutes the true measure of CBOs. Taken together, these small points can create a dazzling brilliance shining on the lives of the *children of the last mile*.

NOTES

1. http://ashokaglobalizer.com/bill-clinton-quote; *and* http://changenation.org/wp-content/uploads/ChangeNation-Introduction.pdf
2. This discussion has been aided by Jeffrey Bradach, "Going to Scale," *Stanford Social Innovation Review*, March 31, 2003. http://www.ssireview.org/articles/entry/going_to_scale/

3. http://www.smallgiantsbook.com/about.html
4. Moses Zulu, conversations with Maya Ajmera.
5. www.irinnews.org/report/97781/analysis-roots-of-polio-vaccine-suspicion
6. http://www.unicef.org/india/nutrition.html
7. "Association Between Economic Growth and Early Childhood Undernutrition: Evidence from 121 Demographic and Health Surveys from 36 Low-income and Middle-income Countries," The Lancet Global Health, Volume 2, Issue 4, Pages e225 - e234, April 2014.
8. Linda Poon, "A Booming Economy Doesn't Save Children from Malnutrition," http://www.npr.org/blogs/health/2014/03/27/29489 5305/a-booming-economy-doesnt-save-children-from-malnutrition
9. Acharya, Nish. (October 28, 2013). *How the Akshaya Patra Foundation Serves 1.5 Million School Lunches Across India Every Day*. Retrieved March 27, 2014 from Skoll World Forum: http://skollworldforum.org/2013/10/28/how-the-akshaya-patra-foundation-serves-1-5-million-school-lunches-across-india-every-day; *and* Dasra. (n.d.). *Akshaya Patra Foundation*. Retrieved March 26, 2014 from Dasra Catalyst for Social Change: http://www.dasra.org/pdf/Elementary_Education/Akshaya_Patra_Foundation.pdf; and Krista McCarthy, Manager of Donor Relations, Akshaya Patra Foundation USA, email message to Clare Dreyfus, July 16, 2014.
10. http://www.akshayapatra.org/sites/default/files/images/harvard_business_school_study.pdf, p.3; and Krista McCarthy, Manager of Donor Relations, Akshaya Patra Foundation USA, email message to Clare Dreyfus, July 16, 2014.
11. Acharya, Nish. (October 28, 2013). *How the Akshaya Patra Foundation Serves 1.5 Million School Lunches Across India Every Day*. Retrieved March 27, 2014 from Skoll World Forum: http://skollworldforum.org/2013/10/28/how-the-akshaya-patra-foundation-serves-1-5-million-school-lunches-across-india-every-day; *and* Dasra. (n.d.). *Akshaya Patra Foundation*. Retrieved March 26, 2014 from Dasra Catalyst for Social Change: http://www.dasra.org/pdf/Elementary_Education/Akshaya_Patra_Foundation.pdf
12. Mitos Urgel, Executive Director, WEAVE Foundation, email message to Maya Ajmera, June 14, 2014; and www.weave-women.org/about-us/
13. Mitos Urgel, Executive Director, WEAVE Foundation, email message to Maya Ajmera, June 14, 2014; and http://www.weave-women.org/early-childhood-development-project/
14. Shining Hope for Communities. (n.d.). *Kibera*. Retrieved March 26, 2014, from Shining Hope for Communities: http://www.shofco.org/locations/kibera; and Jessica Posner Odede, Co-Founder and COO, Shining Hope for Communities, email message to Clare Dreyfus, June 14, 2014.

15. Kennedy Odede, Co-Founder and CEO, Shining Hope for Communities, Interview, March 2, 2012 (Saudamini Dabak, Interviewer); and Jessica Posner Odede, Co-Founder and COO, Shining Hope for Communities, email message to Clare Dreyfus, June 14, 2014.

16. Kennedy Odede, Co-Founder and CEO, Shining Hope for Communities, Interview, March 2, 2012 (Saudamini Dabak, Interviewer); and Jessica Posner Odede, Co-Founder and COO, Shining Hope for Communities, email message to Clare Dreyfus, June 14, 2014; and Shining Hope for Communities. (n.d.). *Our Model*. Retrieved March 26, 2014, from Shining Hope for Communities: http://www.shofco.org/our-model

17. Paul Tough, "The Harlem Project," *The New York Times*, June 20, 2004; *and* Danielle Hanson, "Accessing the Harlem Children's Zone," *The Heritage Foundation*, March 6, 2013; *and* Jessica Hopper, "Person of the Week: Geofffrey Canada Lifts Up Harlem's Students One Block At A Time," *ABC News*, September 24, 2010, retrieved March 26, 2014, http://abcnews.go.com/WN/harlem-childrens-zones-geoffrey-canada-revolutionizes-education-creating/story?id=11719995

18. Danielle Hanson, "Accessing the Harlem Children's Zone," *The Heritage Foundation*, March 6, 2013.

19. Paul Tough, "The Harlem Project"; *and* Danielle Hanson, "Accessing the Harlem Children's Zone"; *and* Jessica Hopper, "Person of the Week: Geofffrey Canada."

20. Priti Patkar and Pravin Patkar, Co-Founders, Prerana, Interview, December 11, 2011 (Saudamini Dabak, interviewer); *and* Pravin Patkar, Co-Founder and Director, Prerana, Interview, January 4, 2012 (Saudamini Dabak, interviewer); *and* www.preranaantitrafficking.org/about/journey.htm

21. news.bbc.co.uk/2/hi/americas/975041.stm., October 16, 2000.

22. Ezequiel Robles, Executive Director, ADEVI, Interview, April 13, 2012 (Saudamini Dabak, interviewer).

23. Ezequiel Robles, Executive Director, ADEVI, Interview, April 13, 2012 (Saudamini Dabak, interviewer).

24. Suparna Gupta, Founder and Director, Aangan Trust, Interview, January 10, 2012 (Saudamini Dabak, interviewer); *and* Ashoka, "Suparna Gupta," 2014. Retrieved March 26, 2014 from Ashoka Innovators For the Public: https://www.ashoka.org/fellow/suparna-gupta

25. Suparna Gupta, Founder and Director, Aangan Trust, Interview, January 10, 2012 (Saudamini Dabak, interviewer); *and* Ashoka, "Suparna Gupta," 2014. Retrieved March 26, 2014 from Ashoka Innovators For the Public: https://www.ashoka.org/fellow/suparna-gupta

26. Suparna Gupta, Founder and Director, Aangan Trust, Interview, January 10, 2012 (Saudamini Dabak, interviewer); *and* Ashoka, "Suparna Gupta," 2014. Retrieved March 26, 2014 from Ashoka Innovators For the Public: https://www.ashoka.org/fellow/suparna-gupta

27. Suparna Gupta, Founder and Director, Aangan Trust, Interview, January 10, 2012 (Saudamini Dabak, interviewer); *and* Ashoka, "Suparna Gupta," 2014. Retrieved March 26, 2014 from Ashoka Innovators For the Public: https://www.ashoka.org/fellow/suparna-gupta

28. https://www.globalfundforchildren.org/partners/atina/

29. https://www.globalfundforchildren.org/partners/atina/; *and* http://atina.org.rs/inicijative_javnog.html; and http://www.global-womens-network.org/wiki/Atina,_Belgrade,_Serbia

30. Abhijit Banerjee, Esther Duflo, *Poor Economics: A Radical Rethinking of the Way to Fight Global Poverty,* Public Affairs press, 2012, pp. 84–85.

31. Priti Patkar and Pravin Patkar, Co-Founders, Prerana, Interview, December 11, 2011 (Saudamini Dabak, interviewer); *and* Pravin Patkar, Co-Founder and Director, Interview, January 4, 2012 (Saudamini Dabak, interviewer).

32. Atul Gawande, "Slow Ideas," *The New Yorker,* July 29, 2013, http://www.newyorker.com/reporting/2013/07/29/130729fa_fact_gawande?currentPage=all

33. George H.W. Bush Inaugural Address, January 20, 1989.

CHAPTER 9

Networking—Strong Voices Made Stronger

There is strength in bonding. Just as individual carbon atoms can become diamonds when joined together, so too can community-based organizations (CBOs) create brilliance when they network. CBOs that talk with each other, share experiences, best practices, and, where possible, pool resources, can create greater efficiencies. They can tap into one another's circles of influence to author a strong, unified voice in support of policies that change the course of vulnerable children. While one voice may resonate clearly, several voices raised together reverberate with strength.

Moreover, networking can bridge the existing development framework by bringing the work at the bottom of that schema, performed by CBOs, closer to the top, where policymakers and thought leaders determine best practices and best approaches. A number of CBOs toil in relative obscurity. Although their work is essential for their communities and they may enjoy freedom from donor mandates, they live outside the funding streams available to larger, more connected organizations. Moreover, the work of these groups is frequently not captured in assessments of conditions impacting the most marginalized. Like the people they seek to serve, these CBOs remain invisible to anyone who is not looking specifically to find them.

CBOs can create webs of influence by aligning together, but this is not always an easy task. The amalgamation of resources, thought, and action can threaten the status quo, and, in so doing, assault existing power structures. Capital does not readily flow to social disruptors. As a result, with

© The Editor(s) (if applicable) and The Author(s) 2016
M. Ajmera, G.A. Fields, *Invisible Children*,
DOI 10.1057/978-1-137-57838-9_9

very few exceptions, networks must be financially creative and find cost-effective ways to communicate and to advocate.

Organizations with targeted agendas supported by focused programs on tight budgets must overcome the stresses and demands of their primary purpose to join willingly with other organizations that may be unknown, distant, or in some cases viewed as competitors. This requires an act of institutional will that puts aside immediate fears and uncertainties in recognition of the potential for greater collective impact.

Yet the tendency among CBOs to consolidate around a consistent goal seems clear. The power and range of these networks is in itself a means of scaling, an avenue through which effective programs can multiply their impact by aligning with others and drawing lessons from one another. Networks can break down territorial silos by expanding a common base of understanding, sharing best practices, and deepening comprehension of the issues. Within effective networks, each member retains its identity, yet becomes part of a stronger whole.[1]

Some organizations link with one another thematically in relationships based on similar missions and common interpretations of one or more particular issues. Other groups link geographically, sharing regional perspectives of social and political situations, exchanging programmatic information that can trigger responses among their colleagues, and developing shared initiatives that span previously siloed issue areas. This can begin with local or regional consortia, which may be completely informal. Such events allow CBOs to realize that their work does not stand alone, that it is in fact an integral part of a quiet swarming effort that may not be apparent on a daily basis. In effect, this networking creates an ecosystem of non-governmental organizations (NGOs) in which separate entities interact as a community within their host environments.

Intermediary Networks

Sometimes the very act of receiving a grant can enlist a CBO into a network that otherwise would be unknown to them. Intermediary grant makers, whose missions entail disbursements to CBOs around the world, have the capacity to create informal networks of their recipients.

As early as 2004, The Global Fund for Children (GFC),[2] which makes investments in small CBOs working specifically with vulnerable children, began to coordinate regional knowledge exchange workshops wherein their grantee partners could come together face-to-face to share successes, challenges, and opportunities for collaboration. Leaders of CBOs, frequently prone to feelings of isolation given the intense nature of their work, can interact with other leaders, finding strength in the notion that they are in fact not alone, and, in so doing, to hatch out new ways to work together. In the end, the ideas and initiatives that emerge from GFC's knowledge exchanges are driven by the CBOs themselves, and not authored in accordance with any preconceived expectations.[3]

Some of the most valuable networking occurs across regions. A series of natural disasters impacted dozens of GFC partners between 2004 and 2006. The South Asian tsunami, Hurricane Katrina, and the Pakistani earthquake demanded localized responses from each group that worked in the areas affected. To share knowledge concerning these emergency responses, and to help develop disaster preparations for CBOs everywhere, GFC brought together the leaders of the groups in these three afflicted areas. Among the outcomes of the knowledge exchange was an understanding that, despite cultural and operational differences, groups had much to learn from one another. Shortly after this meeting, the director of the Dreamcatchers Foundation, which works with vulnerable young people in India, took a one-month sabbatical to spend time in New Orleans with KIDsmART, a group using art to engage young people in learning. The American CBO wanted to draw upon the Indian CBO's experience in dealing with post-traumatic stress from water-related disasters.[4]

Other intermediary grant makers are developing similar approaches. The Firelight Foundation, for example, makes investments in CBOs in sub-Saharan Africa. The organizations that Firelight supports receive more than funding. Each organization becomes part of a consortium of groups, tied together regionally and through the central mission of poverty alleviation. Here, they can draw energy and ideas from one another.[5] Peter Laugharn, Firelight's former Executive Director and current President and CEO of the Conrad Hilton Foundation, explained, "We have ... tried to look at the community-based organizations that we fund as existing within an ecosystem, and not just on their own. When Firelight started ... we were mostly looking just for good reputable organizations that were doing good things for kids in their area. I'd say right now, we're looking for organizations that do that, but have ideas that could be useful to others...Community-based organizations need to be part of a bigger proposition."[6]

CBOs themselves have the deepest understanding of the issues and the most effective responses to them. In situations where they can share their wisdom and help collegial organizations develop their own approaches based on that wisdom, such networks can spawn impressive results.

In-country networks complement this creation of knowledge and generate pathways through which that knowledge can be disseminated and used. Dasra, a strategic philanthropy organization in Mumbai, India, has taken this notion one step further. Based on the conviction that bringing philanthropists and entrepreneurs together can change India's social landscape, Dasra has become a major strategic partner to both the donor and CBO sector throughout India, including many CBOs that focus on innovative ways to meet the educational, health, and protection needs of children.[7] Dasra Social-Impact (DSI) is a comprehensive training program for leaders within the social sector, the largest such training program in India. It encompasses a seven-day residential workshop emphasizing strategic growth, communication and branding, impact assessment, and team development.[8]

In India, Child Rights and You (CRY) partners CBOs, parents, and communities to develop a comprehensive, holistic approach to elevating the plight of children in need. CRY's model builds a coalition of individuals, corporations, media, government, and CBOs to create nurturing environments for the child, his or her family, and their community. CRY members benefit from knowledge and resource sharing that enhances their organizational capacity and emphasizes best practices.[9] Once potential solutions are developed at this level, local governments are engaged and relevant governmental policies that can make these solutions permanent are promoted.[10]

CRY is not an implementer nor is its network based on direct implementation. Instead, CRY is a prime model of an enabling network that enhances the strength of its members. Other such networks exist in other regions, like Starfish Greathearts Foundation in South Africa.[11]

Civic networks can also be significant in driving support to the community level. Rotary International encompasses more than 34,000 local Rotary clubs around the world, composed of more than 1.2 million members.[12] Each of Rotary's recipients, regardless of location, becomes part of a linked network that spans more than 110 countries underwritten by a shared set of community values. As a service organization, Rotary is mandated to play a role in bettering the communities in which clubs are located, and so almost every Rotary club has a grant making function. While grants cover a variety of purposes, many recipients work on issues impacting marginalized young people, including major contributions to efforts to eradicate polio globally. Rotary grants support scholarships and vocational and skills training, and because of the localized decision-making that directs these grants, recipients include CBOs.[13]

Because the conditions of women and children are often closely linked, intersections between women's networks and those working for children are logical. The simple fact that children have mothers and most women have children feeds this dynamic. Accordingly, women's funds operating in many low-income countries sometimes accommodate provisions for children. The Mama Cash Foundation in the Netherlands and the Global Fund for Women have guidelines that embrace programs working with girls in various social levels.[14] And Every Mother Counts is an organization that seeks to address preventable deaths caused by pregnancy and childbirth globally by informing, engaging, and mobilizing action for maternal health and care for the children left behind.[15]

In general, though, the women's movement has not made children, and the interconnectivity between mothers and their babies, a systematic part of their work. There is potential here that is as yet unrealized.

INFORMATION AND RESOURCE NETWORKS

Some networks have formed to collect and disseminate information to broaden understanding and response to the issues affecting the most vulnerable. These networks play a critical role in focusing attention on situations and trends that might otherwise go without sufficient notice.

Global in scope is Child Rights International Network (CRIN), an informational network of more than 3000 child rights organizations around the world. CRIN identifies issues and situations that abuse the basic rights of children and young people, such as unfair criminal sentencing, ethnic discriminations, or adoption and placement issues, and then mobilizes efforts to combat these abuses on both the international and national levels. Internationally, CRIN works with UN officials and regional human rights organizations to push forward discussions of children's rights and information about the violations of those rights. On the national level, CRIN has had success in partnership with local advocacy organizations in addressing specific issues in various countries, including Pakistan, the United States, and Yemen.[16]

The vastness of CRIN's network allows it to penetrate deeply into the corridors of power, and, at times, to assume aggressive tactics in forwarding its messages. Where softer forms of advocacy—such as lobbying, research dissemination, and public campaigns—have failed, CRIN has been able to bring successful legal actions that compel governments to respond to conditions impinging the rights of children. CRIN also helps its partners bring forth legal actions in local jurisdictions around the world. In many cases, the local organizations that pursue these cases would otherwise lack the capacity to do so. Complementing this approach is CRIN's work in summarizing how the UN Convention on the Rights of the Child translates into the legal system in every country in the world.[17]

To both its members and the general public, CRIN provides extensive research and documentation, maintaining a library with 30,000 resources, ranging from UN resolutions to specific court cases to a directory of children's rights organizations in almost every country. The organization also maintains a Children's Rights Wiki as a central repository for information pertaining to children and young people around the world.[18] CRIN has created a worldwide database of the most relevant aspects of thought, law, and policy regarding the rights of children.[19]

The Watchlist on Children and Armed Conflict is a network of NGOs formed in 2001 to advocate for the elimination of children as combatants and their protection within war zones. Using local partners to gather information, Watchlist is able to monitor activities in specific countries. Their work includes documenting abuses, partnering with local CBOs to advocate on behalf of children most at risk, and advising national governments and international governing bodies. The organization strives to equip its partners with the requisite resources to participate in country-wide Monitoring and Reporting Mechanisms through technical support, counsel and the sharing of best practices from its members around the world.[20] Using information gleaned from the fields of conflict, Watchlist has become a major advocate for strategies to protect children at all levels and has regularly presented its findings to key figures within the UN Security Council.[21]

ADVOCACY NETWORKS

Advocacy networks have proliferated over the past decade. These networks allow the voices and perspectives of smaller organizations to be more widely heard and to join with other voices to present a more substantive and unified mass of pressure and issue awareness. Modern technology makes networking available to even the small CBOs working in far-removed outposts, such as rural Zambia or the Amazonian villages of Colombia.

A union of philanthropists, universities, and NGOs, The Coalition for Children Affected by AIDS (CCABA) was formed in 2005 to make children a higher priority in the global response to the disease. CCABA attempts to identify the gaps in knowledge and service systems, and then find ways to plug those gaps by presenting hard data to the public agencies that can take the lead in doing so. Their prominent strategies include engaging global forums at which experts share data and build consensus about the best programs of treatment for children. Significantly, the Coalition brings grassroots organizations to the table, partnering with CBOs throughout the world.[22]

Other networks have coalesced around single issues. End Child Prostitution and Trafficking (ECPAT) headquartered in Bangkok, is working to build a global movement to protect children from sexual exploitation. With 81 member groups, some of which are themselves national or regional coalitions of CBOs, in 74 countries, ECPAT draws from the experiences and wisdom of its partners to influence legislation governing child prostitution, trafficking, child pornography, and sex tourism in the countries where these conditions are most rampant.

The Global March Against Child Labor's mission weds the "right to be free from economic exploitation and from performing any work that is likely to be harmful" with the right "to receive a free and meaningful education." Global March's members are CBOs, trade unions, and teachers organizations from around the world.[23]

Disability Rights International has embarked on a worldwide campaign to end the institutionalization of children. As DRI's Founder and Executive Director Eric Rosenthal explains, "Even though we are a disability rights organization we have common cause with all children because orphanages create disabilities. And a lot of kids are put in not because of the disability, but because their parents are poor.... And so the fine line of who is and who is not disabled doesn't matter to us."[24] Their campaign breaks down silos and broadens their reach beyond a single demographic in order to pursue a common goal for all children consigned to institutional care.

It should be noted that DRI's work is complemented by the substantial efforts which are beginning to arise to transition orphaned or abandoned children from institutional to family life, led by Lumos, established by J.K. Rowling to assist institutionalized children in regaining a family life. Primarily an advocacy organization, Lumos seeks systems change that diminishes the role of institutionalized care and links orphaned children with family structures.[25]

Regional networks can also exert influence on public policy. The National Alliance for the Fundamental Rights to Education (NAFRE), which CRY helped establish, is composed of more than 2000 grassroots entities throughout India. NAFRE has emerged as a major alliance on education, and has used its considerable leverage to influence national legislation, including the ultimate passage of India's 83rd amendment which makes education a basic national right.[26]

FAITH-BASED NETWORKS

Virtually every major faith makes provisions for those in poverty. Faith-based initiatives in service to marginalized children and young people carry great weight and perform immense good. World Vision was established within the Christian faith tradition. American Jewish World Service and B'nai B'rith carry forth this work within the Judaic tradition, and Muslim organizations such as the Rahima Foundation and the Aga Khan Foundation serve people in poverty from an Islamic perspective.

Religions provide their own networks, locally, nationally, and globally. Temples, mosques, parishes, and synagogues connect with one another in relationships that transcend politics or geography. Small churches in California take up collections and send relief to children suffering from malnutrition in South Asia,[27] Jewish Heart for Africa directs funds for solar, agricultural, and education projects,[28] and a mosque in Dallas can underwrite a girls' school in Pakistan.[29] Faith communities have the capacity to connect on the most basic humanitarian level and, through their organizations, can reach across the world to carry forward those compassionate impulses.

The impact of the work of faith-based communities can be profound. In sub-Saharan Africa, where the remnants of colonial structures left huge swaths of indigenous populations ostracized from all government programs, the responsibility of educating black children throughout the region fell to mission schools. In the mid-1920s in South Africa, mission schools were educating in excess of 200,000 black children, with roughly 7000 in state schools.[30] The mission schools provided academic access, but they also instilled feelings of self-esteem that were often squelched in the larger society. Many were multiracial, and so expanded their students' social sensitivities and cultural horizons. Multiple generations of

South Africa's indigenous leadership took their studies at mission schools, including Steven Biko, Oliver Tambo, Robert Sobukwe, Thabo Mbeki, and Nelson Mandela.[31]

The seeds of Lesotho's modern educational system were tilled by mission schools, which flourished throughout the twentieth century. The government, strapped for resources, came to incorporate these schools into their public educational system, underwriting their programs rather than creating their own new ones. Schools that began with, and still maintain, a religious orientation have become the bedrock of Lesotho's ability to educate its young people. This model found fertile ground in Lesotho, an almost entirely Christian nation. The country's Ministry of Education and Training has set a goal of universal free primary education, much of it delivered through these now official public schools run in partnership with the churches. The National University of Lesotho evolved from Pius XII College, established by the Roman Catholic administration of southern Africa, and, in 2006, approximately 90% of the country's secondary schools were owned by churches.[32] The results of this absorption have been noteworthy: at 90%, Lesotho now boasts one of the highest literacy rates in Africa.[33]

Kevin Bartkovich came as a missionary to the remote Bundibugyo district of Uganda in 1997 to found a school. The district had no electricity, no sewage, and no communication with the outside world. Bartkovich founded Christ School, a mission school to serve the children of Bundibugyo and promote community leadership.[34]

Students found a holistic education that included field trips and community service, emphasizing the idea that the students were an integral part of their community's life and were thus obligated to contribute to it throughout their lifetimes. Graduates have gone on to university and have become teachers, medical assistants, and civil service workers. The technicians who put up the first power lines in Bundibugyo were graduates of the Christ School.[35] Once community leadership of this mission school was established, Kevin Bartkovich stepped away and left the people of Bundibugyo to educate their children. Today, years after Bartkovich's departure, Christ School remains strong, with nearly 350 students, many of whom go on to university and then return to give back to their communities. One-fourth of Christ School's teachers are alumni of the school, and many more teach in primary schools throughout the district.[36]

The Aga Khan Foundation, established in 1967 by the leader of Shia Ismaili Muslims, has developed programs addressing poverty, illiteracy, and illness in 30 countries. Aga Khan Education Services targets marginalized young people through the secondary level and operates three academies (India, Kenya, and Mozambique) that seek to provide opportunities for talented and motivated children regardless of economic status. The Aga Khan University in Pakistan has emerged as a premier global institution, encompassing a medical college and a teaching hospital.[37]

Faith-based networks are able to reach further and deeper than large-scale development efforts. Through their congregations, they can delve into issues at the most localized level. J. Mark Brinkmoeller, the Director of USAID's Center for Faith-Based and Community Initiatives, commented, "These networks of congregations existed before USAID was created, and will be thereafter."[38]

The intimacy and sheer number of these efforts gives them the potential to exert a lasting influence on children's development issues. These networks provide scale, according to Brinkmoeller, "but scale meaning lots of smaller bite-sized chunks together, not one big chunk." [39] Faith-based networks provide another access route to the *children of the last mile*, another vehicle in bringing together the 1000 points of light needed to break through the darkness.

BUILDING A MOVEMENT

The networks examined here have multiple impacts—developing and sharing new knowledge, strengthening individual efforts through collective action, providing action-based platforms for public policy advocacy, attracting new sources of funding, and bringing new eyes and minds to the issues that make children vulnerable. Networks expand the capacities of their members exponentially and with great focus and efficiency burrow their work into the deepest corners. In an era of overwhelming numbers of young people at risk and finite resources to bring those numbers down, the power of networks will become increasingly important.

We have seen that, to a large extent, the effect of the efforts to alleviate the conditions of vulnerable young people is less than the sum of its parts. The last two decades—buttressed by advances in technology, communication, and social awareness—have seen the rise of consolidated social initiatives in support of major marginalized demographics. In these cases, the major players within these issues have come together, at least in part, to create major global movements in support of women, single diseases such as HIV/AIDS, breast cancer, and heart disease, and even our pets. What we have not seen is such a movement in support of the millions of children living on society's most distant outskirts.

The recent history of the global women's movement in particular offers lessons for how disparate groups with related agendas can come together to create a powerful momentum that draws both public attention and governmental, multilateral, and private sector resources. From episodes of engagement that go back hundreds of years, a movement has emerged that has had measurable impact on the lives of women and girls in almost every corner of the globe. Such a movement can cut across countries, continents, and cultures to author a unifying call to action.

The UN has been a catalyst of the global women's movement over the past several years. Since its inception in 1945, the UN has had a stated interest in the rights of women, but its early efforts focused on the identification and passage of laws to safeguard those rights rather than the practices and prejudices that created gender inequality. Its work began from a soft foundation: only 30 of the 51 UN charter members allowed women equal voting rights. Quickly it became apparent that laws themselves were insufficient in bringing women to an equal footing, and a more forceful approach would be necessary to compel this reluctant evolution. What followed was a process entailing research, deliberation, negotiation, and messaging. The plight of women was gradually elevated in the public consciousness. Obstacles to advancement were identified, and clear objectives were set. An agenda was in place to guide a consolidated, multicultural approach to women's equality.

In 1995, the Beijing Conference affirmed that "women's rights were human rights," [40] that all relations between the genders had implications in the role and station of women, and that gender equality was an issue of universal concern. The Conference adopted the Beijing Declaration and Platform for Action that has guided the development of gender equity programs to this day. More than 17,000 governmental and NGO representatives attended, spanning 189 countries of origin. An NGO Forum held in conjunction with the conference drew another 30,000 participants. The Beijing Declaration was subsequently adopted and put into action by all member states.[41]

The issues summarized in the Beijing Declaration bear a close resemblance to similar issues impacting vulnerable children. The elements of underdevelopment, the politics of marginalization, and the economic struggles that attend social isolation run parallel in both groups. The women's movement had cultivated a small momentum through the scattered and uncoordinated efforts of its actors, but it received a huge boost from the focus afforded to it by the UN, which necessarily elevated its importance on the individual agendas of the UN's member states. The UN was able to consolidate and focus the disparate efforts of the movement and issue a call to action with credibility, leverage, and presence.

The global women's movement continues today, with high visibility, strong and powerful voices, and a basic realization in most cultures that equality and acceptance is the right thing to do. This movement took root through a variety of factors and a compendium of individual and institutional commitments. But it could well be argued that it was not until a major global body took the issues of the cause under its wing and made them priorities that a true movement emerged. In the end, a global community adopted the assumptions of the movement, compelling it to recognize the conditions of marginalization and exclusion that the movement addresses, and has been motivated to special action around those central themes.

Children, though, continue to be the focus of efforts that are largely disjointed, separate, and uncoordinated. They do not benefit from a recognizable, compelling champion, nor are they effectively organized within the agendas of many governments, development agencies, and multilaterals. They are underrepresented and underacknowledged as their own demographic, yet the condition of children and young people exerts a huge impact on development indices and economic performances in both high- and low-income countries and exacts an immense human toll.

They need a movement of their own.

CREATING A VOICE FOR CHILDREN

For children who have little voice themselves, networks that base their work on children's advocacy offer a vehicle through which their issues might be heard. While their work is invaluable, it is an incomplete solution.

Networks such as those profiled here are frequently the collective embodiment of groups working on single issues. There are exceptions, such as CRY or CRIN, but as such they are as siloed as the groups themselves, as bound by the limits of particular issues, conditions or geographies as those NGOs with single emphases. They may speak well, passionately and compellingly about their field and what they present can carry immense weight. But what they present often does not, and cannot, break down the silos that keep issues separate and resources isolated. They cannot present a consolidated voice for children whose conditions transcend the boundaries of place or issue.

The most compelling voices to have emerged on behalf of children are those of young people themselves. Well before the Taliban tried to assassinate her in October 2012, Malala Yousafzai was an outspoken advocate for girl's education in Pakistan. She had been blogging for the BBC since the age of 11, providing firsthand accounts of the impact of the Taliban's reemergence in her home territory, a reemergence that, among other things, denied girls the right to go to school. Malala received recognition from international children's rights groups, including a nomination from Desmond Tutu for the International Children's Peace Prize awarded by the KidsRights Foundation in the Netherlands. By 2012, the prime minister of Pakistan directed the establishment of an information technology campus in the Swat Degree College for Women at Malala's request, and that same year a secondary school in the region was renamed in her honor.[42]

When she returned to the country to resume her education, she was targeted by the Taliban and shot on her bus ride to school in October 2012. The assault was well publicized and became an event of global note. The brutality did nothing to quell her voice. In fact, Malala Yousafzai has since emerged as one of the world's most forceful, articulate, passionate, and well-reasoned voices for the rights of all children to have access to education, to aspiration, and to fulfillment, culminating in her receipt of the 2014 Nobel Peace Prize. She embodies the value of children and young people, and her voice rings clearly.

Malala was not the first such voice. In 1987, at the age of four, Iqbal Masih was bonded by his parents to work as a carpet weaver to pay off a loan of $16. Chained to a loom, Iqbal worked 14 hour days, seven days a week. Six years later, he managed to escape his bondage and found refuge with the Bonded Labor Liberation Front. He subsequently found his voice as an activist and traveled around the world addressing the issue of bonded child labor. Shortly after returning from a trip to the United States, he was shot and killed in mysterious circumstances near his home village in Pakistan. He was 12 years old when he died. Iqbal's life inspired the formation of several groups, including Free the Children in Canada, Good Weave in the United States, and the Iqbal Masih Shaheed Children's Foundation in Pakistan. In 2009, the US Congress established the Iqbal Masih Award for the Elimination of Child Labor.[43]

Does it require tragedy for a child's voice to be heard? And, in the absence of these voices, who speaks for the dispossessed, the marginalized, and the vulnerable young people that remain as unheard as they are unseen?

It would be hard to argue that, in recent years, a consolidated movement on behalf of marginalized children and young people has been put in place. The most powerful and widely heard voices articulating the conditions impacting the young have been children themselves—Malala and Iqbal and Ishmael Beah, whose memoir of his experiences as a child soldier in Sierra Leone, *A Long Way Gone*, rose to international prominence.

Yet even the most compelling children's voices will be incomplete. Marginalized children and young people need adult voices to carry their messages and represent their interests. Their marginalization itself makes them invisible, easy to be ignored and inconvenient to be heard. Many of these children, such as Malala, live in conditions and situations that put them at risk should they choose to speak out. Young children who suffer from extreme poverty or malnutrition are incapable of giving voice to their problems.

To be sure, strong adult voices carry forth the plight of these young people, and some do it exceptionally well. But, as is the case in international development in general, much of their efforts are siloed, focusing on one problem, or one region, or too often on the work of one organization. The most visible spokespeople on children's issues are too often identified singularly with one aspect of a broad, multilayered problem, and their representations most often speak to that aspect at the expense of an overriding message conveying the complexities of marginalization.

Leaders of major international NGOs, whose primary responsibility is to the financial and programmatic health of their organizations, speak on behalf of their own issues, focusing on their groups' individual need for recognition and funding. Moreover, organizations receiving any government funding or grants have limited capacity to be critical of government policies and efforts.

The result is a fractured effort, devoid of any central compelling spokesperson or any consolidated set of aspirations. While the advance of a particular organization may yield some quantifiable good, and may well change the lives of a set of young people in desperate situations, it does little to raise the visibility and awareness of the compendium of conditions that overlap and reinforce one another to consign hundreds of millions of young people to lives of vulnerability and neglect. In a very real sense, the children most affected by poverty and violence and dispossession are leading the way. Adult voices have yet to ring as clearly.

NOTES

1. http://ecpat.net/what-we-do
2. Author Maya Ajmera is the founder of the Global Fund for Children, which she subsequently led for 18 years, until 2012.
3. https://www.globalfundforchildren.org/gfc-2010-knowledge-exchange-south-america/
4. Global Fund for Children Annual Report 2008–2009, p. 39. https://www.globalfundforchildren.org/wp-content/uploads/2012/01/Why-The-Global-Fund-for-Children.pdf; *and* KidSmArt Annual Report 2007–2008   http://www.kidsmart.org/images/2007-2008_Annual_Report.pdf; and Sonali Ojha, email message to Clare Dreyfus, June 16, 2014.
5. http://www.firelightfoundation.org; *and* D. Wu and N. Hawley, *The Fire Behind the Brand: Firefight Founder Kerry Olson, from Grassroots to Public, November 2, 2012.* Retrieved March 26, 2014 from Notes on the Road: http://www.notesontheroad.com/kerry-olson.html; and Peter Laugharn, email message to Clare Dreyfus, July 16, 2014.
6. Peter Laugharn, former Executive Director, Firelight Foundation, Interview, August 28, 2013, transcript pp.3–5. (Maya Ajmera and Clare Dreyfus, interviewers).
7. http://www.dasra.org/Portfolio-Organizations
8. http://www.dasra.org/DSI + interview Deval Sanghvi, CEO, Dasra, January 3, 2012.
9. GFC. *Annual Report: 2001–2002,* p. 7, 12, 17. Retrieved March 27, 2014 from Global Fund for Children: https://www.globalfundforchildren.org/wp-content/uploads/2012/01/GFC_AnnualReport_2001-02.pdf
10. http://www.cry.org/projects/storiesofhopen.html
11. https://www.starfishcharity.org/our-work/capacity-building.aspx
12. https://www.rotary.org/en/rotary-international
13. https://www.rotary.org/en/about-rotary
14. http://www.mamacash.org/what-we-do-2/grantmaking/; and http://www.globalfundforwomen.org/what-we-do/how-we-grant
15. http://everymothercounts.org/learn/#
16. http://www.crin.org/en/home/what-we-do/advocacy
17. http://www.crin.org/en/home/what-we-do/research
18. http://www.crin.org/en/home/what-we-do/worldwide-database
19. http://www.crin.org/en/home/what-we-do/crinmail
20. http://watchlist.org/who-we-are/; *and* http://watchlist.org/influencing-the-agenda/monitoring-and-reporting-mechanism/; *and* Watchlist. (April 2012). *No one to trust: Children and Armed Conflict on Colombia.* Retrieved March 26, 2013 from Watchlist on Children and Armed Conflict: *http://www.protectingeducation.org/sites/default/files/documents/no_one_to_trust.pdf*

21. http://watchlist.org/who-we-are/; *and* http://watchlist.org/influencing-the-agenda/monitoring-and-reporting-mechanism/; *and* Watchlist. (April 2012). *No one to trust: Children and Armed Conflict on Colombia*. Retrieved March 26, 2013 from Watchlist on Children and Armed Conflict: *http://www.protectingeducation.org/sites/default/files/documents/no_one_to_trust.pdf*

22. http://www.ccaba.org/our-projects/research/; and Peter Laugharn, email message to Clare Dreyfus, July 16, 2014.

23. http://globalmarch.org/campaign/page/whats-new; *and* http://globalmarch.org/node/212

24. Eric Rosenthal, Founder and Executive Director, Disability Rights International, Interview, July 25, 2013, p. 3, (Maya Ajmera and Clare Dreyfus, interviewers); *and* Laurie Ahern, President Disability Rights International, email message to Clare Dreyfus, July 16, 2014.

25. http://wearelumos.org/the-solution

26. http://www.cry.org/projects/storiesofhopen.html

27. http://www.santacruzsentinel.com/aptos/ci_24761129/aptos-twin-lakes-church-feeds-hungry

28. http://greatnonprofits.org/reviews/jewish-heart-for-africa

29. Kamal Daya, India Education Fund, Dallas, TX, Interview, October 2013. (Gregory Fields, interviewer).

30. http://www.nytimes.com/2013/12/28/us/mission-schools-ambiguous-legacy-in-south-africa.html

31. http://www.nytimes.com/2013/12/28/us/mission-schools-ambiguous-legacy-in-south-africa.html

32. http://www.mapsofworld.com/lesotho/education/

33. https://www.cia.gov/library/publications/the-world-factbook/geos/lt.html

34. Kevin Bartokovich, Founder, Christ School, Interview, March 19, 2012 (Saudamini Dabak, interviewer).

35. Kevin Bartokovich, Founder, Christ School, Interview, March 19, 2012 (Saudamini Dabak, interviewer).

36. Kevin Bartokovich, Founder, Christ School, email message to Clare Dreyfus, June 12, 2014.

37. Aga Khan Development Foundation, http://www.akdn.org/programmes.asp

38. J. Mark Brinkmoeller, Director, Center for Faith-Based and Community Initiatives, USAID, Interview, April 26, 2013, transcript p. 6 (Maya Ajmera and Clare Dreyfus, interviewers).

39. J. Mark Brinkmoeller, Director, Center for Faith-Based and Community Initiatives, USAID, Interview, April 26, 2013, transcript p. 2 (Maya Ajmera and Clare Dreyfus, interviewers).

40. First Lady Hillary Rodham Clinton, Remarks for the United Nations Fourth World Conference on Women, Beijing, China, September 5, 1995. http://www.un.org/esa/gopher-data/conf/fwcw/conf/gov/950905175653.txt

41. http://www.un.org/womenwatch/daw/followup/session/presskit/hist.htm

42. Sumera Khan, "National Peace Prize Named After Malala Yousafzai," *Express Tribune*, December 20, 2011; cf. Mehsud, Saud, "Malala Yousufzai: Pakistani Schoolgirl Had Defied Threats from Taliban for Years," *Christian Science Monitor*, October 10, 2012.

43. http://www.dol.gov/ilab/issues/child-labor/iqbal/

CHAPTER 10

Enabling the Work on the Ground— Supporting Children at the Grassroots

Any effort to address the issues impacting vulnerable children and young people is necessarily enabled by factors that consolidate resources, ideas, logistics, tools, and energy into programmatic action. These enablers influence the capacity of on-the-ground efforts like community-based organizations (CBOs), and, in most cases, determine their reach and, ultimately, their effect. Each sector has its own agenda and its own purpose, and each is itself subject to a variety of influences that impact its role in children's development issues.

Taken together, these enablers carry immense potential to change the facts and figures that define the plight of marginalized children. The challenge of consolidating their interests around a central core of actions focused on young people has yet to be met, but individually each of these actors has had, and will continue to have, profound influence on the world's capacity to elevate the conditions of its invisible children.

TECHNOLOGY

Technology in all its forms has become a tool permeating almost every aspect of our daily lives. As such, its applications permeate the ability of every sector to respond to the issues and challenges affecting vulnerable children.

Through technology, the distant has become accessible, and the once strange has become familiar. The incredible transnational flow of

© The Editor(s) (if applicable) and The Author(s) 2016
M. Ajmera, G.A. Fields, *Invisible Children*,
DOI 10.1057/978-1-137-57838-9_10

information, impressions, and messages on a daily basis defies quantification as trillions of bytes pass through cyberspace from one device to another. Transmission of ideas that once took days now takes seconds and almost no part of the planet is truly out of reach.

We have seen in the last two decades how technology has reshaped the way high-income countries live on a day-to-day basis. We have created a world of instant communication, with conveniences unimaginable just a few years ago. We can access our homes remotely, and turn lights off and on from miles away. At our jobs, we can view our computer screens from the next continent. Technology has found ways to treat complex diseases, such as cancer or heart disease, with minimal invasion and minimal trauma. Technology has built vast fortunes and created immense, almost immeasurable wealth.

But to this point, it has done far less for children in poverty. The potential exists, and we can see it. What must come next are the creativity and the will to employ technology for humanistic purposes that reach the last mile. If we fail to do so, we run the risk of creating another form of marginalization, a technology gap that might augment and deepen the divides between the haves and the have-nots.

We have in our hands tremendously powerful tools for rewriting the way both high- and low-income societies interact with and support the most marginalized. The melding of social applications with technology has been stammering, and the promise of our continual technological evolution provides opportunities to rework the lives of children in poverty that are bounded only by the limits of social thought and imagination. This in itself constitutes a platform for change that, quite simply, has never existed before.

Technology allows the immediate sharing of information so that conditions or situations in one quarter can become responses in another. An American example is Change.org, a progressive political site which reacts to singular events and makes them national, coalescing responses and pressure from across the country on the basis of what might be happening locally.

Websites determine the public identity of any group. For even the most remote CBO, a good website can bring an intimacy that is often compelling and is always quite human, translating complex social issues into accessible situations and conditions. Most sites have become interactive rather than stagnant. Dialogs can ensue, stories can be shared, and a deeper understanding that can impel action or response can be created. All of this broadens participation and brings much higher levels of public awareness to the issues at hand. And any good website will have a "Donate" button that gives anyone who happens by the chance to have an impact on the organization's work.

Social media such as Twitter can be hugely valuable in lending CBOs a voice and giving them a platform to use it. Most of the networks referenced in these pages have active and widely followed Twitter accounts as well as Facebook, Tumblr, Instagram, and Flickr presences.

Girls Not Brides, a global partnership of more than 450 organizations in over 70 countries addressing child marriage, has utilized these technology applications to great effect. The organization knits together its members, which span every inhabited continent, and is able to advocate with a collective voice on behalf of the 15 million girls under the age of 18 married each year in accordance with a well-stated, detailed theory of change. At the same time, they maintain active presence on all major social media sites and issue regular calls for collective action. Blogs—first-person accounts of child brides and those who avoided early marriage, and substantive news updates on developments in their constituents' countries— dominate the website. In all, Girls Not Brides has tapped technology as an essential tool in building a strong and sustainable issue-based network.[1]

In Liberia, still one of the lowest-income nations in the world and recovering from years of brutal civil violence, rural health care is almost nonexistent. The civil war destroyed most of the health facilities outside the capital, and professional health workers left the country in hordes. Even today, Liberia has less than 100 physicians, which would be equivalent to all of Manhattan having only 15 doctors. Essential health services for those in rural areas are generally out of reach, with a two-day walk usually required for those in the most remote districts to find even a basic clinic.[2]

To combat this reality, Liberian American Raj Panjabi founded Last Mile Health (LMH). Rather than rely on doctors, nurses, hospitals, and the other rare commodities of formal health care, LMH recruits the villagers themselves to become frontline health-care workers able to provide essential primary-care services for the lowest-income children and their families. LMH trains them in fundamental practices such as administering immunizations, first aid care, preventive measures, and simple hygienic treatments. LMH monitors frontline health workers' progress and provides ongoing training while supplying them with the basic supplies needed to maintain a base level of community health, in essence professionalizing them and making the quality of their interventions consistent. By doing so, LMH is helping communities better reach the *children of the last mile*.

The model is driven by simple technology strategically applied so that the "last mile villages," as Panjabi calls them, can be accessed and serviced. Liberia's telecommunications company, Cellcomm, has partnered with the organization to provide cell phone service to the frontline health workers. More significantly, the frontline workers can get consultations on treatments, general diagnoses, and insights from partnering physicians and nurses across the country.[3]

The partnership with Cellcomm, which was instrumental in building the network capacity to reach previously unserved rural villages, and the gift of land from the Liberian government upon which Cellcomm could place their transmission tower, has facilitated the development of LMH's treatment network, while demonstrating the benefits of public–private cooperation. Private philanthropy prepaid for the first two years of network usage to guarantee Cellcomm enough revenue to make it worthwhile for the company to go into an underserved market. At the same time, LMH is able to generate job creation at the village level by paying its frontline workers a small salary.[4]

Education for All

In a world where millions of young people are out of school and have no access to systematic education, technology offers a solution: long-distance learning. Information-communication technology has the potential to place knowledge at the fingertips of children whose current educational opportunities are far less than ideal.

Khan Academy, founded by Sal Khan, has developed specific lessons on a wide range of topics, all of which can be accessed online without charge. Khan has enlisted premier educators to develop lessons across their specialties. Lessons take three forms: tutorials with videos, simulations, and exercises; practice problems; and real-time class instruction. Videos are 5–20 minutes in length to be easily digestible and are presented in a conversational rather than lecturing style. Khan lessons can be a central learning platform, or they can be supplemental to established curricula, depending on the needs of the student and teacher. Through Khan Academy, learning can happen anywhere, from a formal classroom to the corner of a bedroom. Thousands of videos are accessible from the Khan Academy website and are available in 18 languages including Xhosa, Swahili, and Bengali.[5]

The greatest significance of Khan Academy is the accessibility it promises. Anyone with Internet access anywhere in the world can learn math, science, and other subjects from the most basic level to the most sophisticated, contingent solely upon his or her own curiosity rather than on whether a school is nearby or, if it is, whether the child is allowed to attend it.

Long-distance learning, despite its youth, has already begun to take root in new forms. Neil D'Souza, who had worked both with Khan Academy and as a software engineer at Cisco, founded Zaya in the belief that any space can be a place of learning. Zaya provides personalized learning programs for children half a world away. Each student interacts with Zaya's learning management system, which creates lesson suggestions from various resources, including Khan Academy, and several other remote learning programs. The content adapts automatically to each student's pace of learning. This individual approach is complemented by larger group instruction where teachers and students can pursue concepts together in a classroom setting.[6] Zaya is currently supporting 20 learning labs inside schools and care centers in India, Indonesia, and Mongolia, all of which have a high incidence of children living in poverty with limited educational opportunities.[7] While Zaya's approach is designed to work anywhere in the world, its emphasis is on those at the bottom of the social pyramid.[8]

Child Protection

Communications technology is emerging as a critical ingredient in providing immediate assistance to children and young people in emergency situations. In Mumbai in 1996, the CHILDLINE India Foundation launched CHILDLINE, a toll-free number for children in distress. Through 2013, more than 30 million calls had been serviced through an expanded network that now encompasses 291 cities in 30 states and more than 540 partner organizations that respond to the children in need. CHILDLINE has answered the calls of street-connected children, child laborers, runaways, commercial sex workers, those needing emotional support, and children in every sort of trauma.[9]

In responding to the calls it receives, CHILDLINE can often alleviate hidden or unseen conditions that impact more than the caller. In Kolkata, a young girl aimlessly roaming the streets was apprehended by the police who then called CHILDLINE for assistance. The girl was a resident at a shelter home run by a nongovernmental organization (NGO), and, upon questioning, she revealed that almost all the residents were victims of sexual exploitation. A subsequent rescue operation coordinated by CHILDLINE, the police, India's Child Welfare Committee, and two other NGOs rescued 28 young people, half boys and half girls, out of the home, after which they were safely resheltered to safe and well-monitored facilities.[10]

In the United States, AMBER Alerts are broadcast via electronic media, social media, and emergency text messages to help locate missing children. The program is a voluntary collaboration between law enforcement, electronic media, and transportation agencies to offer immediate responses to child abductions. Through early 2014, AMBER Alerts have rescued more than 675 children, including a one-year-old girl inside a car that was stolen in Georgia and an eight-year-old boy in Ohio who was kidnapped by his noncustodial father. Both children were rescued when public citizens responded to AMBER Alerts and notified local authorities.[11]

Birth Registration

The benefits of communication technology can begin at birth. We have seen how the absence of an official birth registration turns a newborn invisible, lacking identity with the state, and all that identity entails. The process of birth registration in Senegal, for example, is rife with bureaucracy and inefficiency. Village chiefs in Senegal's countryside must travel physically to national offices to provide birth documentation. Even when those journeys are made, documentation can be lost or mislaid. Under the best circumstances, it may be months before an official registration finds its way back to a remote rural village. Compounding these pitfalls, many rural Senegalese have few notions about the importance of even registering their child's birth, unaware of how the lack of birth registration can limit access to education, health care, and financial services for their children in the future.[12]

In response to the ongoing problem of lack of birth registration among children in poverty in Senegal, Aide et Action, a Swiss-based NGO, is using technology to register newborns, employing widely accessible technology to facilitate the birth registration process. In 30 remote villages, the organization, in conjunction with the French telecommunications company Orange, provided mobile phones to the chiefs, each equipped with special software that could capture birth information and send it directly to the Senegal State Registrar. The adaptation of this software was a logical step for Orange, which had already developed an application to communicate the immediate market price of sesame seeds to buyers. Exchanging sesame seeds for babies was an easy coding transition. At the same time, Aide et Action and Orange supplied the registration office with specific equipment to receive the rural transmissions. Registrations are processed physically, in paper form, and electronically in the registrar's database. An official registration number is then transmitted back to the village chief to give to the parents. The child is thus officially registered, and the parents can collect a hard copy of the birth certificate at any time from the registrar's office.[13]

Mobile registrations are also underway in parts of Uganda, which has more than five million children under five without birth registrations and an unregistered rate of 70%. UNICEF's Innovation Unit has partnered with all of Uganda's telecommunications providers to give registration access to both rural leaders and remote hospitals using open-source technology developed by UNICEF. Wherever needed, hospitals were given Internet access along with a web-based registration application. In the villages, chiefs and other registration officials were given access cards to register local births. Birth certificates could then be printed locally, at the hospitals or regional administrative offices.

Within the first two months of UNICEF's implementation of this system in Uganda, all 300 births at the three government hospitals and six local government catchment areas where this new process was being tested were properly registered. Rollout of the system continued throughout 2012 to 131 hospitals and 61 local jurisdictions around the country. During that time, 145,411 births—80% of the total throughout the participating regions—were successfully registered.[14]

There is a deep, untapped reservoir of technological applications that can directly address the situations and conditions that create vulnerability. CBOs are only now beginning to tap into the far-reaching opportunities that will enable them to reach further and to dig deeper into their communities. These applications can be as vast as our imaginations allow, and no aspect of marginalization—education, health, exploitation, violence—is beyond the reach of technological innovations to alleviate these conditions. One necessary byproduct of these advances is the increasing cooperation between the public and private sectors, between those who create and own the technology and those who can employ it for social benefits. And, as we have seen, in some cases, corporations are not waiting for CBO partners. They are assuming the work themselves through an enlightened corporate mandate that effectively and efficiently links the profit motive with social gain and, in so doing, puts them at the front of these innovations. The civil sector would do well to seek out new partnerships increasingly to harness this creativity.

PHILANTHROPY

Resources drive development in all its forms. The best, most effective initiatives lie fallow without funding streams to give them life and depth. Funding from governments and multilaterals comprises a huge component of the resources being directed to global children's issues, but increasingly significant investments are now arising from private donors. Philanthropists giving abroad wrestle with the same questions and evaluations that drive domestic giving: cost-efficiency, return on investment, impact, and, quite critically, how well those investments make their way to those who most benefit from them.

In the international arena, philanthropy has the potential not only to feed existing avenues of support but also to help author new pathways that bring essential resources within reach of the most dispossessed. Support for community-based initiatives has risen in recent years, and this support, with its commensurate results, has marked a subtle shift in the philanthropic landscape. More and more donors are looking to localized giving opportunities, with the result being an elevation in awareness and participation, thereby creating a momentum of its own.

How then to channel these resources to the most effective initiatives for vulnerable children and young people? The increase in online giving is indicative of the role of the individual in seeking to establish a more personal relationship with the beneficiaries of his or her philanthropy. In the international arena, the GlobalGiving Foundation emerged as one of the first such mechanisms. GlobalGiving puts forward on its website a host of development projects which have undergone a thorough due diligence. Donors pick their giving targets, GlobalGiving processes their gifts to one or more community-based projects the donor has most likely never seen and of which he has likely never heard. Since its inception, GlobalGiving has processed more than $116 million from 395,000 donors to 10,324 projects around the world.[15]

It is important to note, though, that GlobalGiving does not build networks, nor does it emphasize any set of issues beyond the general rubric of international CBOs. GlobalGiving, and other websites that have arisen similar to this model, is a tool rather than a strategy. But it is still notable that any individual with an Internet connection and at least $10 can have the capacity to impact directly an organization working with some of the world's most vulnerable people.

Some individuals at the top of the economic scale have consolidated their concern for low-income populations through visible philanthropy meant to inspire others to make investments at similar levels. When Warren Buffett committed much of his fortune to the Bill and Melinda Gates Foundation in 2006, the world's wealthiest took notice, and some came to evaluate what course they might take with their assets. In June 2010, a campaign—the Giving Pledge—was officially launched to urge the wealthiest families and individuals to dedicate the majority of their wealth to philanthropy. Initially focused on those in the United States, subsequent response and interest has brought in wealthy individuals from several countries, including China and the UK. More than 120 individuals have committed to the Giving Pledge, all of them billionaires.[16]

This initiative does not pinpoint specific issues or methods of giving, nor does it entail a legal commitment. Its strength is in the moral imperative that compels its participants, each of whom has his or her own giving mechanisms and program priorities. Some have criticized the Giving Pledge as mere public relations, with no pressure to reveal to whom or how much is given and no enforcement for actual participation.[17] But if the actions of some of the world's wealthiest in support of philanthropy "to change the world" can elevate the awareness and discussion of giving possibilities, then the Giving Pledge carries great weight aside from the value of any funding that it ultimately delivers.

Several major private foundations have guidelines that incorporate children's concerns and long histories of significant investments in programs that seek to address children's issues. Most of this support has been for top-down initiatives; CBOs are rarely the focus of their giving.

There are exceptions to this model. Comic Relief UK seeks to use high-visibility entertainment to raise funds for vulnerable young people. Established in 1985, Comic Relief has raised nearly £1 billion, or $1.7 billion. Much of its disbursements go to small and medium-sized organizations working in areas of extreme poverty. The organization will provide small funding for pilot testing to local groups with limited resources, then seek to build its funding over time while helping its partner scale their work. Comic Relief will also support the work of intermediary grant makers who fund CBOs.[18]

The Bernard van Leer Foundation (BvLF), based in The Hague, specifically grants funding to CBOs improving opportunities for socially and economically underdeveloped children up to the age of eight. BvLF focuses on education, reducing violence and ameliorating child poverty.[19] The Jacobs Foundation in Zurich supports innovations in child and youth development globally, bridging research with localized programs addressing education, especially early childhood education, and youth employment.[20]

The Children's Investment Fund Foundation (CIFF), a London-based foundation, works to improve the lives of children in low-income countries through programs of large-scale, sustainable impact, usually through government partnerships. CIFF seeks to transform traditional approaches to development. The organization's founder, Jamie Cooper-Hohn, has stated that CIFF "is committed to successfully marrying the acumen and discipline of the private sector with the best thinking and evidence of what works in development. We are aware that our approach is a substantial divergence from the norm of development funding."[21] Focusing on the areas of neonatal survival, the prevention of mother-to-child HIV transmission, early learning, and acute malnutrition, CIFF seeks partners that can bring their designs to scale and impact the greatest possible number of marginalized young people.[22] But even Ms. Cooper-Hohn admits that CIFF does not reach the most marginalized children: "In order to get scale needed for government to invest, you can't reach the poorest kids— the numbers are too small for the high cost."[23]

Funders such as van Leer, Jacobs, and CIFF are exclusively supporting efforts on behalf of children and young people. But they are among the very few who do so. Others exist with this singular focus but only work domestically in the United States, and still others have guidelines that burrow into the particular issues of education, child health, and nutrition or violence.

The Freedom Fund came into being in 2013 to "mobilize the capital and knowledge needed to end slavery." Their work focuses on community-level interventions with an eye toward scaling those that are most effective.[24] Intermediary organizations have been able to identify effective CBOs working on this issue, and it remains to be seen whether a new group such as the Freedom Fund will build on this existing collective knowledge or seek to reinvent the wheel. With startup support of $30 million dollars from three major philanthropic groups and a laudable intention, Freedom Fund must develop the expertise needed to identify and sustain small, often hidden, community-based work around the globe.[25]

Major multifaceted foundations also support initiatives for children's development, although their work here is part of larger diverse portfolios. The Bill and Melinda Gates Foundation, for example, has given hundreds of millions of dollars to immunization efforts that target children globally, along with a host of initiatives that address education and health both domestically and abroad.[26] The John D. and Catherine T. MacArthur Foundation has offices in India, Mexico, Nigeria, and Russia to find and maintain relationships with effective organizations promoting human rights and international justice, girls' secondary education, and reproductive health.[27] Ford, Rockefeller, Mott, and dozens of other major players also maintain offices overseas to monitor and address conditions in the developing world that indirectly affect children and young people.

When funders take risks in their giving, good things can happen at the community level. Judith-Ann Walker, a native Trinidadian who had settled in Nigeria, began her own organization, development Research and Projects Center (dRPC). (She explains that the small "d" represents development software, as opposed to big "D" development hardware, which in her mind has not worked.) dRPC became an intermediary funder for groups that were far too small to be noticed by mainstream funding sources but whose work embodied social change on behalf of some of Nigeria's most marginalized children. In 1995, the MacArthur Foundation took a chance on Judith-Ann and dRPC, awarding a grant of $98,000 to be overseen by one of MacArthur's existing West African partners so that they could support dRPC's regranting to 80 small organizations throughout northern Nigeria.

The risk paid off. After initial dRPC grants ranging from $500 to $1000, most of these groups found solid footing and were able to grow their work. Judith-Ann explains the impact on these groups and those who led them: "Not only are they still active and present, but their leaders have also moved into development work, and they are the ones the international organizations have co-opted as staff, and they are the ones who now have the insights to see the importance ...of working with the grassroots."[28] MacArthur's nontraditional, risk-filled investment spawned a network of healthy CBOs working throughout Northern Nigeria, a region embroiled both then and now in sectarian violence, economic underdevelopment, and lingering child poverty.

But the approach of most major foundations to children's issues is not holistic, nor is it comprehensive. The resources they invest are too often siloed, reaching children affiliated with the conditions they have identified as priorities, but they do not focus on children as a giving target. Moreover, the visibility of these foundations within the giving community, their sizeable assets, and the pursuit of programs which have some indirect application to children's conditions can fuel a fallacious public perception that assistance is in fact reaching all marginalized children, and that different types of investments are not needed. For example, if Gates is directing hundreds of millions of dollars annually to Sub-Saharan Africa, then what else needs to be done?

Local Philanthropy

Philanthropy is rising in places other than the United States, and Western Europe, including India, Brazil, and South Africa. Countries that have previously lacked a rich philanthropic tradition are now beginning to become more active in strategic social investing, and indigenous philanthropy has emerged as a critical resource for programs that previously tended to look overseas for their support.

Community foundations create giving mechanisms that channel local and regional philanthropic resources to local solutions. This unique approach recognizes an often overlooked resource in building local capacity. While community foundations have long been a part of the philanthropic landscape in the United States, they are beginning to emerge as a special factor on the global scene. More than 1500 community foundations are working in nearly 50 countries, incorporating much of Central and Eastern Europe, Mexico, Kenya, South Africa, Brazil, and Thailand. Significantly, local foundations are best positioned to identify and support programs that effectively reach deeply into their communities and stand the best chance of finding the *children of the last mile*.

Diaspora giving has emerged as a major conduit for development funds. The American India Foundation, for example, has become a visible bridge between the Indian community in the United States and social needs in India.[29] Similarly, Africans in the Diaspora mobilize Africans living abroad to support grassroots organizations throughout the continent fostering economic development.[30] Because expatriates who send money back to their homelands are usually doing so in response to close family or community ties, their gifts are more likely to find their way to CBOs that may be unknown to more formal giving mechanisms but are valued organizations within the communities left behind. At this point, it is impossible to know with precision the total funds given in this way, but according to the Hudson Institute, remittances sent overseas in 2011 from the United States surpassed $100 billion, or more than three times the level of all official US foreign assistance programs.[31]

Funds, then, are being directed to children's issues by philanthropists at various levels, and clearly philanthropy has the potential to be a major factor in redirecting a global approach to the marginalized young. But significant challenges are still ahead.

While considerable philanthropic funds are going to children's programs, this funding is extremely disorganized. Philanthropists are huddled in many of the same silos as the programs they support. Funding can be isolated, and, therefore, less impactful than if it were coordinated with related efforts or initiatives, such as the natural linkages referenced earlier between education, nutrition, health care, and community development. The result of this lack of coordination, this lack of communication among philanthropists, is that efforts are often fragmented rather than focused.

We have often seen the good intentions of funders in throwing money at intractable, complex problems in the belief that those funds would find a way to change long-set social dynamics. Money sent forth on the basis of quantity of investment rather than quality can be diluted, ineffective, and, at worst, squandered.

The philanthropic sector has immense potential to author sustainable systematic change if it can coalesce its scattered efforts. Very few donors are targeting the work of CBOs, and, in many cases, philanthropic funds that find their way to CBOs have to pass through several filters and middlemen, many of whom exact fees for their own services that dilute the impact of the original investment. Moreover, the sector as a whole tends to be risk-averse. Especially among long-standing funders with established programs of giving that span several decades, the courage necessary to make departures that can propel funding in new directions is often lacking. It becomes much easier to rely on tried-and-true giving patterns rather than venture into new funding opportunities that may be riskier, although they may achieve results not seen before.

The Private Sector

Corporations, especially the multinationals, have increasingly come to the conclusion that social engagement for the development of the communities in which they work is good business. Quite simply, people living in poverty do not have the financial resources to purchase most goods and services, and their marginalization can destabilize regions of strategic corporate interest. Social unrest in Nigeria, for example, can jeopardize Coca Cola's distribution network, and bands of roving youth with nothing to do can eliminate incentives to do business near Brazil's *favelas*.

In line with the private sector's primary role to drive an economic engine for the benefit of its shareholders, corporations have directed larger portions of their in-country budgets to corporate social responsibility (CSR) efforts. Many corporations have willingly developed partnerships to ensure the cost-effective implementation of their CSR investments address specific problems related to their keenest corporate interests.

The corporate sector has always been the smallest component of the philanthropic community and likely will remain so for the foreseeable future. But philanthropy has become more complex, and what passed for philanthropy in years past—the simple, charitable act of making gifts—has become more sophisticated. Philanthropy has taken new forms, including venture philanthropy, focused on measurable results, long-term investment and hands-on social management, and strategic philanthropy, linking for-profit identification with nonprofit initiatives. The wealth generated by the dotcom boom, driven by new thinkers who thought outside the box to create new technologies and new fortunes, has created a new generation of philanthropists who see things differently and often reject the traditional avenues of giving. As they continue to grow into their roles as social investors, their potential impact on children's issues should become more apparent in the years to come.

The corporate sector has altered its approach for the better. While the sector still makes gifts and grants, it is far more likely now to make investments that generate social returns that can lead to stability, increased markets, and safe working environment for its employees while expanding the corporation's brand in the most positive way possible.

Corporations have tended to partner with large-scale, highly visible international nongovernmental organizations (INGOs) as the safest pathway for social investments. But as corporate investment strategies continue to evolve, the role of CBOs has come increasingly into play. Many major multinationals have adopted a decentralized giving policy. Citicorp was one of the first to place local investment decisions into the hands of its separate country operations rather than from its headquarters in New York City. Citicorp came to rely on its local leadership to select partnerships consistent with the corporation's guidelines and finance those decisions centrally. Because of this approach, Citicorp has come to support CBOs working in education and health in many of the countries in which it has a strong presence. Other major corporations, including Bertelsmann Stiftung in Germany, Toyota Motors in Japan, and HSBC in the UK, have adopted this strategy in an effort to deepen their corporate brands in local markets while maximizing the impact of their CSR investments.

The Swedish corporation IKEA has adopted a visible policy of ensuring that no IKEA product is manufactured through child labor. Aside from demanding that its suppliers and subcontractors adhere to this ethic, IKEA has entered into, and financially supported, relationships to mitigate the impact of child labor abuse, including partnerships with UNICEF and local and international NGOs, like Save the Children. IKEA has its own Children's Ombudsman,[32] whose responsibility it is to ensure that the company complies with the United Nations Convention on the Rights of the Child (CRC). They also have a department in India to work specifically on child labor issues and social projects. Again, IKEA considers this level of engagement to be good business: "We firmly believe that the best way IKEA can help to improve the situation for children is through active business co-operation. Our presence gives us the possibility to raise the awareness and put demands in countries where child labor is part of today's reality."[33]

In recent years, IKEA partnered with UNICEF to create a three-year-long child rights project in 200 villages in the Northern India, state of Uttar Pradesh, seeking to prevent child labor by addressing the causes. The program gradually broadened, and more organizations were brought into the process in the states of Punjab, Haryana, Gujarat, Maharashtra, and Rajasthan. As a result, more than 65,000 children have been moved out of child labor and into classrooms, and more than 16,000 children between the ages of 15 and 18 received alternative vocational skill training.[34]

In the Indian state of Bihar, Unilever is partnering with the CIFF, referenced above, to address handwashing—a simple hygienic practice with major public health implications. More than two million children die each year from diarrhea and pneumonia, which can be countered through handwashing. In rural India, though, only 1% of mothers washed their hands with soap after defecation, and only 11% washed before handling food.[35] Partnering with another NGO, Socio Economic Unit Foundation (SEUF), Unilever embedded small microchips into Lifebuoy soap that was distributed to low-income communities to gage actual soap usage by children. While not all those who discovered chips in their soap were pleased,[36] Unilever used the survey information to design a handwashing campaign for school children that has proven it can change the behavior of the household for the benefit of community health. Unilever's "School of 5" program is pending approval to be implemented across 28,000 schools over five years in Bihar, reaching nine million school children, their mothers, and families.[37]

CIFF's role in this partnership is to support appropriate strategic decision-making and to assist Unilever in bringing this initiative to lower social levels, which CIFF's partners can access but are out of Unilever's reach. Beyond this, CIFF will secure targeted grants that shift the financial burden of project sustainability from a for-profit corporation to a scalable nonprofit initiative, managed by CIFF to bring Unilever's findings and subsequent handwashing campaign to broader social segments. Essentially, CIFF is charged with bringing down the cost of this initiative, which they have done.

The results transcend dollars and cents: Unilever projects an initial impact of 12,200 under-five lives saved. An estimated eight million cases of diarrhea will be averted, which will contribute not only to the mortality reduction but also to a reduction in stunting as each episode of diarrhea increases the chance of becoming stunted.[38]

Accordingly, creative partnerships between the private sector and CBOs that offer lessons in creative problem solving and the efficient use of resources to lift conditions of marginalized young people have emerged. Nike's Grassroots Girls Initiative directed substantial resources to community-level approaches that address the plight of vulnerable girls working through reliable intermediaries. Nike's initial partners in the Grassroots Girls Initiative—the American Jewish World Service, EMpower (The Emerging Markets Foundation), the Firelight Foundation, the Global Fund for Children, the Global Fund for Women, and the Mama Cash Foundation—authored a multiplier effect for Nike's investments. They ensured that the funding emanating from a major multinational corporation with no expertise in community-based grant making reached the ground fully and completely. This funding reached invisible lives, altering the trajectories of girls and the communities in which they live. Through a consortium, Nike was able to transform top-down funding into efficient and effective bottom-up, grassroots initiatives. Nike's emphasis on building knowledge from this model can inform other major funders who might also develop funding networks to reach deeper levels of society than their own directly administered philanthropy can reach.

The Rise of Private Schools

Public–private partnerships have created more than new relationships: they have authored new configurations that creatively merge the resources of both the private and public sectors to generate new systems and structures that broaden the opportunities reaching the most marginalized. Because governments in low-income countries often have insufficient resources to educate all their children, other options for educational access have arisen to fill the void. We have seen informal educational programs directed by CBOs and NGOs in various countries that afford opportunities for millions of children in poverty. These efforts are being increasingly complemented by the rise of affordable private schools run by local entrepreneurs.[39] Most of these schools are for-profit businesses run by individuals on a small scale.

The impact of private schools on educational access for young people in poverty is increasingly quantifiable. A two-year longitudinal study in India, Ghana, Nigeria, and Kenya found that, in each low-income area surveyed, the majority of students attended private schools. Only 35% of the schools functioning in the slums of Hyderabad in India were government schools. In the low-income Ga district of Accra, only 25% of the schools were government run, and in the three lowest-income districts of Lagos, Nigeria, that figure is 34%. The remainder of schools in each location was private, run by individual proprietors and receiving no government funding.[40] Moreover, student achievement at these private schools often runs higher than at government schools. In Hyderabad, for example, mathematics scores were 22% higher than at government schools.[41]

The NGO sector is also becoming involved in providing private alternatives to low-quality public schools. BRAC began as The Bangladesh Rural Advancement Committee in 1972 as a small grassroots organization to bring relief and development assistance to that newly independent and ravaged country. In the 1980s, BRAC established its first nonformal schools for disadvantaged children to transition to public schools. Over the next three decades, BRAC has built a system of schools outside the formal educational structures in seven countries educating more than 1.25 million young people. Nearly five million children, most of them girls, have graduated from BRAC schools. BRAC has become the largest secular nongovernmental educational system in the world.[42] Its structure allows it an operational freedom that is not common in educational systems even in high-income societies. BRAC's goal is for its students to transition to government schools within five years.

The phenomenon of private schools for the lowest-income students is being reproduced all over the world. In rural Africa, Village Schools International (VSI), a Canadian faith-based group, is managing 29 secondary schools in Tanzania and Malawi, with another ten under construction.[43] Omega Schools educate more than 6000 students at ten schools throughout Ghana using concepts developed by James Tooley, Professor of Educational Policy at the University of Newcastle in the UK.[44]

The evolution of private schools for children in poverty is just one manifestation of the creativity that has developed from the partnerships authored by different social and commercial sectors. Private schools fill critical voids left by inadequate government education systems. Many subsidize the education of their lowest-income students in the form of scholarships or fee waivers. But significantly, these schools go where government schools do not. Private schools can go further down the road than do government schools, and, in so doing, bring opportunities to young people with no other alternatives.

As the private sector continues to interact closely with NGOs, multilaterals, and the public sectors, new configurations will continue to emerge that channel resources, both human and financial, to the ground in strategic ways that attack the root causes of poverty and marginalization.

Increasingly, the private sector has embraced the notion that involvement with CBOs is consistent with corporate pressure to maximize profit. Industries driven by customer service, such as the telecoms, and those based on consumer demand, such as pharmaceuticals, have found benefit in these new configurations. Even corporations with their own well-defined giving mechanisms are finding ways to engage with local communities in the areas around the world where they are doing business. What this means is that the private sector, more so than ever before, has the capacity to contribute to systemic change on behalf of those living in extreme poverty.

Multilateral Organizations

The channel for much of the world's collective effort in addressing the conditions of poverty and social alienation has been the multilateral organizations coordinated through the United Nations (UN) or those created jointly among and between separate governments. The UN in particular has been instrumental in consolidating broad-based efforts for defined issues and conditions. These multilaterals will, and must, continue to be major players in any movement going forward to deepen and expand support of the most marginalized.

As noted earlier during the discussion of the development framework, the multilaterals occupy the top level, along with major donor governments. Because of this, they are in a unique position to coordinate middle-level efforts (those of major INGOs and relief consortia) while offering leadership on the general issues of child marginalization. This is both an opportunity and a responsibility that the multilaterals have yet to grasp fully. Despite their size and their reach, there remains a lack of consolidation and outspoken advocacy for those they seek to help.

The UN multilateral structure covers wide territory. The organization with the most direct relation to and longest history with children's issues is, of course, UNICEF, established in 1946 as the United Nations International Children's Emergency Fund. But it is not the only multilateral whose work impacts these issues.

Other UN multilaterals—UNDP (United Nations Development Program), UNHCR (United Nations High Commissioner for Refugees), UNFPA (United Nations Fund for Population Activities), UNAIDS, UNWomen, WFP (World Food Program), WHO (World Health Organization) and ILO (International Labor Organization)—all pursue work directly impacting the condition of children around the world. Each of these agencies exists on the strength of member nations contributions, and each operates in accordance with well-defined programmatic guidelines. Between them, these five multilaterals carry combined annual budgets exceeding $16 billion. Some of these funds support the health, nutrition, safety, and general well-being of young people in various desperate circumstances, even though none of these agencies has a singular mandate to assist children and young people as a separate demographic.[45]

UNICEF remains the principal actor in the global effort to elevate the status of marginalized children. Its history confirms a long-standing impact and includes such highlights as a Nobel Peace Prize in 1965 and the adoption of the Convention on the Rights of the Child (CRC) in 1989. Its annual State of the World's Children, noted earlier, is a comprehensive data-driven summary of children's conditions globally, including indices for health, education, mortality, and other salient measurements. Periodic summits on children and children's issues have provided a steady drumbeat of information that leverages concern among nations and substantiates the plight of invisible young people.[46] Their contributions have been enormous, and, with a reliable budget and high credibility worldwide, their potential to continue to impact children's lives remains considerable.

UNICEF's current focus areas are child survival and development, basic education, gender equality, HIV/AIDS, child protection, and policy advocacy.[47] Its structure, with 150 offices globally and thousands of staff, allows UNICEF to work with all sectors and to aspire to large-scale projects and anticipate large-scale results. Yet its intergovernmental nature can prevent controversial or nontraditional interventions that member nations might find objectionable or that might challenge long-standing cultural, ethnic, or religious realities in areas of need.

While UNICEF functions on a big stage, it effects change at the local level by influencing government action. For example, UNICEF's project in China helping low-income, disadvantaged children in urban areas by creating early childhood centers and safe spaces resulted in leveraged resources from the Chinese government by demonstrating how it can be done. The government has also replicated child-friendly spaces in rural areas for left-behind children that provide preschooling and nutritional support. Geeta Rao Gupta, Deputy Director of UNICEF, explains that this kind of systemic change is best possible through a major multilateral working in partnership with a government committed to such change.[48]

The UNICEF Innovation Unit, referenced in Chap. 4 as an example of an impactful foreign assistance mechanism, acknowledges that programs need to be designed in the field from the ground up, as local context and cultural nuance are key to sustainability. Technology-based projects that the Innovation Unit has tried to build from its New York headquarters have almost always failed.[49] So when an idea originates, a team is sent to the field to partner with local governments and local NGOs in developing a product built from the ground up through a human-centered design[50] process that incorporates the norms of the communities in which it will be implemented.[51]

UNICEF, as well as all multilaterals, has the potential to consolidate large amounts of resources, reach governments, and, in so doing, help set global priorities.[52] By entering effective partnerships with local CBOs, multilaterals can help close the gaps in service distribution. For example, the WFP provides food supplements to many groups working with the most marginalized children in public–private partnerships that have worked smoothly for many years.[53] Accordingly, these multilaterals must necessarily be a major player in determining the global response to children's issues.

All multilaterals by their very nature are large bureaucratic systems. As such, multilaterals can be inflexible, wedded to processes and programs that are slow to change. Moreover, their collective approach is siloed— WFP deals with food supplies and food security, UNDP works with economic development, and so on.

Such an approach can lead to parallel efforts, overlaps, and gaps in coverage. WFP, for example, has food distribution systems in place in more than 70 countries, thus constituting an impressive infrastructure to get food into the hands of those who need it. But under an agreement with UNICEF, WFP addresses "moderate acute malnutrition," while UNICEF focuses on "severe acute malnutrition."[54] The result is a splintered effort that runs the considerable risk of leaving hungry children behind because they do not fit comfortably into either one of these categories. At the same time, overlaps of service and duplicate infrastructures can waste valuable resources.

UNICEF itself has separate divisions working with separate issues, including child protection, education, and child survival. Add to this the changing dynamics of globalization. UNICEF is intergovernmental, but it is increasingly societies and individuals that are interacting, not governments, fueled by citizen engagement driven by information and communication technology.[55] We see this in the work of CBOs and in political movements such as the Arab Spring. The world is increasingly being moved from the bottom up.

The Sustainable Development Goals

As discussion continues concerning global development, both UNICEF, along with the other multilaterals, and the major INGOs are assuming strong voices in determining what can reasonably be accomplished through the coming decades. The Sustainable Development Goals (SDGs), discussed in Chap. 4, provide a working context for these collective efforts, framed in specific targets to mitigate specific issues. And, as noted, the conditions of marginalized children and young people receive stronger notice in the SDGs than they did in the Millennium Development Goals (MDGs).

It could well be argued that the entirety of the SDGs contribute to the well-being of children. All of the goals, including those that speak to the environment, to societal infrastructure, or to accessible energy, will impact the world's children in some way. But this is just more of the same rationalization that has typically placed the concerns of marginalized young people under the broader umbrella of more general issues. While the SDGs pay marginally more heed to the plight of the poorest of the poor, the specific conditions impacting vulnerable children and young people require focused and systematic redress.

At their best, the SDGs provide an actionable platform from which multilateral organizations, major global NGOs, and the world's governments can take steps to alleviate beyond past efforts to address the factors that place children at risk. Most likely, these efforts will still be unable to reach the *children of the last mile*. Still, the SDGs can propel action that push this work further down the road. They represent both hope and possibility, but only if they are taken seriously by their signatories and if funding to implement their steps can be made adequate.

INGOS

The major INGOs clearly have a significant role to play in elevating the status of marginalized children. With their resources, delivery networks, and experience in reaching afflicted areas relatively quickly, the INGOs are well suited to immediate emergency response. They also provide indispensable work in long-term displacements, especially for refugee and internally displaced populations in need of essential services. INGOs run a wide gamut of services feeding rehabilitation, reconstruction, and long-term development.

Yet the same inconsistencies of service delivery, overlap, and replications that plague the multilaterals apply in perhaps even greater measure to the INGOs. Not all organizations carry the same capacities or emphases. But in chasing the considerable sums of money offered by the United States Agency for International Development (USAID), the Department of State, and UNHCR among others, lines become blurred, and these organizations chase the same funding even if the purpose of that funding falls beyond the organization's mandate. An INGO's raison d'etre can easily become procuring grants and contracts rather than developing an efficient operational strategy. Seduced by the immense amount of dollars at stake, organizations often find themselves spending time and resources chasing their funding, then making up programs to spend the funds they've raised. They work in reverse, without planning beyond the next round of grants or Requests for Proposals (RFPs).

Significantly, many of the INGOs are decentralized enough so that their individual country affiliates may operate differently, or in accordance with different priorities, than does their central body. Save the Children Sweden, for example, develops its own emphases within the broader framework of Save's central mission, paying greater attention to issues impacting children and young people who have immigrated to Europe and face discrimination or racial violence.[56] Country-based affiliates often have their own boards and their own localized sources of financial support. This provides some level of independence and a capacity to respond to situations close at hand without undue bureaucratic considerations.

The resources at the disposal of major INGOs, all of whom pursue vital and life-changing work in various forms, are critical in shifting the social dynamics that place children at risk. They will continue to be major actors as the ongoing drama unfolds. But without a centralized focus on children and young people as a priority development target, their work will be all the more difficult. And without mechanisms that drive support to the community level, much of the assistance offered will fail to find the most marginalized children. In fact, because of their draw on major funding resources and their general reluctance to hand over programmatic control to local groups, INGOs can be competitors rather than enablers in the process of moving more support to the community level.

GOVERNMENTS

The approach of national governments around the world to the issues of development is nearly as diverse as the governments themselves. With substantial resources that can be directed to social and economic enhancements and the capacity to set policy and priorities, governments wield enormous influence in determining the trajectory of international response to marginal conditions impacting hundreds of millions of lives.

The US Government

Those governments with the most resources for social investment and the vehicles through which to deliver those resources are obviously critical players in aid delivery. Among them, the United States stands at the top. The US government enacts development policy through a number of channels, all of them relatively well-financed and capable of exerting immediate impact on the ground.

As noted in Chap. 4, USAID drives the US government's foreign development and assistance investments. As a government entity, USAID must reflect US government interests. And so there is risk in working with grassroots networks. Because CBOs are localized and approaching issues on their own terms, the chance always exists that someone might end up being connected to something the US government does not like. Funding community-based interests allows those communities to make their own decisions, which sometimes are not completely aligned with US national interests.[57]

When USAID does go into another country, its contracts often go to US-based implementing partners such as CARE. This consumes much of the budget at the top end. USAID's desire to work with more local partners in practice results in funneling support though US organizations down to more localized levels because USAID works at a much larger scale. Very little of this support, though, ever reaches the community level. It becomes difficult for them to winnow the size of their grants down to the level that works for local CBOs.[58]

Still, there are instances in which USAID has been successful in getting support to the community level. Madalo Samati was working as a researcher for a USAID-funded project in Malawi, Girls' Attainment in Basic Literacy and Education (GABLE). As such, she traveled from village to village to learn different applications of girls' education. Drawn to the power of communities, she and five colleagues formed a new local organization, the Creative Center for Community Mobilization (CRECCOM). Through a number of initiatives, including research into community issues, facilitating community dialog, role modeling, and communication, including the use of theater, CRECCOM impels communities to develop their own solutions to localized issues. USAID provided an initial funding component. The GABLE program from which Madalo came was managed by an INGO, but since CRECCOM evolved out of GABLE, USAID eventually transferred some of the GABLE funding to CRECCOM.[59]

This process of localization remains inefficient. INGOs typically approach local NGOs to partner because many USAID grants now mandate work with local partners. But INGOs receive the biggest chunk. In recent USAID-supported programs, INGOs have subcontracted a small portion of their grants to CRECCOM and other local partners. The local partners who implement the project in schools and communities receive disproportionally little of the project funds. For example, as part of two early grade reading projects run by INGOs—one with a $24 million grant and one with a $12 million grant—CRECCOM received only $2 million and $250,000, respectively for the entire community involvement component. With only a fraction of the total budget, CRECCOM is implementing the program in ten districts reaching out to over 2000 school communities for the former and 52 school communities for the latter. In Madalo's words, "This is just ridiculous."[60]

There are many layers to this desire for increased localization of USAID assistance, and the challenges of finding legitimate, efficient, and effective implementation partners at the local level are obvious. To do so well will require input and cooperation from USAID's subdivisions, its existing partners in the field, and the INGOs that have knowledge of and access to local players. For example, USAID's Center for Faith-based and Community Initiatives (CFBCI) has the capacity to connect USAID funding with effective CBOs around the world. While CFBCI is not a funder, it can help CBOs build their capacity to become more competitive for USAID grants through recommendations or specific implementation strategies. USAID's functional bureaus—Food Security; Economic Growth, Education, and Environment; Democracy, Conflict, and Humanitarian Assistance; and Global Health—will adapt this new strategy into their own programs of operation and work through existing channels to find suitable implementation partners.[61]

Within USAID's Bureau for Economic Growth, Education, and Environment is its office for women, which seeks to integrate gender equality systematically across all of USAID's programs. No such office exists for children, although in 2012, USAID created the office of Special Advisor and Senior Coordinator on Children in Adversity. Dr. Neil Boothby was the first to serve in this position, which also supervised the Interagency Working Group on Highly Vulnerable Children (HVC).[62] The Working Group's mandate is to coordinate US government programs "to eliminate the causes of vulnerability; strengthen families, communities, and national systems to minimize exposure to cumulative risk factors...; and strengthen protective factors and build capacity to help children recover and prevent a recurrence." This group represents the first concerted effort in the United States to coordinate children's issues across multiple government agencies.[63]

The Center on Children in Adversity initiative began with great promise. It identifies itself as "the first-ever whole-of-government strategic guidance for US Government international assistance for children."[64] But results to date have been limited. In a report to Congress in October

2014, Robert Horvath, who replaced Neil Boothby as Special Advisor on Children in Adversity, listed accomplishments spanning all US government agencies.

And while the effort is to be applauded, the results were meager. Across all aid programs, a total of 90,000 children were diverted from child labor conditions, and another 1000 were relocated from institutional to family-based housing. Roughly 2.7 million children received nutritional assistance through the Department of Agriculture's McGovern-Dole International Food for Education and Child Nutrition Program, which distributes US-based agricultural products to infant and child nutrition efforts. Another 76,000 households caring for orphaned or vulnerable children received financial stipends.[65]

A review of these numbers against the immensity of children in need leads to the conclusion that even the largest purveyor of global aid cannot reach those at the end of the last mile. A further review of the Children in Adversity program indicates that intentions alone may not be enough to surmount the considerable bureaucratic and administrative hurdles of coordinating millions of dollars of aid in a targeted way across sprawling independent US government agencies.

Moreover, the *children of the last mile*, and those who work and advocate for them, remain left out of the policy and allocation decisions made by the Children in Adversity initiative, which relies on the same top-down delivery patterns discussed earlier. To be truly effective, this program must incorporate the programs that genuinely reach those children in the greatest adversity and who are otherwise unseen. From such promising beginnings, this program appears now to be another component of a still-flawed system, relying on contractors, subcontractors, and major suppliers, with too little of its already scant resources ever reaching the community level.

The Displaced Children and Orphans Fund (DCOF) began in 1989 through USAID's Office of Democracy, Human Rights, and Governance to improve the lives of children at risk, including orphans, unaccompanied minors, children affected by armed conflict, and children with disabilities. Implementing USAID grants and agreements, DCOF provides programmatic support and technical assistance for initiatives that provide care, protection, and services for especially vulnerable children, including those impacted by armed conflict, street-connected children, and those otherwise living outside established systems of care. Currently supporting programs in 31 countries, DCOF is one of USAID's most child-centric initiatives, even though it does not specifically support CBOs.[66] In April 2014, DCOF merged with the Center on Children in Adversity.[67]

The new emphasis on localization, however flawed, has also generated a spirit of innovation at USAID. Grants are flowing from specific USAID initiatives in different directions than they have before. For example, Duke University's Social Entrepreneurship Accelerator program (SEAD) program[68] received a $10 million USAID grant to spur global health entrepreneurship, including innovative research, and collaborative activity to develop models crossing business, global health, and health-care delivery sectors.[69] In late 2013, USAID made a $2 million matching grant combined with an additional $2 million from General Atlantic, Newman's Own Foundation, The Pershing Square Foundation, and Rockefeller Philanthropy Advisors to Echoing Green for a three-year partnership to invest in young global entrepreneurs who are devising new models to address global development issues.[70]

This innovative spirit has fueled the launch of the US Global Development Lab, a USAID initiative launched in April 2014 to produce new development solutions by engaging nontraditional stakeholders, building cross-sector partnerships and employing new science and technology applications to address long-standing development challenges. While the returns on this new initiative are still uncertain, the Global Development Lab is based on bringing together new perspectives on previously intractable issues.[71]

As a multibillion dollar agency, USAID carries immense presence in international development. It is the 800 pound gorilla that cannot be ignored. But for all its intentions, USAID struggles with issues of efficiency, and its size prohibits it from reaching the most basic community levels. In essence, its hand is too large to reach through the small doorways that lead to the children and young people in struggling communities.

As noted earlier, USAID has yet to develop transparency and accounting protocols that show clearly where the pathways of its funding ultimately lead. While billions of dollars are in fact allocated to poverty alleviation, nutrition, health, and other measures that impact positively the lives of children, it is impossible to know with any precision or confidence how much of that funding reaches the community level and how much is subsumed in implementation agreements with contractors and subcontractors.

As independent agencies, both the Inter-American Foundation (IAF) and the African Development Foundation (ADF) are distinct within the

US foreign assistance framework. Given the impact of their work, where that work is focused, and their modest budgets, these two groups are the best kept secrets in US international development. Both agencies enjoy bipartisan support and exist through separate Congressional budget appropriations. They work independently from the major governmental departments, and, as such, have a relatively high level of operational flexibility while remaining accountable to their Congressional funders. Their ability to direct support to the community level in some of the world's most economically stressed situations sets them apart from other US initiatives.

IAF channels development assistance directly to grassroots groups in Latin America and the Caribbean. Since 1972, IAF has awarded almost $710 million in grants to more than 5000 local organizations. IAF encourages proposals from traditionally marginalized groups, especially indigenous peoples, African descendants, women, and persons with disabilities.[72]

IAF's emphasis on grassroots engagement is distinctive within US government assistance programs, but IAF is also one of the few efforts within US systems that reach directly to the community level. Responding to local initiatives creates a certain tension for an agency that must remain reflective of US interests, though IAF argues that thriving local communities in Latin America and the Caribbean are themselves in the US national interest because they mean more stable societies and better partners. At the same time, Robert Kaplan, IAF's President and CEO, explains that empowerment has risks for donors. "Others often use the terminology, but what they really mean is just participation—get local people to participate so everyone feels good about the decisions that the donor wants to make. The donors don't actually want to give up control which is what can and should happen when people are empowered."[73]

Similarly, ADF, an independent government agency established in 1980 to work directly with low-income communities throughout Africa, focuses on locally designed solutions. ADF provides grants totaling approximately $22 million annually to community groups pursuing social and economic development at the local level. All recipient organizations must be 100% African owned and managed and legally registered within their home country. ADF has made grants ranging between $50,000 and $250,000 in more than 20 countries and manages an annual portfolio of more than 540 projects.[74]

Shari Berenbach, ADF's former President and CEO, discusses the advantages of ADF's community-based approach. "[We] must look at the whole ecosystem. You can't just separate and train youth and expect them to become entrepreneurs when food, water, health, power, and so on, isn't there. [We] need to strengthen families and communities to increase economic growth and opportunity. But just waiting for the economy to take care of itself is not going to reach marginalized kids."[75]

Western European Governments

The United States is not the only government with well-developed programs for international assistance. The governments of Western Europe have crafted their own responses to development questions and assumed increasingly visible positions on the global stage. And, in fact, many European governments are far ahead of the United States in crafting assistance programs that deliver support to the grassroots level.

The Department for International Development (DFID), the UK's international assistance arm, binds its work to the CRC although it lacks a specific programmatic focus on children. A significant portion of their funding supports education, reproductive health, and human rights, but without a clear children's issue mandate it becomes difficult to measure DFID's impact on marginalized young people.[76] Even so, it would be natural to conclude that DFID's investments, which exceed £10 billion annually, or $16.87 billion, have some positive impact on marginalized children.[77]

DFID's assistance is decentralized, managed by regional offices throughout the world. As a result, funding decisions are made largely on the basis of priorities established in each office. Some locations, notably Bangladesh, Nepal, and Zimbabwe, are specifically using child rights as a point of entry for programmatic funding.[78]

In Germany, the Deutsche Gesellschaft fur Internationale Zusammenarbeit (GIZ), or German Society for International Cooperation, has a clear commitment to children's rights. Much of their funding is directed to orienting legal systems to protect children and young people and promoting dialog between governments and NGOs to develop sustainable structures for child protection. GIZ has directed funding to 130 countries, with 21% of their budget supporting work in Sub-Saharan Africa, and nearly 18% of all funding supporting education projects.[79]

Irish Aid's Civil Society Fund (CSF) is an integral part of Ireland's national policy for international development, termed "One World, One Future." With an emphasis on reducing hunger, advancing educational opportunities, building sustainable development, and food security, the CSF makes grants to NGOs working in the world's lowest-income regions, 85% of which were directed to Sub-Saharan Africa.[80] Most of Ireland's overseas development assistance is channeled through local NGOs rather than bilateral or multilateral configurations.[81] Significantly, Irish Aid also provides funding in Ireland's schools for an increased awareness of global development issues.[82] The country has also created an official Ombudsman for Children, among whose duties is providing high level policy advice to the Prime Minister concerning children's issues, both domestically and globally.[83]

The Norwegian Agency for Development Cooperation (NORAD) directs support for women's and children's health, education, and HIV/ AIDS, all of which has a positive impact on children in their geographic funding areas. NORAD's budget surpasses 27.8 billion krone, or roughly $4.5 billion. Norway devotes more than 1% of its GDP to development and assistance, the highest such percentage of any country in the world.[84]

Taken together, the efforts of donor governments to bring assistance support to lower-income regions has become a powerful tool in reaching children and young people beset by deep-seated, localized problems. Most of these efforts face the challenge of translating top-down strategies into community-level interventions, and, despite good intentions, most are beset by some measure of inefficiency, duplication of efforts, and waste. Governments, due to their resources and their ongoing role on a global stage, have tremendous potential to alter the course of the world's neediest children and young people. But they must do a better job in focusing those resources and identifying ways to channel them to the communities that most need them.

Government Policies to Protect Children

Perhaps the most effective and sustainable response to the marginalization of children is the prevention of that marginalization before it can take root. National governments especially (but also regional and local governments) have the capacity to develop and enact policies that prevent and respond to violence, abuse, exploitation, and unnecessary separation from family while fostering children's survival, development, and well-being. As part of the social contract that legitimizes all governments, protection is, or should be, a central function of even the most underdeveloped government.

The role of social protection entails several levels, all of which pertain to even the most vulnerable populations. UNICEF has developed a Protective Environment Framework (PEF) defining the eight elements critical to full protection. These include: a governmental commitment to protection, reflected in appropriate budgets and policies; relevant legislation and enforcement of that legislation; attitudes, traditions, and customs that value children; the open discussion of social issues through the engagement of media; the development of children's life skills; the capacity and competence of those who work with children; basic protective services; and monitoring and oversight.[85] Clearly, policies protecting children can be essential in mitigating the other risks that lead to the issues discussed in these pages. National social systems and policies that protect children and provide them access to justice through legal frameworks can offset the most vicious and persistent negative influences. In the end, implementing protection policies prove to be more cost-effective than addressing the ills that these policies might have prevented, as noted in Chap. 3.

Some countries obviously do this better than others. In India, the Ministry of Women and Child Development spearheaded the creation of an Integrated Child Protection Scheme (ICPS) which came into being in 2009. With a stated goal of both providing for children in need and reducing the risks and vulnerabilities that lead to abuse, neglect, exploitation, and abandonment, ICPS has coordinated central protective services and raised public awareness about children's rights and needs. Their role within the central government has led to increased capacity for service delivery by child-focused agencies, and they have been able to extend this coordination to both the regional and local levels. CHILDLINE, referenced above, is a major ICPS partner, as are dozens of other protective agencies throughout the country.[86]

The 1994 Rwandan genocide compelled that country to reevaluate its social and governmental structures, processes which continue to this day. In 2011, Rwanda established the National Commission for Children (NCC) to create a national plan for child protection and to safeguard their basic rights. In concert with the NCC, Rwanda adopted a National Child Care Reform Strategy to deal more compassionately with those who had lost family during the genocide by deinstitutionalizing their care wherever possible. Starting with a national review where orphaned children voiced their concerns over the level of their care, this initiative led to significant reductions in institutionally based care as children and young adults were moved to family-based settings. At the same time, the NCC sponsored the training and education of 14 new social workers and 14 psychologists to work with these young people.[87]

Despite the examples set by India, Rwanda, and other countries with developed social protection policies, governmental attention to child protection is uneven, especially in less stable countries. The US Center for Disease Control and Prevention commissioned a study of seven countries— Cambodia, Haiti, Kenya, Malawi, Swaziland, Tanzania, and Zimbabwe— regarding incidents of sexual violence between 2007 and 2013. What they found reinforces the perceived lack of systemic protection for young people: among those aged 13–24 in these countries, the average prevalence of sexual violence exceeded 25%, and of those abused, only 10% received state-provided services for their trauma.[88]

There can be no denying the inherent power of governments to establish a protective landscape for childhood and adolescent development. The improvements in access to education, cited in Chap. 4, underscore what can happen when governments focus seriously on broadening development opportunities. Significantly, many of these improvements have come about as the result of public–private partnerships (BRAC, VSI, and others mentioned above) in recognition that the capacity of governments, especially poor ones, to develop new approaches that better the lives of children is best exercised through networked resources. But regardless of resources, or political coalitions, or social movements, every government has the capacity to establish a protective environment for its youngest and most vulnerable. Without this, any effort at development is built upon shifting sands.

NGO-State Relationships

The manner in which any state regards its NGO community will dictate in large part the role of that community and its ability to do its best work. States who maintain stability based on inequality of resources, participation, and rights, often consider the civil sector as threatening and work to suppress NGOs, usually at great cost to their most desperate citizens. States that regard NGOs as assets in providing services and relief that the state may not have the resources to offer itself, or see NGOs as advocacy partners for issues of special concern, will provide nurturing environments for NGO growth or at least stay out of their way.

There are states that value self-preservation over the welfare of its own people. In Ethiopia, in 2010, the central government, led by Meles

Zenawi, withheld famine relief from those not affiliated with the ruling party. A portion of foreign assistance for the famine found its way not into the stomachs of hungry political opponents but into Zenawi's coffers. William Easterly refers to the *Tyranny of Experts*, whom he defines as development economists, cold war strategists, and some "postindependence African leaders," who design and deploy assistance in top-down methods often ignoring the political and economic rights of those they are seeking to assist. The impulse among philanthropists and humanitarians to improve the living standards in desperate countries has fed this "tyranny" while paying too little mind to the actual conditions on the ground.[89]

Government attitudes in response to the civil sector can range from noninterventionist to active encouragement of their work to a desire for control. Predictably, NGOs and CBOs working for poverty alleviation or improved health in remote areas are more favorably regarded than those advocating for an unwelcome refugee or ethnic community or those seeking structural changes. In all cases, this NGO–government relationship is a determining factor for the civil sector's scope of work.

Local organizations that are able to develop collaborative relationships with their governments are more likely to scale their operations. We have seen the impact of government embrace of NGO efforts in the scaling of Akshaya Patra, whose programs expanded exponentially once the Indian government saw the unique value of their work and how it reached constituencies that their own resources could not serve. These local organizations are better able to utilize government resources for broader impact or to move their work into other corners of the country.[90]

THE LAW AND LEGAL SYSTEMS

Laws regulate social behavior. Their construction establishes the limits and boundaries of actions, defines consequences for overstepping those boundaries and, in so doing, brings order, reason, equity, and balance to pluralistic societies. For children and young people to act equitably, the law must protect their points of vulnerability and ensure respect for their persons and for their dreams.

People in poverty in particular are especially subject to violence, suffering from what Gary Haugen and Victor Boutros call *the Locust Effect*: "the unique pestilence of violence and the punishing impact it has on efforts to lift the global poor out of poverty."[91] Yet laws are not protecting children from this violence. Enforcement is sketchy, and legal systems are not sufficiently responsive to the situations impacting the most marginalized. Rape and assault in developing societies can go unpunished because legal systems are neglected and beset by ineffective police, bureaucracy based on outdated laws or precepts, and naked corruption. In many societies, it is only the wealthy who can afford to pay for operative legal services. People in poverty are left at the mercy of very flawed systems.[92]

It is not difficult to find examples of failed legal systems compounding the conditions that place children and young people in jeopardy. An epidemic of sexual assault in Guatemala, wherein as many as a third of all girls between 14 and 18 had experienced some form of sexual assault within the past year, led the government there to bolster its legal response. Guatemala introduced new protocols for prosecutors of sex crimes and designated a special police unit to combat sexual assaults. But the courts could not keep up with this new activity, and so only 10% of all cases received indictments, and only 5.8% were ever successfully tried.[93]

And so the victims, unsupported by an inadequate legal system, are prone to homelessness, sex trafficking, gangs, and addiction. Many choose to flee altogether: up to a quarter of all child migrants from Guatemala, Honduras, El Salvador, and Mexico have experienced abuse by a caregiver.[94] It is estimated that 58% of all children from these countries detained crossing the US border have legitimate claims to seek international protection from violence in their homes or communities.[95] The current child immigration crisis in the United States, where up to 85,000 unaccompanied minors cross its borders illegally each year, stems in no small part from the failure of Central American legal systems to protect their children.[96]

The CRC sets forth more than 40 principles to which signatories agree to abide. All member nations except Somalia and the United States have put their signatures to the CRC, so, at least in theory, a comprehensive global construct for the legal recognition and protection of children and young people already exists. The UN Committee on the Rights of the Child monitors the implementation of the CRC by member states; so, again in theory, a mechanism is in place to impel compliance with these comprehensive rights.

The CRC has been an effective tool in compelling member states to incorporate human rights principles into legislation, promoting discussions of children's rights, with some direct action, including the establishment of Ombudsman for Children and developing national agendas for children.[97] It has come to be viewed as a paramount universal statement confirming the role of states in protecting its youngest and most vulnerable citizens. But enforcement of its principles is ragged, sometimes nonexistent, and implementation of its ideals has been uneven at best. In too many places, the CRC is little more than a piece of rhetoric, something which can make a signatory feel good about its public commitment to the lives of children but not compelling any tangible action that might be either inconvenient or too expensive.

Given the levels of poverty, abuse, violence, and marginalization affecting hundreds of millions of children, it would be easy to conclude that the CRC has failed. But perhaps a more accurate conclusion would be that the CRC has had to state its noble principles against an incredible momentum of social, economic, cultural, and political factors that are intricate, complex, and deep-seated. Until the impact of those factors is reduced, it will be impractical to judge the success of the CRC.

All legislation, like politics, is local. In the end, it is contingent upon each country, each state, each locality to enact and enforce proper legislation protecting the well-being of children and young people. Watchdogs such as Child Rights Information Network and Human Rights Watch are committed to protecting and defending children's rights and more than eager to shine light on those situations where legal systems fall short in protecting the young. A community of NGOs works to change laws from the bottom up, such as Adolescent Girls' Legal Defense Fund (AGLDF) at Equality Now, which supports and publicizes strategically selected legal cases representing the most significant human rights abuses of adolescent girls. AGLDF is currently pursuing cases in countries ranging from Ethiopia to Yemen to Pakistan to Brazil.[98] UNICEF has also joined in the effort to spotlight abusive systems and change them at the root.[99]

Legal systems can abuse children in various ways. Systems can criminalize children caught in desperate circumstances that force destructive behaviors. Children are often sentenced according to the same criteria as adults and incarcerated with adults, leading to abuse. Children can be treated as inconsequential witnesses, and their stories discounted, often to the advantage of those stories' perpetrators. Their complaints can be dismissed, and their testimony often carries less weight than that of any adult.[100]

Take, for example, the sentencing in the United States of young people to life sentences without parole. Currently, there are 2500 juveniles with such sentences.[101] Most of these were imposed by judges who have no leeway for individual circumstances, who are obligated to impose this harsh sentence by state law. The children sentenced are most often themselves the products of violence. Nearly 80% have witnessed violence in their homes, and more than half witnessed regular violence in their neighborhoods. With no hope of living outside prison walls, their lives lose direction and aspiration while the violence around them continues: 80% of all girls and nearly half of all children sentenced to life without parole are physically abused.[102]

In situations where there is no rule of law, such as during conflicts, natural emergencies, or in ungoverned spaces, children fare even more poorly. In such situations, it becomes imperative for children to have advocates who will stand up for them until legal systems can be made functional and some semblance of order restored. Major INGOs, such as the International Rescue Committee, have recognized and assumed this responsibility as a clear mandate in their disaster alleviation work.[103]

As noted in Chap. 3, civil conflict too often leads to the creation of "ungoverned spaces," territory outside the rule of law or convention, subject only to the actions of the combatants themselves. Even in areas previously considered socially or economically advanced, the process of war can quickly break down all authority and leave the citizens within those regions at the mercy of violent conflict. The ongoing violence in Syria, for example, has broken apart sections of a once functioning society, compromised any sense of order, and negated the rule of law. Parts of Syria have become little more than battlefields. In such ungoverned territories, even basic humanitarian relief can be held hostage to those who would fight their wars on the backs of civilians.[104]

Children in these ungoverned spaces are at particular risk, but the rule of law in itself does not guarantee protection. Siddharth Kara, Director of the Human Trafficking and Modern Slavery Program at the Harvard University Kennedy School of Government, considers the law and legal systems to be only a part of the solution of child protection. Genuine movement occurs at the community level. Especially where the majority of a population may not support an existing law, enforcement at the local level becomes key. This is where gradual change of long-standing social problems can be enhanced by legal systems with proper local enforcement.[105] Priti Patkar, one of Prerana's founders discussed earlier, has spent much time working with local police and judges to improve enforcement of existing laws, to which she attributes a large measure of Prerana's success.[106]

In the last analysis, laws cannot guarantee behavior or assure that those under the law's protection will in fact enjoy that protection. But they can set in clear and definitive terms the value placed on all members of a society, especially the youngest and most vulnerable, and thereby create a solid framework that impels their security.

ACADEMIA AND RESEARCH INSTITUTIONS

Colleges and universities throughout the world serve as intellectual incubators for those who emerge into leadership positions within the various fields of international development. Academia prepares those who will become the authors of policy and programs pertaining to the social, economic, cultural, and political interactions impacting children and young people. As such, academia has both the opportunity and the responsibility to ensure that those it teaches are well versed in the intellectual underpinnings of what their work entails.

There are research initiatives that are in fact providing critical insights into the issues that place children at risk. The *Young Lives* study at Oxford referenced earlier is breaking new ground concerning the causes and consequences of childhood poverty in developing countries. Employing a multidisciplinary research team coordinated through Oxford's Department of International Development, *Young Lives* tracks the lives of around 12,000 children in four low and middle-income countries across the globe reflecting different levels of development over a 15-year period. The work is ongoing, and the conclusions are evidence-based.[107]

As a longitudinal study, *Young Lives* seeks to generate in-depth analysis of low-income children's lives and the coping strategies they and their families adopt. The research focuses on four countries—Ethiopia, India (in Andhra Pradesh and Telangana), Peru, and Vietnam. These were chosen to reflect a wide range of cultural, economic, geographical, political, and social contexts. The children come from households experiencing varying degrees of poverty and marginalization, caused by disparate factors. *Young Lives* employs quantitative and qualitative methods, including surveys of children and their caregivers, complemented by substudies on early childhood care and development, family lives and environment, and other topics to create an overview of development factors that affect the changes measured quantitatively.[108]

Jack P. Shonkoff, MD, Director of the Center on the Developing Child at Harvard University, bases his work on what the science of early childhood development tells us about how children's brains develop and how early experiences literally get into the body and influence learning, behavior, and health for a lifetime. The science presents a powerful reason, Shonkoff asserts, to break down silos across sectors and enter a new era of innovations in policy and practice that can benefit children facing adversity worldwide. As he and his coauthors state: "Ministries of health prioritize child survival and physical well-being, ministries of education focus on schooling, ministries of finance promote economic development, and ministries of welfare address breakdowns across multiple domains of function. Advances in the biological and social sciences offer a unifying framework for generating significant societal benefits by catalyzing greater synergy across these policy sectors."[109] This cross-sectoral approach shows promise as a framework for evaluating what can be done both to respond to and to prevent early childhood adversity.

Shonkoff's work entails cross-referencing scientific influences, such as the impact of social stress on brain plasticity, with social interventions such as the provision of nutrition and health care. He employs his conclusions to suggest changes in policy and practice to broaden access to the factors that dictate positive human development: "Science tells us that the foundations of lifelong health and learning are built in the earliest years of life. Therefore, the time has come to match continuing progress in the global reduction of child mortality with greater investment in the universal promotion of early childhood development, particularly in the poorest nations."[110]

In 2003, the Economics Department at the Massachusetts Institute of Technology launched The Abdul Latif Jameel Poverty Action Lab (J-PAL) to reduce poverty by ensuring that policy is based on scientific evidence. In the years since, J-PAL has developed a global network of researchers employing various methods, including randomized evaluations, to investigate critical policy questions in the fight against poverty, much of which involves poverty's impact on children and young people. Among J-PAL's evaluations are the impact on children's health of chlorine in water systems in Zambia and the effect of vocational training for disadvantaged youth in Colombia.[111] Innovations for Poverty Action (IPA) uses a similar approach and was in fact sired by some of the same individuals who launched J-PAL.[112]

Pratham, which conducts the Annual Survey of Education Report referenced in Chap. 8, has participated in a J-PAL evaluation of the impact of a community-based literacy program in which young volunteers conduct evening classes to teach literacy to younger children. The results were stunning: all previously illiterate children were at least able to recognize letters, and those who began with some level of literacy were far more likely to be able to read a short story by the end of the classes.[113]

Think-tanks play such a role in creating and disseminating knowledge of children's development issues. The Center for Strategic and International Studies, a public policy research institution, in partnership with the International Youth Foundation and Hilton Worldwide, has developed a *Global Youth Index* to measure the well-being of young people in individual countries. On the basis of six indices—citizen participation, economic opportunity, education, health, information and communication technology, and safety and security—the Global Youth Index seeks to inform policymakers, donors, professionals in the field, and the general public of the relative standing of young people across the globe.

The Youth Index reveals some noteworthy findings. In all, young people are doing rather poorly and experience relative low levels of well-being. Young people score strongest concerning health issues and weakest concerning economic issues. How young people themselves feel about the quality of their lives often does not match what the data indicates, implying a disconnect between reality and perception.[114]

Other think-tanks engage in issues pertaining to children and youth in poverty. The Center for Universal Education at the Brookings Institution focuses on issues of access and quality, with an emphasis on girls. The Center for Global Development delves into areas related to global poverty and inequality. Others exist, and each in its own way contributes to the body of knowledge informing global children's development.

The One Health Initiative (OHI) came into existence in the late 2000s to expand interdisciplinary collaborations touching upon aspects of health care for humans, animals, and the environment. OHI seeks to accelerate biomedical research, enhance public health, and improve medical education and clinical care by sharing research and hard data across disparate fields of study. Participating organizations include the American Medical Association, the American Veterinary Medical Association, the Centers for Disease Control, and the US National Environmental Health Association. In all, OHI points toward holistic responses that embrace all relevant components of scientific and social thinking concerning humanistic development.[115] This is especially relevant when we consider the example of siloing, discussed in Chap. 5, in which the distribution of free livestock without referral to proper animal hygiene and husbandry led to outbreaks of epilepsy among children.[116]

Academic research regarding children's issues in the United States tends to be US-centric. Given the paucity of comprehensive programs at the university level and the ongoing tendency to think in silos,[117] academia in the United States is missing an opportunity to engage itself more deeply into global children's development. Said Jo Boyden of Oxford University: "There are some really serious gaps, and I think in the States the strong focus on national issues has narrowed the field to the States to some degree. So it's surprising how few American scholars are really familiar with the political economy of childhood poverty in Egypt or Pakistan or Nigeria or wherever."[118]

If academia is truly to prepare the next generation of leaders who can apply their skills and wisdom to international development issues, it cannot ignore young people as a comprehensive and complex demographic. Courses must identify and analyze the issues impacting children and young people distinctly, and not as part of other demographics. Academia must break down its tendency to draw lines around children's issues, to silo them in tight boxes, or to fold them into broader issues where the singularity of influences on children and young people lose their clarity. They need to offer more courses focused on children in international development that are not only relegated to schools of education, public health, or social work, similar to the way women in international development has become its own field of study recognized by public policy and international studies programs.

The *Young Lives* study discussed above focuses on the demographics rather than the CBOs that work with those demographics. The other research efforts referenced here have great value, but they do not deal directly with CBOs. Despite increasingly visible examples of CBOs that have devised effective interventions, and have in many cases scaled those interventions, there is a lack of evidence-based research on the work of CBOs. Ruchika, for example, referenced in Chap. 6, has grown from a small presence on Bhubaneswar's train platforms to a major social service organization reaching thousands of India's most marginalized children in that city with a variety of programs.

It is quite difficult to conduct research in remote or underdeveloped community settings, especially with groups focused on survival that have few resources to direct to the processes that such research might entail. Even hosting an outside researcher can strain programs operating on razor-thin budgets. It can also seem unduly expensive to undertake research in areas with an underdeveloped infrastructure. But there are lessons to be learned through CBOs, and academia would do well to turn an eye toward extracting those lessons formally.

THE MEDIA

Many of the stories profiling the young people caught in desperate situations reviewed earlier in these pages would not have come to us except for the splendid work of journalists digging into the lives of those others cannot see and the circumstances that render them invisible. Nicholas Kristof, Orla Ryan, Fred de Sam Lazaro, and dozens of others have developed an acuity for seeing these children and telling their stories. We owe them a debt of gratitude. The media, both print and electronic, can play a defining role in bringing us to the realization of what is truly happening at the grassroots level.

The nature of media is to capture public attention. Spectacular events get play, and disasters and emergencies become central media events. Journalists, editors, and producers struggle with the public's short attention span and rush from event to event and from story to story, often treating the subjects of these stories perfunctorily without going into sufficient depth to analyze the causes of their situations or the effects those situations create.

But, as Nicholas Kristof says, "As many infant girls die unnecessarily every week in China as protesters died in the one incident at Tiananmen [Square]. Those Chinese girls never received a column inch of news coverage, and we began to wonder if our own journalistic priorities were skewed... When a prominent dissident was arrested in China, we would write a front page article; when 100,000 girls were routinely kidnapped and trafficked into brothels, we didn't even consider it news."[119]

One could argue that the condition of marginalized children is riveting enough to warrant deep coverage. Indeed, the profile of Dasani by Andrea Elliott in *The New York Times*, referenced in Chap. 1, garnered much attention. It also spurred response in official governmental circles. New York City's mayor reached out to Dasani's mother and, more significantly, pledged a review of the city's policies regarding the homeless.[120] The media has the power to impel change, or at least consideration of these uncomfortable issues, by illustrating the human impact these issues carry with them.

But as compelling as these stories may be, they still fight for space in the public forum. The media clutches and grabs at whatever is closest at hand, despite the lingering weight of issues impacting children and youth. Compounding the challenge is the notion of compassion fatigue from a media that is saturated with images of war, violence, poverty, and want from various arenas around the world. According to Oxford's Jo Boyden, "Nowadays, we're lucky to get a sound bite onto a news item. You cannot get a whole program focusing on these issues... But there's a real loss of momentum in the field. So I think it's really important to think about how you can capture people's attention because frankly... people have seen too many pictures of starving children."[121]

Problematic, too, is the manner in which marginalized children are depicted on those occasions when they are covered at all. A focus on trauma, loss, and disaster can ironically deepen the invisibility of the children affected. The children shown become the gimmicks of the story, and pity-invoking portrayals that sensationalize complex issues, situations, or problems do little to foster understanding or promote solutions. They translate to ratings, but they rarely translate to action.

The responsibility of the media is not limited to high-income countries or to media outlets with broad readership. Indigenous media within low-income societies have the distinct advantage of being closer to the stories. They must bring them out for a wider world to see. In fact, it is local journalists that have vantage points and perspectives that outside journalists rarely attain. One of the most powerful developments in local journalism is the evolution of Integrated Regional Information Networks (IRIN) which arose in 1995 to report on on-the-ground conditions following the Rwandan genocide. Headquartered in Nairobi, IRIN reports now from 82 countries with an emphasis on humanitarian stories from regions that are traumatized, war-torn, or overlooked by more traditional media.

The changing face of media in general provides another opportunity for invisible children to be made visible. Journalism has taken new forms, and social media continues to expand in new ways. Every day we can access more blogs by regular citizens who have new stories to tell. Social media outlets such as Facebook, Instagram, and Twitter can give anyone with Internet access a public voice. Almost anyone can post a video on YouTube and show the world what he sees. These vehicles offer a cost-effective way to develop a web presence as opposed to a formal website, which often carries expenses that CBOs cannot easily bear.

With the amazingly rapid pace of social and communication-based technological advances, it would be difficult to predict how the media will look 5, 10, or 20 years in the future. But its role in bridging disparate worlds will not likely change, no matter what vehicles are employed to fill that role. The media, in the end, has the capacity to shine lights into the hidden corners that we do not easily penetrate and bring forth the stories of the invisible.

Each of the sectors that plays a significant role in enabling the world's response to vulnerable young people has unrealized potential in making that role more effective. Moreover, these actors most often work independently, finding cooperation and cooperative arrangements almost by accident rather than through overriding strategy. As well, the tendency to silo the issues impacting children limits their effectiveness in dealing with these complex influences.

Yet each sector is undeniably a major influence in determining how effectual the work of those on the ground will be toward alleviating trauma, suffering, and detachment. They remain the fundamental building blocks in crafting a progressive response to changing the lives of dispossessed children and young people.

NOTES

1. http://www.girlsnotbrides.org/
2. http://www.who.int/bulletin/volumes/88/7/09-071068/en/ and Rajesh Panjabi, Co-founder and CEO, Last Mile Health, email to Maya Ajmera and Clare Dreyfus, July 5, 2014.
3. http://www.forbes.com/sites/samanthasharf/2013/11/17/last-mile-health-training-rural-liberians-to-save-lives/; and Rajesh Panjabi, Co-founder and CEO Last Mile Health, Interview, January 14, 2014. (Maya Ajmera and Clare Dreyfus, interviewers).
4. Rajesh Panjabi, Co-Founder and CEO, Last Mile Health, Interview, January 14, 2014, transcript p. 6. (Maya Ajmera and Clare Dreyfus, interviewers); and Rajesh Panjabi, Co-founder and CEO, Last Mile Health, email to Maya Ajmera and Clare Dreyfus, July 5, 2014.
5. https://www.khanacademy.org/about and http://khanacademy.desk.com/customer/portal/articles/329337-is-khan-academy-available-in-other-languages-
6. http://social.yourstory.com/2013/11/zaya-learning-labs-education-revolution-happening-cloud-starring-kids-dharavi/
7. http://www.changemakers.com/project/teach-class
8. http://zaya.in/approach/learningmodel/ and http://zaya.in/approach/locations/

9. http://www.childlineindia.org.in/1098/1098.htm; and Nishit Kumar, Head of Communications & Strategic Initiatives at CHILDLINE India Foundation, email message to Clare Dreyfus, June 26, 2014.

10. http://www.childlineindia.org.in/1098/csa-28-minors-kolkata.htm

11. National Center for Missing and Exploited Children, http://www.missingkids.com/amber and http://www.missingkids.com/amber/success

12. http://techpresident.com/news/wegov/24165/two-mobile-birth-registration-programs-piloted-senegal-and-uganda

13. "Mobile Birth Registration in Sub-Saharan Africa: A case study of Orange Senegal and Uganda Telecom solutions" by GSMA Mobile Identity Team, p. 8. http://www.gsma.com/mobileidentity/wp-content/uploads/2013/05/Mobile-Birth-Registration-in-Sub-Saharan-Africa.pdf

14. http://techpresident.com/news/wegov/24165/two-mobile-birth-registration-programs-piloted-senegal-and-uganda; cf. "Mobile Birth Registration in Sub-Saharan Africa: A case study of Orange Senegal and Uganda Telecom solutions" by GSMA Mobile Identity Team, p.8.

15. http://www.globalgiving.org/aboutus/

16. http://givingpledge.org

17. Eleanor Goldberg, "The Giving Pledge Is Just a Glorified Tax Break: Critics," http://www.huffingtonpost.com/2014/02/13/giving-pledge-critics_n_4776265.html

18. http://www.comicrelief.com/about-us; amd http://www.comicrelief.com/our-grants/international/how-we-fund

19. http://www.bernardvanleer.org/English/Home/Mission.html

20. http://jacobsfoundation.org/what-we-do/

21. http://ciff.org/about/approach/

22. http://ciff.org/priority-impact-areas/

23. Jamie Cooper-Hohn, President and CEO, Children's Investment Fund Foundation, Interview, October 16, 2013, transcript p. 13. (Maya Ajmera and Clare Dreyfus, interviewers).

24. http://www.freedomfund.org/about-us/#Mission

25. http://www.freedomfund.org/about-us/#Mission

26. www.gatesfoundation.org/What-We-Do

27. http://www.macfound.org/about/#sthash.wQwVICqh.dpuf

28. Judith-Ann Walker, Director, development Research and Projects Center, Interview, December 13, 2013, transcript p. 5–6. (Maya Ajmera and Julia Wallin, interviewers).

29. http://aif.org/about/about-aif/

30. http://africansinthediaspora.org/

31. http://www.hudson.org/content/researchattachments/attachment/1229/2013_indexof_global_philanthropyand_remittances.pdf, p. 29.

32. According to the UN, an ombudsman is a "designated, independent neutral" person who investigates complaints and provides impartial advice and assistance.
33. Ikea's Position on Child Labour, Issued by IKEA Services AB, March 2003, p. 1. http://www.ikea.com/ms/de_AT/about_ikea/pdf/ikea_position_child_labour.pdf
34. http://www.savethechildren.net/about-us/our-corporate-partners/ikea-foundation
35. Dr Adam Biran PhD et al., "Effect of a Behaviour-Change Intervention on Handwashing with Soap in India," The Lancet Global Health, Volume 2, Issue 3, Pages e145–e154, March 2014. http://download.thelancet.com/pdfs/journals/langlo/PIIS2214109X13701608.pdf?id=caamNObnjENV_aecDmgAu
36. "Chip-Sandwiched Soaps Create Panic" http://articles.timesofindia.indiatimes.com/2011-12-11/thiruvananthapuram/30504229_1_soaps-survey-police-officer
37. Sonny Bardhan et al. "Reducing Child Mortality in Bihar Through Improved Handwashing Behavior," March 11, 2013, pp. 1–2.
38. Sonny Bardhan et al. "Reducing Child Mortality in Bihar Through Improved Handwashing Behavior," March 11, 2013, pp. 1–2 and Jamie Cooper-Hohn, President and CEO, Children's Investment Fund Foundation, Interview, October 16, 2013, transcript p. 6–7. (Maya Ajmera and Clare Dreyfus, interviewers).
39. Josh Kwan, "Private Schools for the Poor," *Stanford Social Innovation Review*, Spring 2012.
40. James Tooly and Pauline Dixon, 2005. Private Education is Good for the Poor: a Study of Private Schools Serving the Poor in Low-Income Countries, CATO Institute, p. 1–2.
41. James Tooly and Pauline Dixon, 2005. Private Education is Good for the Poor: a Study of Private Schools Serving the Poor in Low-Income Countries, CATO Institute, p. 1–2.; cf. "Rich Pickings: Bad State Education Means More Fee-Paying Schools in Poor Countries," *The Economist*, March 17, 2012.
42. Josh Kwan, "Private Schools for the Poor", *Stanford Social Innovation Review*, Spring 2012, p.50.
43. Josh Kwan, "Private Schools for the Poor", *Stanford Social Innovation Review*, Spring 2012, p. 52.
44. http://www.omega-schools.com/history.php *and* http://www.spectator.co.uk/features/independent-schools-september-2013/9009861/distance-learning-2/
45. cf. specific agency pages at https://www.un.org/en/aboutun/structure/
46. http://www.unicef.org/about/who/index_history.html
47. http://www.unicef.org/whatwedo/

48. Geeta Rao Gupta, Deputy Executive Director, UNICEF, Interview, December 19, 2013, transcript p. 12–13. (Maya Ajmera and Clare Dreyfus, interviewers).

49. Erica Kochi, Co-Lead, UNICEF Innovation, Interview, February 28, 2014 (Maya Ajmera and Clare Dreyfus, interviewers).

50. Human-centered design is a process in which the needs, wants, and limitations of end-users are given priority at each stage of programmatic development.

51. Erica Kochi, Co-Lead, UNICEF Innovation, Interview, February 28, 2014 (Maya Ajmera and Clare Dreyfus, interviewers).

52. Geeta Rao Gupta, Deputy Executive Director, UNICEF, Interview, December 19, 2013, p. 8 (Maya Ajmera and Clare Dreyfus, interviewers).

53. http://www.wfp.org/partners/non-governmental-organizations

54. http://www.wfp.org/nutrition/how-wfp-fights-malnutrition

55. http://www.unicef.org/innovations/

56. http://www.raddabarnen.se/

57. Robert Kaplan, President and CEO, Inter-American Foundation, Interview, December 19, 2012, transcript p.17–19. (Maya Ajmera and Clare Dreyfus, interviewers); and Manuel Nunez, Managing Director, Office of External & Government Affairs, Inter-American Foundation, email message to Clare Dreyfus, July 15, 2014.

58. Shari Berenbach, former President and CEO, African Development Foundation, Interview, December 3, 2013, p. 6 (Maya Ajmera and Clare Dreyfus, interviewer).

59. Madalo Samati, Director of Programs, CRECCOM, Interview, October 31, 2013, transcript pp. 16–18. (Maya Ajmera and Clare Dreyfus, interviewers); and Madalo Samati, Director of Programs, CRECCOM, email message to Clare Dreyfus, July 16, 2014.

60. Madalo Samati, Director of Programs, CRECCOM, Interview, October 31, 2013, transcript pp. 19–21. (Maya Ajmera and Clare Dreyfus, interviewers); and Madalo Samati, Director of Programs, CRECCOM, email message to Clare Dreyfus, July 16, 2014.

61. J. Mark Brinkmoeller, Director, Center for Faith-Based and Community Initiatives, USAID, Interview, April 26, 2013, transcript p. 2. (Maya Ajmera and Clare Dreyfus, interviewers).

62. http://www.childreninadversity.org *and* http://www.childreninadversity.gov/about/who/usaid-center-on-children-in-adversity

63. Third Annual Report to Congress on Public Law 109-95. The Assistance for Orphans and Other Vulnerable Children in Developing Countries Act of 2005, December 2009, page 11.

64. http://www.childreninadversity.gov/about/why/architecture-of-u-s-government-assistance

65. Robert Horvath, http://www.childreninadversity.gov/docs/default-source/annual-reports/pl109-95_hvc_final.pdf?sfvrsn=4

66. http://www.docdatabase.net/more-dcof-955289.html

67. http://www.childreninadversity.gov/news-information/newsletter/news-of-note---june-2014

68. Author Maya Ajmera was appointed the 2014 Social Entrepreneur in Residence at Duke University.

69. "Duke Receives $10 M Grant from USAID to Fund Social Entrepreneurship Program": http://www.dukechronicle.com/articles/2012/11/09/duke-receives-10m-grant-usaid-fund-social-entrepreneurship-program

70. http://www.usaid.gov/news-information/press-releases/dec-9-2013-usaid-convenes-partnership-prime-pump-social-entrepreneurship

71. http://www.usaid.gov/GlobalDevLab/about

72. http://www.iaf.gov

73. Robert Kaplan, President and CEO, Inter-American Foundation, Interview, December 19, 2012, transcript p. 19. (Maya Ajmera and Clare Dreyfus, interviewers) and Manuel Nunez, Managing Director, Office of External & Government Affairs, Inter-American Foundation, email message to Clare Dreyfus, July 10, 2014.

74. http://www.usadf.gov/index.html

75. Shari Berenbach, former President and CEO, African Development Foundation, Interview, December 3, 2013, transcript pp. 7–9. (Maya Ajmera and Clare Dreyfus, interviewers).

76. Maguire, S. (2007, Sept). *A Study of the Child Rights Climate within the UK's Department for International Development.* Retrieved March 8, 2014, from DFID Publications: http://webarchive.nationalarchives.gov.uk/+/http:/www.dfid.gov.uk/Documents/publications/child-rights-climate.pdf

77. https://www.gov.uk/government/news/uk-provides-schoolbooks-for-a-generation-of-children-in-lebanon

78. Maguire, S. (2007, Sept). *A Study of the Child Rights Climate within the UK's Department for International Development.* Retrieved March 8, 2014, from DFID Publications: http://webarchive.nationalarchives.gov.uk/+/http:/www.dfid.gov.uk/Documents/publications/child-rights-climate.pdf

79. SEEK Development. (2013, November). *Country Profile Germany.* Retrieved March 8, 2014, from Donor Tracker: http://donortracker.org/sites/default/files/SEEK20Donor%20Profile%20Germany%20November%202013.pdf

80. Government of Ireland. (2013). *One World, One Future: Ireland's Policy for International Development*. Irish Aid, Department of Foreign Affairs and Trade. Dublin: Irish Aid, p. 31. https://www.irishaid.ie/media/iris-haid/allwebsitemedia/20newsandpublications/publicationpdfsenglish/one-world-one-future-irelands-new-policy.pdf

81. Irish Aid. (n.d.). *Where the Money Goes*. Retrieved March 8, 2014, from https://www.irishaid.ie/what-we-do/how-our-aid-works/where-the-money-goes

82. Irish Aid. (n.d.). *Development Education Funding*. Retrieved March 8, 2014, from Irish Aid: https://www.irishaid.ie/what-we-do/who-we-work-with/civil-society/development-education-funding

83. Ombudsman for Children. (2014). *Ombudsman for Children*. Retrieved March 8, 2014, from http://www.oco.ie

84. The Norwegian Agency for Development Cooperation: http://www.norad.no/en/front-page *and* http://www.norad.no/en/tools-and-publications/norwegian-aid-statistics

85. http://www.unicef.org/tdad/index_56031.html

86. http://www.childlineindia.org.in/Integrated-Child-Protection-Scheme-ICPS.htm

87. http://www.unicef.org/rwanda/protection.html

88. http://www.cdc.gov/mmwr/preview/mmwrhtml/mm6421a1.htm

89. http://www.theguardian.com/global-development/2014/mar/20/william-easterly-tyranny-experts-development-dictators; cf. William Easterly, "Stop Sending Aid to Dictators," *Time*, March 13, 2014, http://time.com/23075/william-easterly-stop-sending-aid-to-dictators/

90. Garilao, E. (1987). Indigenous NGOs as Strategic Institutions: Managing the Relationship with Government and Resource Agencies. *World Development,15*, 117.

91. Gary Haugen and Victor Boutros, *The Locust Effect* (Oxford University Press, 2014) p. xi.

92. Gary Haugen and Victor Boutros, *The Locust Effect* (Oxford University Press, 2014) p. 36.

93. Holly Burkhalter, "Curb the Child Migration Crisis Begins with Combatting Sexual Abuse", *Washington Post*, June 27, 2014; http://www.washingtonpost.com/opinions/holly-burkhalter-curb-the-child-migration-crisis-begins-with-combating-sexual-abuse/2014/06/27/00fd58d8-fd5c-11e3-b1f4-8e77c632c07b_story.html

94. UNHCR, 2014. Children on the Run: Unaccompanied Children Leaving Central America and Mexico and the Need for International Protection, p. 4–7. www.unhcrwashington.org/sites/default/files/UAC_UNHCR_Children%20on%20the%20Run_Full%20Report.pdf Cf. Holly Burkhalter,

"Curb the Child Migration Crisis Begins with Combatting Sexual Abuse", *Washington Post*, June 27, 2014; http://www.washingtonpost.com/opinions/holly-burkhalter-curb-the-child-migration-crisis-begins-with-combating-sexual-abuse/2014/06/27/00fd58d8-fd5c-11e3-b1f4-8e77c632c07b_story.html

95. UNHCR, 2014. Children on the Run: Unaccompanied Children Leaving Central America and Mexico and the Need for International Protection, p. 4–7. www.unhcrwashington.org/sites/default/files/UAC_UNHCR_Children%20on%20the%20Run_Full%20Report.pdf Cf. Holly Burkhalter, "Curb the Child Migration Crisis Begins with Combatting Sexual Abuse," *Washington Post*, June 27, 2014; http://www.washingtonpost.com/opinions/holly-burkhalter-curb-the-child-migration-crisis-begins-with-combating-sexual-abuse/2014/06/27/00fd58d8-fd5c-11e3-b1f4-8e77c632c07b_story.html

96. Holly Burkhalter, "Curb the Child Migration Crisis Begins with Combatting Sexual Abuse," *Washington Post*, June 27, 2014; http://www.washingtonpost.com/opinions/holly-burkhalter-curb-the-child-migration-crisis-begins-with-combating-sexual-abuse/2014/06/27/00fd58d8-fd5c-11e3-b1f4-8e77c632c07b_story.html

97. http://www.unicef.org/crc/index_30229.html

98. http://www.equalitynow.org/AGLDF

99. Erica Kochi, Interview, February 28, 2014 (Maya Ajmera and Clare Dreyfus, interviewers).

100. http://www.crin.org/en/library/publications/stop-making-children-criminals

101. http://fairsentencingofyouth.org/wp-content/uploads/2013/04/The-cost-of-incarceration-INFOGRAPHIC-pdf.pdf

102. http://sentencingproject.org/doc/publications/jj_The_Lives_of_Juvenile_Lifers.pdf. p. 10.

103. http://www.rescue.org/our-work/child-youth-protection

104. Eliza Griswold, "Can General Linder's Special Operations Forces Stop the Next Terrorist Threat?", *The New York Times Magazine*, June 13, 2014; http://www.nytimes.com/2014/06/15/magazine/can-general-linders-special-operations-forces-stop-the-next-terrorist-threat.html?module=Search&mabReward=relbias%3Ar%2C%5B%22RI%3A6%22%2C%22RI%3A18%22%5D

105. Siddarth Kara, Interview, March 17, 2014, transcript pp. 4–5. (Maya Ajmera and Clare Dreyfus, interviewers).

106. Priti Patkar and Pravin Patkar, Interview, December 28, 2011 (Saudamini Dabak, interviewer) *and* Pravin Patkar, Interview, January 4, 2012 (Saudamini Dabak, interviewer).

107. http://www.younglives.org.uk

108. http://www.younglives.org.uk/what-we-do/research-methods

109. Shonkoff, Jack, et al. "An Integrated Scientific Framework for Child Survival and Early Childhood Development," *Pediatrics: Official Journal of the American Academy of Pediatrics*, March 27, 2012, abstract. http://pediatrics.aappublications.org/content/early/2012/01/02/peds.2011-0366.full.pdf

110. Shonkoff, Jack, et al. "An Integrated Scientific Framework for Child Survival and Early Childhood Development," *Pediatrics: Official Journal of the American Academy of Pediatrics*, March 27, 2012, p. 9. http://pediatrics.aappublications.org/content/early/2012/01/02/peds.2011-0366.full.pdf

111. http://www.povertyactionlab.org/evaluations and http://www.poverty-actionlab.org/evaluation/effect-information-and-subsidies-chlorine-usage-zambia   and   http://www.povertyactionlab.org/evaluation/vocational-training-disadvantaged-youth-colombia

112. www.poverty-action.org

113. Banerjee and Duflo, *Poor Economics: A Radical Rethinking of the Way to Fight Global Poverty*, p. 86.

114. https://csis.org/publication/global-youth-wellbeing-index

115. http://www.onehealthinitiative.com/index.php

116. Cate Dewey, "Pigs, Poverty, and Epilepsy," in *Sick! Curious Tales of Pests and Parasites We Share with Animals*, Elizabeth Arnold Stone, editor, Ontario Veterinary College, 2014, pp. 95–99.

117. Based on 2013 review of course lists, professor biographies, majors and concentrations, and syllabi available on websites of all top ranked public and private International Studies and Public Policy schools in the USA, as well as affiliated schools of Law, Education, Public Health, and Social Work, conducted by research coordinator Clare Dreyfus on behalf of the authors.

118. Dr. Jo Boyden, Interview, July 17, 2013, transcript p. 5 (Maya Ajmera and Clare Dreyfus, interviewers) + email.

119. Nicholas Kristof and Sheryl WuDunn, *Half the Sky: Turning Oppression into Opportunity for Women Worldwide* (New York: Vintage Books, Random House, Inc., 2009) p. xiv. *Cited in:* Gary Haugen and Victor Boutros, *The Locust Effect* (Oxford University Press, 2014) p. 50.

120. "De Blasio Invites Mother Of 'Invisible Child' To Inauguration," http://www.huffingtonpost.com/2013/12/31/de-blasio-inauguration-_n_4523714.html

121. Dr. Jo Boyden, Interview, July 17, 2013, transcript p. 16 (Maya Ajmera and Clare Dreyfus, interviewers).

CHAPTER 11

Fulfilling the Promise—Changing the Systems That Can Change the Lives of Children

Each day the sun rises on young faces that know no hope. There are hundreds of millions of them, and we have tried to see them in these pages, despite the invisibility which cloaks their lives.

Consider again the numbers: 100 million street-connected children, 215 million children working in hazardous conditions, 38 million refugee children, 33 million child migrants, 18 million orphans, and 1.2 million children trafficked annually in the sex trade.[1]

We have tried to look at why they are where they are and what the forces are that keep them consigned to lives of poverty, dread, abuse, and despair. But merely seeing them, recognizing who they are, is no answer. Rather, it is an acknowledgment of their humanity and a first step toward authoring relief for the conditions that have placed them on society's edges.

To change the dynamics that imperil children and systematically keep them from realizing the potential, wonder, and aspiration that should be attend to every childhood requires a new way of thinking. With good intention, governments, organizations, multilaterals, and philanthropists have struggled to find effective remedies to the plight of marginalized young people. And despite every good intention, their efforts have come up short. It is time to reevaluate and find new ways to move forward.

© The Editor(s) (if applicable) and The Author(s) 2016
M. Ajmera, G.A. Fields, *Invisible Children*,
DOI 10.1057/978-1-137-57838-9_11

THE ENTIRETY OF CHILDREN—CHANGING OUR THINKING AND BREAKING DOWN SILOS

As we have noted, the issues impacting vulnerable young people are multilayered. We cannot pigeonhole them, nor can we bind them into tidy, issue-specific packages that lend themselves to clean solutions.

While we might wish to provide educational opportunities for children in poverty by building a school, we know that hungry children cannot learn well, so a school in itself is only one part of what we need to do. We need to feed them. And some of the children may well have a home life filled with violence or abuse. We need to protect them. Others may have no home life at all and live on the streets. We need to bring them in. Still others might be forced to work during the day to provide income for their families. We need to provide evening classes or find another source of income for their families so that their children can go to school. Some children in the community may face ethnic or religious prejudices and so are not welcomed at the school. We need to break through these exclusions. Others may be too sick to go to school. We need to treat them and immunize them against future diseases. Others might not see any relevance to an education that does not hone their skills for future employment. We need to supplement basic education with skills development and training for the jobs available in their country.

In such a situation, it would not be uncommon to find an educational initiative building that school, a nutrition program providing meals, a health organization offering periodic medical checkups and immunizations, and a vocational training or skills program working with laborers and their families. There may be yet another group equipping that school with books and computers. We see separate groups with separate programs, perhaps competing for separate resources, all trying to address one community with multidimensional problems. The result may be progress for that community (or it may not), but the way those results are reached reflects duplicated effort, conflicting goals, and wasted resources.

Recommendation 1: Reconsider the ways in which children's issues are defined, and see children holistically as a distinctive demographic

We cannot draw hard lines around the issues that marginalize the young, nor can we seek to address their conditions through single-focus responses. We can no longer content ourselves with working in silos.

Children's issues have been cut up, sliced up, and categorized, the factors defining their lives pitted against one another in tug-of-wars for limited funding. Groups mark their territory and define their constituencies, labeling the children they reach in tags that are too narrow, restrictive, and incomprehensive.

The first step, then, is to recognize the entirety of children and young people, to confirm that their lives do not fit into neat boxes, easily classified categories, or statistical tables. This simple realization can and should be the basis governing the interactions of all sectors involved with the plight of marginalized young people. We need to acknowledge the importance of dealing with boys as well as girls, and not segment them by gender. We need to see how a well-meaning effort to educate a young girl or provide skills training to a young boy has repercussions that cross issue-based boundaries.

Our propensity to label, isolate, and silo for the sake of convenient categorizations dilutes resources, limits our vision, and precludes the development community from addressing any more than one segment of a compendium of factors at a time. We need to view children and young people differently. We need to see them in all their complexity as embodiments of intersecting influences that cannot be unraveled into singular threads.

SUPPORTING HIGH-IMPACT COMMUNITY-BASED ORGANIZATIONS

We have seen examples of community-based organizations (CBOs) developing innovative, cost-effective solutions to the deeply embedded issues compromising the lives of the young. By their nature, effective CBOs are integral components of the communities they serve. Their local leadership and programs are emanations of social, cultural, political, and spiritual nuances that assure embrace by the community, and maximize the chances for sustainability.

The proliferation of CBOs around the world—there are more than three million nongovernmental organizations (NGOs) in India alone supporting a broad spectrum of social issues, and, among them, tens of thousands of CBOs that operate under the radar [2]—provides an opportunity to reach children and young people that have not been accessible. CBOs are the mechanism through which donors and donor governments can reach the *children of the last mile*.

But they cannot do so if they remain undervalued and undercapitalized. CBOs do not draw from the same resource pools as the large-scale, top-down programs that are imported with the best of intentions yet often fail to take root, their seeds of change falling on culturally resistant stone. Small localized organizations struggle for resources and recognition, yet we have seen no better pathway to the children who are truly invisible.

Recommendation 2: More investments in, and more money for, CBOs. This includes regular and predictable operating support for CBOs and capacity building within the CBO sector to support leadership development, infrastructure development, and strategic planning

The impact of CBOs globally is limited by the paucity of resources directed their way. This must change. Philanthropy is a large part of this solution, and philanthropists must increasingly direct their investments down channels that ultimately result in on-the-ground interventions. Two or three strategic commitments from those who have taken the Giving Pledge could redirect the flow of funding to CBOs, and we urge the truly major philanthropists who have taken this Pledge to consider the human impact of cost-effective giving at the community level.

While it is possible for philanthropists to find effective CBOs, it is also risky. Without proper expertise in identifying and vetting legitimate CBOs—often small in scale, set off in remote locations, and lacking organizational transparency (e.g., few CBOs have the resources to generate an annual report detailing their finances)—philanthropists face a difficult task in finding suitable community-based investments. It can be done, but great care must be exercised to avoid the pitfalls of ineffective organizations, those with short shelf lives, or, in the worst case, those that are merely shells and providing little or no service at all.

Traditional approaches to funding, program development, and outcome measurement bind us to familiar pathways. We cannot be afraid of taking chances, finding new interventions that bring intellectual, physical, and financial resources together into new configurations, or reaching new implementing partners on the ground. We cannot be afraid of seeing investments fall short when the new formulas we are trying to create do not quite add up. Quite simply, we will never find new approaches—the ones that override those that have failed to reach millions at daily risk—unless we take the risk of innovation.

CBOs by their very nature are based in such risk. Their approach tends to be holistic, focused on the child as a complete person impacted by a compendium of factors. Their work addresses the child, not the issue. And so the street-connected child who is also a child laborer, and who might be a young girl living in a society where girls are not valued, who might have a physical or emotional disability, and is not attending school can find assistance that goes beyond any one of these conditions through a CBO that sees her for who she is instead of fitting her into a category that can never be as inclusive or comprehensive as she needs it to be.

We cannot ignore the impact of CBOs that are flexible enough to incorporate approaches that step outside established service delivery patterns or theories. While they do not have the resources of major top-down efforts, and never will, they fill an incomparable role that requires both respect and expansion. According to Sarah Thomas de Benitez of the Consortium for Street Children, "You need top down and bottom up together, it's not an either or—UNICEF is pushing for better child protection systems, which are needed, but you still need CBOs working on the ground."[3]

We have seen dozens of examples in these pages of organizations and their leaders who transformed the old way of doing things to find new ways to reach their children on the ground, thus creating lasting, sustainable solutions to their problems. These leaders, and the CBOs they have built around their visions, merit the same level of risk-taking from those that fund these processes, analyze their results, and make public policy on the basis of their issues. We owe them the same bravery they show us every day.

Within the last three decades, a growing number of intermediary funders have arisen that can direct gifts efficiently to CBOs in virtually any part of the world. Philanthropists can engage these intermediary grant makers with confidence and can be assured that their investments will in fact find the ground and do good work. More than this, they can become engaged with the beneficiaries of their investments and in the process be active learners concerning the issues that govern their work. They can make themselves aware of best practices, and they can broaden their own understanding of the complexities of children's issues.

For example, The Global Fund for Children has distributed nearly $40 million in grants to more than 600 CBOs in nearly 80 countries.[4] The Global Fund for Women employs a similar model for CBOs supporting girls and women. Within sub-Saharan Africa, the Firelight Foundation identifies CBOs working to support "the health, resilience, and education of children."[5]

Donors working with intermediaries have the opportunity to develop intimate knowledge of the groups being supported by their investments and the range of issues that these groups are addressing at the community level. At the same time, they can be assured that their investments are being directed to groups that have been thoroughly examined, evaluated, and ultimately vetted as legitimate organizations doing good impactful work. There is no guesswork in supporting intermediary grant makers and minimal risk that investments will be squandered or fall into the wrong hands.

Similarly, support of national and regional grant making consortia and intermediaries can be a critical step in strengthening community-level interactions. Groups profiled earlier, such as dPRC in Nigeria and CRY in India, channel support to small groups that are invisible except to the closest observer. Given its reputation and its thorough knowledge of effective on-the-ground programs, the Afghan Institute of Learning could well coordinate support for other CBOs in Afghanistan, a region that is extremely difficult for international organizations to reach. Enlightened investments in groups such as these, from US-based intermediaries to regional and national grant makers, can have a multiplier effect on the strength of the CBO sector.

Small amounts of funding strategically placed can do great things. It does not require a multimillion dollar investment to send children to school in rural Uganda. It can be done for much less if the right partner is engaged, and that right partner is bound to be a CBO. Traditional development thinking places a higher value on a program reaching 5000 young people than it does on one that only reaches 100. But if that smaller program is in fact providing more than a single service to those 100 children, if it is engaging them holistically, and if it is demonstrably changing the way they live their lives, if those children have absolutely no other alternative, then how can we possibly make that judgment? The elegance of CBOs is in the children they reach, whom no one else seems to be able to find, and in the cost-effective ways in which they change those formerly unreachable lives.

With enormous amounts of funding directed to top-down interventions over the past several decades, and too little in the way of lasting impact coming out of these investments, the conclusion is inescapable that new ways of developing and implementing social solution are needed. CBOs provide this, and their work wraps itself around a community's most diseased roots and stays there until the roots are made healthy. It becomes, then, axiomatic that the more resources expended through this pathway, the more lasting, sustainable good can be done. As one of the best investments for international development, CBOs require more funding. We do not need to add more money to the already sizable pool of funds expended for international development. We merely need to spend these funds more wisely so that they penetrate to the community level.

CBOs face the same organizational struggles that affect other types of institutions. Most come into being with a great idea but a poor or nonexistent infrastructure. During a CBO's early stages, the efforts to build a program, root it within a marginalized demographic and find the resources needed for even rudimentary implementation, often crowd out concerns for building a lasting structure or securing the capacity to carry that work forward. Many CBOs end up dying for lack of resources, infrastructure, or administrative capacity.

We cannot regard capacity building and infrastructure costs as irrelevant to the central work of any organization. These are legitimate expenses. Moreover, CBOs with their focus on programs, often have little in the way of understanding of even the most basic business principles needed to stabilize and ultimately grow an organization.

To survive in an increasingly competitive environment where resources are precious, CBOs must be able to develop their institutional capacities. They need to build strong infrastructures through dedicated investments that recognize the value of organizational stability. These investments must be coupled with professional services that help CBOs understand and implement their own organizational structures.

One of the best examples of localized capacity building is Dasra, whom we considered earlier as a broker between the donor community and effective CBOs throughout India. Dasra's work also entails capacity building for CBOs, including the identification of new funding relationships, strategic development and planning, and leadership training.

During its relatively short lifetime (founded in 2000), Dasra has strengthened the core of 500 NGOs in India and trained hundreds of CBO leaders. Their model would not be hard to reproduce in other countries with strong NGO communities. In the end, organizations survive through their structural strength and through the ability of their management to navigate the changing currents of funding, administration, personnel, policy, advocacy, and community presence in a volatile social environment. Leadership acumen is essential to keeping these unique and valuable organizations in full function. Under any circumstances, the capacity building needs of groups with ideas that are stronger than their structures should not be ignored.

Recommendation 3: Include CBOs in policy discussions, knowledge exchanges, seminars, and virtually any forum at which children's issues are discussed on any level

CBOs operate on the front lines of the battle against poverty, violence, abuse, and alienation. Their perspectives on the issues that affect vulnerable children and young people, and their understanding of the root causes of these issues, afford them an authority of immense value. Outside expertise cannot replace their unique perspective.

As a result, CBO leadership provides a unique resource in any evaluation of public policy affecting the marginalized young. While many CBOs, as we have seen, have developed vigorous and influential advocacy programs, and many others are called upon in discussions of public policy within their issue areas, these are too often the exception rather than the rule.

Host governments, whatever their politics, must recognize the value of the perspectives that can be offered by CBO leadership if indeed they are serious about developing and implementing public policies that stand a chance of striking at the causes of marginalization. Many governments ignore CBOs, or, worse, see them as threats to their stability. Such a view is shortsighted and counterproductive. The remarkable leaders who have grown these organizations carry with them an expertise that cannot be duplicated. They must be heard within the corridors of power.

Recommendation 4: Make CBOs more accessible to donors, policymakers, thought leaders, academics, and other players in international development through networking at both the national and international levels

The CBO sector as a whole is strengthened when it can be brought together to exchange ideas, challenges, and successes. It is further strengthened when its work is brought out of the shadows and put before the international development community, philanthropists, academics, and the public at large.

Too often, though, CBOs are afterthoughts, regarded as small, out of the way or inconsequential when groups are brought together to highlight development work or to formulate policy. Major networking events, such as the Global Philanthropy Forum, the Clinton Global Initiative, the Synergos Institute's *University for a Night,* and the Philanthropy Workshop provide excellent opportunities for the work of CBOs to be highlighted and for leaders in the field to be exposed to the innovations and energy that dictate the work on the ground. Networking can also occur on smaller scales. Donor forums or public policy seminars can provide similar platforms for CBO leaders to gather, to share their work and, in the end, to generate greater visibility.

Such events are complementary to knowledge exchanges within and among the CBOs themselves. Knowledge exchanges, either based on regional or thematic emphases, allow leaders to brainstorm, and, in many cases, to form new alliances or partnerships. These exchanges should be horizontal, encompassing multiple sectors, including CBOs as well as relevant government agencies or representatives, multilaterals, and the private sector. In this way, new ideas can formulate and new relationships can be built.

The power of networks is clear, as shown earlier. While operational networks such as ECPAT and Global March Against Child Labor have been effective in bringing together CBOs with similar mandates, networking must extend beyond operations. Donors, academics, and policy leaders network too. CBOs need to be a part of that. They are too important to be relegated to spectator status.

In short, CBOs must come to be regarded as primary partners in the efforts to alleviate the conditions of children and young people living in poverty, and, as such, afforded the financial, intellectual, and capital resources commensurate with this standing. CBOs have shown themselves to be cost-effective, creative, and a credible actor within the development spectrum. They are able to reach the *children of the last mile*, those young people who remain invisible.

They merit money, position, access, and voice.

REIMAGINING THE ROLE OF THE US GOVERNMENT

In every country, governments carry unrivaled influence in determining the tone of discussion and reaction to social issues. This may be self-evident, but it bears noting that the control of public monies and the capacity to establish official policy positions affords every government a dominant perch from which to direct each country's response to all segments of its society, including the most vulnerable.

Any blueprint, then, in revising approaches to children in poverty must include specific steps by the government, applicable to every country that has a stake in redefining these conditions. And while every government is different and strives to maintain its own identity, its own values, and its own methods of functioning, every government carries a responsibility to address the needs of those on its outer margins. Without the full and willing participation of government in dealing with children and young people, all other efforts will be necessarily incomplete.

As keepers and distributors of public monies, each government has the power to direct financial resources to the issues it deems most immediate and of the highest priority. Donor country governments have taken seriously this responsibility to try to find ways to lift up the parts of global society that are lingering behind the development curve. We have noted some of these efforts, all of which merit applause. The financial contributions of governmental agencies tasked with international development have been significant, and they continue to grow.

But essential questions linger concerning where this money goes and how it is directed. Does in fact a flood of resources better the plight of children and young people, and is at least a portion of it able to reach the most marginalized children?

The United States is the largest international assistance donor in the world, sending more than $30 billion to other countries in various forms and through various programs. As such, its structures for delivering this assistance provide lessons for policy changes that, taken together, will benefit the most marginalized.

We have reviewed the major mechanisms through which the United States provides international assistance. While impressive in terms of dollar value and intent, US government efforts require adjustment if they are to reach the most marginalized children on the ground. As the largest player in the international arena, US policies have considerable influence on the actions and programs of other donor nations. What the United States does in terms of international assistance reverberates throughout the world and compels complementary actions on the part of other countries. Accordingly, the US government has the ability to influence the ways in which the global community seeks to reach the children and young people it has so far been unable to engage.

Money alone is not the answer, nor has it ever been since the dawn of international development assistance. We do not need to flood the world with funding. What we do need is to direct that funding in strategic ways that find and support children and young people who have heretofore been invisible.

What we are suggesting is a rethinking of US funding priorities for its international development assistance supported by new structures that streamline investments at the community level.

Recommendation 5: Create the Children's Global Investment Trust as a separate US government agency empowered to make grants to CBOs working with the most marginalized children and young people

The deepest problems can only be solved through bold dreams coupled with bold action. We need a new approach to reach the marginalized *children of the last mile*.

We suggest the creation of the Children's Global Investment Trust (CGIT) as a separate US government agency. CGIT would consolidate community-level support for groups working directly with the most vulnerable children around the world. Like the Inter-American Foundation (IAF) and the African Development Foundation, this new group would be an independent body with a separate budget appropriation from the US Congress.

This need not, and should not, be an overly large, bureaucratic body, nor should it entail new dollars. Its work could be accomplished by redirecting a small portion of existing development funding from the USAID pool. An annual appropriation between $25 and $50 million would allow initial inroads to be made with CBOs across the globe. CGIT's model would rely upon distributing small amounts of money strategically to groups at the community level. It would bypass middlemen and subcontractors and directly and completely feed the work on the ground. With its own management structure, CGIT would have the sole decision-making authority in disbursing its grants. With that authority would come the responsibility for intense oversight of grants made and due diligence of potential partners.

Relationships would be established with legitimate, vetted groups working in the field, with established intermediary grant makers who have systems in place for identifying and supporting these types of groups, and with policymakers in the countries where these groups work. The CGIT would provide monetary support for CBOs through the counsel of existing intermediaries, who in turn would monitor the impact of these investments and continue to evolve effective strategies of grassroots engagement. From its relatively modest starting point, funding for CGIT could increase on the basis of demonstrated impact.

The growing trend toward community involvement in development processes makes the CGIT a logical next step. All major funding bodies, including multilaterals, European governments, and the US government itself, are beginning to pay attention to sustainable interventions occurring at the local level. The CGIT feeds this trend, and makes it more systematic, allowing the US government to make strategic community investments and broaden its presence at the most basic societal levels. It begins the process of establishing formal governmental policy that mandates the delivery of services for children and young people rooted in local communities rather than from the top-down.

Recommendation 6: Refine agencies within the US government's foreign assistance structure to facilitate funding of CBOs dealing with children's issues. These agencies include, but are not limited to, the Inter-American Foundation, the African Development Fund, the Displaced Children's and Orphans Fund, and the Center for Faith-Based and Community Initiatives

If political realities delay the establishment of a Children's Global Investment Trust, the US government cannot wait to redirect development assistance to the community level. There are steps that can be taken right away, and, regardless of whether the CGIT comes into being in the near future, these steps are worth taking on their own merit.

We introduced the IAF and the African Development Fund (ADF) as two of the best-kept secrets in US foreign assistance. Both the IAF and the ADF provide effective models for delivery of funding to grassroots indigenous efforts. Each of these initiatives channels money to grassroots programs, which is laudable, but neither has a special prescription for children and young people. While these groups need increased funding, they also require an expansion of their missions to specifically incorporate and emphasize the plight of children and young people underserved by other initiatives.

Though it has yet to reach its full potential, the Displaced Children and Orphans Fund (DCOF) is a model worth refining and expanding. Its mandate is to deliver aid to the most vulnerable children at the community level. That alone merits expansion, but with $14.7 million annually, the current funding levels are ridiculously inadequate to meet this mandate. More funding needs to be directed through this USAID initiative, which itself must be clearly focused on bringing these funds directly to the grassroots instead of contracting with large international NGOs (INGOs).

The Center for Faith-based and Community Initiatives (CFCBI) has been able to identify for USAID effective community-based and faith-based initiatives around the world, but it has no funding authority. It can only make recommendations instead of grants. To support the component of community-level work being driven by the numerous faith-based and community organizations around the world, CFCBI should be given funding authority. Grants would be small, and in fact much smaller than USAID's usual grant range. But CFCBI would be able to identify and support groups that otherwise would fly under the radar.

Most CBOs lack the structure and resources to successfully apply for USAID funding. They are at a huge competitive disadvantage, even though their work is cost-effective and reaches children no one else can. Consequently, models of successful community-level investments need to be evaluated and applied to other programs throughout USAID so that its laudable intention to direct more funding closer to the ground is matched with effective programs that ensure these funds make their way properly to the grassroots. USAID can employ these strategies geographically, as through IAF and ADF, or thematically, as through DCOF. Other opportunities exist to tailor standing programs, or to create new ones, so that higher percentages of aid flow directly to overlooked demographics of marginalized young people. For example, we suggest the creation of an Asian corollary to IAF and ADF so that the three agencies working in partnership can steward policies of grassroots support and engagement that reaches every corner of the globe.

Beyond this, USAID would do well to empower its USAID Innovation Unit to fund entrepreneurial intermediary grant makers directly. If in fact the agency has a commitment to supporting more localized initiatives, then there is no better way to do so than to rely on the collective experience, wisdom, and networks of highly effective intermediaries.

Recommendation 7: Recognize children's issues as a foreign policy imperative

Providing support for the most marginalized young people makes sense from a humanitarian perspective and from a policy perspective. Joseph Nye coined the term "soft power" in the 1980s to describe a government's ability to persuade new alliances by using assets that generate attention and illustrate shared goals. As Nye writes, "Seduction is always more effective than coercion, and many values like democracy, human rights, and individual opportunities are deeply seductive."[6] Delivering effective humanitarian support for children and young people previously left out of the development arc can be extremely seductive, and aside from changing forever the lives of those impacted, can co-opt rather than coerce. This represents soft power at its best.

But it also represents an amalgam of approaches that former Secretary of State Hillary Clinton referred to as "smart power." She has stated,

"I began my tenure as US Secretary of State by stressing the need to elevate diplomacy and development alongside defense—a 'smart power' approach to solving global problems."[7] Development, and especially the development of children and young people in poverty, provides a compelling tool in redirecting societies, and those who help author that redirection stand to benefit both politically and strategically.

Children's issues are not about charity or about lifting for the moment the conditions of those in need. They revolve around the concept of sustainable development, which has deep-seated implications for the nature of the societies that development creates.

Nor can children's issues be subjugated to narrow political concerns. The fact that the United States, with its potential to be a global leader in elevating the conditions of the poorest and most marginalized, is one of only two UN member countries (along with Somalia) not to have ratified the Convention on the Rights of the Child is nothing short of a disgrace. Ratification has been blocked by political posturing and single-issue responses that have suspended any consideration of ratification. The United States cannot lead if it assigns the issues affecting vulnerable children to narrow political arguments.

The incidents of violence brought about by marginalized, despondent, essentially hopeless segments of populations in poverty underscores the need to rethink how we consider issues affecting children and youth. We see too often that hopelessness leads to despair, which in turn can lead to acts of desperation. We see, too, that a society with economic and social weaknesses at their foundation hold back our collective trajectory, that underdevelopment in any part of the world sucks financial and intellectual resources, compromises political stability, and invites dissolution. We have struggled with the effects of underdevelopment for decades.

And if we fail to provide for our children, if we cannot elevate them into the mainstream flow of social processes where they can reasonably expect to play a productive role in the world around them, then these costs are carried forward from generation to generation.

Children's issues transcend the humanitarian impulses that give them preeminence. They also represent a foreign policy consideration impacting both national security and global identity. As such, all of us need to treat these issues with greater seriousness than we have in the past. Children need to be part of foreign policy discussions.

Recommendation 8: Create an Ambassador-At-Large for Children within the US Department of State

The state of children's welfare globally needs to be regarded as a component of foreign policy, and therefore children merit their own ambassador. Such a position within the US Department of State could exist to coordinate the various efforts and initiatives across the department, including USAID and its subordinate programs. It would also serve as an official governmental voice representing the interests of marginalized children, following the precedent of State's Ambassador-at-Large for Global Women's Issues. A Special Advisor for Children's Issues already exists at State, but elevating this position to ambassadorial status would deepen its credibility, broaden its platform, and target its already compelling messages more clearly.

Wielding this voice effectively could be a powerful tool in reauthoring the ways in which children's issues are regarded. An Ambassador-at-Large would be able to articulate government policy concerning development, support, and assistance initiatives to all audiences. He or she would be able to state clearly the need to break down issue-based silos and make the case for philanthropic engagement around children's issues, including building more stable markets through the engagement of the corporate sector. The Ambassador would also be able to impel academic or research-based activities on behalf of children, and to oversee and advocate for all official efforts that turn policies into action.

Aside from the administrative responsibilities of coordinating the threads of children's development programs, an Ambassador-at-Large would be a spokesperson who could elevate the visibility of these issues and compel response, or at least recognition, from various social sectors. Such a position would provide by its very nature the credibility of the government's engagement with children's issues, and focus attention on the most marginalized, including those whom we do not see.

Recommendation 9: Create a White House Special Advisor for Children

Married to the notion of an Ambassador-at-Large for Children at State is the need to create a Special Advisor for Children at the executive level. This position would be the President's point person on all matters pertaining to children and youth domestically and abroad. As such, he or she would be responsible for collecting relevant information and data to inform policy decisions. More significantly, this position would be the public voice of the executive branch, articulating the President's policies and programs, and representing the country at the highest level at international gatherings, seminars, and policy summits.

The Special Advisor would be more than a public relations position. By providing a focal point for policy considerations, the Advisor would add emphasis to the significance afforded issues impacting children and young people, including the status of children in the United States. This would in turn be a factor in compelling a more comprehensive, strategic response by the executive branch regarding these issues. The Special Advisor for Women's and Gender Issues at the White House provides a precedent and a model for how this position would function. Adapting this model for children strengthens the hand of the executive branch.

These recommendations apply to the US government's role in children's development globally. As such, they are country-specific. But the principles of these ideas apply universally. Each country, regardless of its governmental structure or its past involvement in development, can adapt these ideas appropriately.

The goal of each of these recommendations is the further elevation of children's issues within the priorities of the governments that have the capacity to alter our collective response. Each government has a role to play. The creation of any movement begins with recognition. If a global movement on behalf of invisible children is to take hold, governments must step up and assume their role.

STRENGTHENING MULTILATERALS

The United Nations (UN) should by all logic be a focal point for consolidating policy, resources, and attention directed to children's issues. The adoption of the Millennium Development Goals (MDGs) in 2000, and the impetus to refine those goals into the Sustainable Development Goals (SDGs), provides theoretical guideposts for what needs to be done. It also provides a call to action for member nations to adopt these goals, treat them seriously, and direct sufficient resources to maximize the chances that these ambitious goals might be met.

But a call to action does not guarantee action itself, and we have seen that both the MDGs and SDGs are incomplete. We have also seen that, despite their lofty intentions they have not compelled responses that reach the *children of the last mile*. There remain millions of invisible children beyond the grasp of any program, theory, or UN goal.

UN Secretary General Ban Ki-moon called upon the working group developing the SDGs to ensure that these new goals focus on the most marginalized and the young.[8] Yet it is obvious from the results of the deliberations of this group that the agenda for their work is too crowded, encompassing issues of energy, security, and good governance. Without aggressive advocacy, children run the risk of being just another talking point, just another component of siloed goals.

Recommendation 10: Incorporate CBOs into UNICEF's overriding strategies for funding, strategic development, and public relations

No UN agency has more potential, or a clearer responsibility, to lead the charge against the factors of marginalization of children than UNICEF. With its long history, extensive financial resources, operational infrastructure encompassing thousands of professionals in almost every country in need, and the credibility of a UN-based platform, UNICEF stands as an unqualified leader in global endeavors on behalf of children and young people.

Much of UNICEF's work has pioneered initiatives that have ultimately proven to be of great value. Its global efforts for clean water and sanitation, malaria prevention, HIV/AIDS mitigation, and nutrition have saved countless lives. Its Innovation Unit has established a spirit of creativity that has helped author and sponsor new technological solutions to longstanding problems. Its work in helping corporations meet their social responsibility goals and its aggressive use of sponsorships with public figures, sports teams, and artists have brought messaging into new arenas. UNICEF in all its work is an asset of inestimable value.

Still, UNICEF has not filled the role of spokesperson for the most marginalized children and young people. UNICEF's leadership has been prominent but less than vocal concerning the more uncomfortable topics attending invisible children. It is one thing to be the face of the organization to donor nations, corporate leadership, and knowledge seminars, and quite another to be a vocal advocate for policies and programs that will shift the development paradigm in the direction of those it has yet to reach. This takes courage, and it takes huge reservoirs of leadership.

UNICEF is necessarily dependent on the financial resources and policy approval of its member states, and so must walk a fine line between acquiescence and advocacy. This is particularly true when that advocacy may ruffle the feathers of donor states that are either the center of some of the issues in question, those who ignore the existence of the most intractable problems, or pursue policies that work against potential solutions. At times, the need for diplomacy and tact no doubt outweigh the need for brutal honesty of putting forward the realities of policy failures, neglect, and brutality. It is always easiest to rely on programs that are already in place rather than agitate for programmatic departures. We acknowledge that rethinking existing systems is an ongoing challenge that mixes delicately with maintaining relationships with funders who expect predictable results based on established formulas, even when those results fall short of what they could be. Given the nature of its funding and its composition, UNICEF clearly is in a delicate position dependent upon many separate interests.

But while UNICEF has done exemplary work, it has not created a movement. UNICEF has not emerged as a global spokesperson advocating for the most unreachable children, the hundreds of millions of children worldwide that remain without a voice. UNICEF's Executive Director needs to step up and be that voice.

Beyond this, UNICEF must recognize the power and potential of CBOs to perform the tasks on the ground that UNICEF currently consigns to major, top-down investment partners. We have seen that CBOs are cost-effective, far-reaching, and lean. They merit a stronger role in UNICEF's funding and partnership strategies, not merely as implementation subcontractors but as targeted conduits with specific programmatic deliverables that tie into UNICEF's broader mission.

UNICEF's recognition of CBOs must go farther than funding and partnerships, though. As the preeminent actor in global children's issues, UNICEF has great influence in determining who gets heard. Quite simply, they choose who sits at the table when policies and programs are discussed with governments, other multilaterals, and the INGO community. CBOs have not been part of these discussions, and the voices of the children with whom they work have not been well represented in UNICEF's evaluations. This must change. UNICEF needs to include all segments of those working on behalf of the most marginalized, including and especially those closest to the ground. CBOs need to be squarely on UNICEF's radar as funding recipients, as program partners, and as policy contributors.

Recommendation 11: Create an Undersecretary for Children and Youth at the UN that would coordinate all UN programs and interventions impacting children

While UNICEF may take the lead in the collective work on behalf of the young, it is not the only UN entity pursuing these efforts, as noted above. The UN has a plethora of agencies whose programs touch upon children's issues, even if they do not maintain those issues as a focus. As a result, the risk for duplication of services, inefficiency, and miscommunication is always present.

An Undersecretary for Children, responsible for coordinating efforts that impact the conditions of vulnerable children and young people across all UN programs and reporting directly to the Secretary General, would lend efficiency and coordination to the various initiatives that now exist within the UN's separate agencies. Such a position would also be expected to present a strong public voice on behalf of the most marginalized.

The work of UNDP, UNHCR, UNFPA, UNAIDS, UNWomen, WFP, WHO, ILO, and other entities provide critical contributions to the welfare of children and young people. But much of what they do is incidental to their primary missions. This does not demean its importance, but it does certainly underscore the need for coordination. A new Undersecretary for Children would fill this role, which would no doubt expand as the position matures and finds its legs.

Moreover, if the new SDGs are to incorporate a stronger emphasis on the young, then that emphasis must be represented at the highest organizational level. The implementation of the SDGs will be a central focus for all UN work moving forward. For the SDGs to succeed, or at least for them to be maximally effective, CBOs must be part of the service equation. CBOs can reach children that no one else can find. To incorporate a bolder role for CBOs in UN service provision consistent with the new SDGs, coordination will be imperative, and these CBOs will need a champion to represent their impact and compel their participation with bodies that have heretofore looked past them. This should be a central part of the new Undersecretary's portfolio.

In all, the Undersecretary for Children would comprise a central administrative function as an integral part of the Secretary General's cabinet. He or she would oversee existing program implementation, help develop new programmatic directions capitalizing on each agency's strengths and expertise, and add a compelling voice to the global discussion of vulnerable children.

Change to extensive bureaucratic organizations does not come easily. The finest, most carefully crafted programmatic or administrative enhancements can be met with intransigence and fear. The prospect of change sometimes makes weaklings of us all. But the UN occupies an unparalleled position in the global endeavor to alleviate the traumas of the young. Accordingly, the role of children within the UN must be made more central.

Earlier the suggestion was put forth that the United states, in particular, should establish major positions within its executive branch to coordinate and advocate sophisticated responses to children's issues. At its simplest, these positions are prototypes that other governments can adapt in their own way. The collective impetus of these new types of positions, and the gravity they impart to policy and program implications for children, can overcome any reluctance on the part of the UN to find ways to conform to this new emphasis. Because the United states is the UN's largest donor nation, it carries a certain amount of leverage with the body as a whole. The creation of the Ambassador-at-Large and the White House Special Advisor positions may make the UN more apt to add positions with similar mandates on a global level. Embracing these changes on the national level can contribute to a new global structure.

ACADEMIA AND RESEARCH INSTITUTIONS—MAKING THE CASE FOR CHILDREN

The global academy has a role to play in changing the lives of disenfranchised children. Academia has the capacity to research, teach, and inform. Without their participation, the intellectual underpinnings of any children's movement will be tenuous.

Recommendation 12: Encourage global academic research— evidence-based, cross-sectoral, child-centered, and focused on the work of CBOs—within academia and think-tanks that expands the parameters of traditional thinking concerning the social development of children

Research is a key component to determining which types of interventions work best. Academia has long delved into aspects of children's issues, and that characteristic must continue and deepen. The type of research engaged, though, must be child-centric. Much research to date has placed children within their usual silos, as malnourished or homeless or under-educated, and so on. For *children of the last mile* to get the interventions they need, these silos must be broken down.

Research must be evidence-based, relying on hard data measuring social conditions, interventions, and outcomes. We would also benefit from more research that is based in the science of children, from brain development to the stresses imposed by both physical environments and emotional trauma. Research that incorporates a global perspective and crosses disciplines would assist the rethinking of children's issues that is the basis of most of these recommendations.

There are, of course, various methods through which research pertaining to marginalization, violence, poverty, abuse, and the host of issues attending the vulnerable young can be mined. What matters is that the best methods come to the fore, and that the issues are seen through a child-centered focus that strips away entanglements with auxiliary influences. The academic community should heed the work of premier researchers such as Boyden and Shonkoff, referenced earlier, certainly for the information they produce, but as much for the methods through which they produce it and the thinking that generates those methods. There are strong lessons that can be learned which can guide deeper, more relevant, and meaningful research into these complex issues.

As noted in Chap. 10, academic models of global development have looked past CBOs. But research focused on the unique impact of CBOs in addressing complex children's issues, their characteristics, their leadership, and their innovative interventions would provide immense value to the body of knowledge informing international development. Academic research has too often relied on traditional delivery systems as primary resources and the basis for analysis. The goal of the highest quality research, though, is to push the boundaries of knowledge outward, beyond existing bases and reference points. Academia can offer a tremendous service to the international development community, the government sector, philanthropists, and all engaged in redirecting the lives of vulnerable children by turning a sharp eye to the work of CBOs.

Recommendation 13: Leading academic institutions must expand their curricula to embrace systematic study of global children's issues

The paucity of substantive courses addressing the international development of children was noted earlier as a shortcoming of the academic sector. That failing can be corrected readily through the creation and regular offering of programs of study related to children's issues. These courses need to stand alone and not be incorporated into broader disciplines. Children and young people merit this emphasis, and their issues require evaluation on their own.

Within the teaching of international children's development, the role of CBOs must begin to receive special focus. We have seen how communication technology can bridge even the most remote regions. There can no longer be an excuse for not including these unique groups in the formal academic analysis of what works and what does not. The lessons are increasingly at hand as CBOs become more visible, and their work becomes more accessible. Any international development course dealing with children and young people will necessarily be incomplete if the CBO sector is not featured in some way

Academia needs to teach this material. It needs to train the next generation of leaders who will go into the field, direct efforts on the ground, develop relevant and effective public policies, and engineer new approaches to mitigate social, economic, and cultural influences that rob children and young people of their future. Academia needs to train and inform those who will lead organizations that channel resources to this work, research the impact of these collective efforts, and, in sum, fill the roles necessary to elevate the position of children worldwide.

This is not a minor field, nor should it be considered on the academic periphery. For the hundreds of millions of children who need this leadership, the academic discipline of international children's development is the most critical science, the most essential art.

ADVOCACY—ELEVATING THE VOICES

Most advocacy stems from NGOs themselves and increasingly from the CBOs that are closest to the ground. Because their voices are clearest, we would do well to channel them, to bring them together, and to create a crescendo. At present, there is no agency or organization that can do this. Neither is there an NGO whose primary mission is advocacy from the community level.

Recommendation 14: Create a global child advocacy organization that represents forcefully the issues of marginalized children and young people from the ground up to policymakers, to philanthropists, to academia, and to the public at large

Some organizations, such as the newly formed Global Alliance for Children, have a distinctive mission that encompasses advocacy. Global Alliance strives to "support the development of country ownership, information systems, national and international cooperation, science and learning."[9] While this is laudable and necessary work, it does not channel resources from the ground up, nor does it rely on the insights of CBOs or grassroots leadership, which are the most compelling and inescapable voices in the field.

Other organizations that have a single-issue focus are sometimes quite loud and quite visible, but their work is their own and not on behalf of the most vulnerable children in general. The leadership of these organizations must prioritize their groups' agendas—including fund raising and programmatic expansion—so their messages are usually narrow. They cannot speak for the field, and, as regular recipients of government grants, they are not free to be a critical voice when needed.

If a comprehensive child advocacy organization does not exist, it is time to create one. This has to be done through philanthropic investments from the private sector. Any organization reliant even in part on public funding will lack the independence to speak freely, to agitate for governmental action, or to goad public agencies into needed action. Such an organization cannot be a subcontractor. But such an investment from the private sector makes sense because advocacy and the creation of a public voice can in fact leverage support, recognition, and visibility for all actors in the field.

Failing that, the responsibility for coordinating the various CBO voices from the field may fall to an existing organization that already has a broad global network encompassing grassroots organizations in multiple low-income countries and the credibility that allows it to be heard in corridors of power, the media, and the public at large. Given its presence among CBOs in nearly 80 countries and its high reputation, it is easy to suggest The Global Fund for Children[10] assume this role, but other possibilities exist, too. What matters is that one of these organizations steps up to assume this mantle, to coordinate and channel the compelling voices from the field to deepen the impact of the messages sent forward, and create a public awareness of the realities that affect the lives of marginalized young people.

THE BLUEPRINT FORWARD

Breaking Down Silos

1. Reconsider the ways in which children's issues are defined, and see children holistically as a distinctive demographic

Increasing Support for Community-Based Organizations

2. More investments in, and more money for, Community-based Organizations (CBOs). This includes regular and predictable operating support, and capacity building within the CBO sector, including leadership development, infrastructure development, and strategic planning

3. Include CBOs in policy discussions, knowledge exchanges, seminars, and virtually any forum at which children's issues are discussed on any level
4. CBOs must be made accessible to donors, policymakers, thought leaders, academics, and other players in international development through networking at both the national and international levels

Reimagining the Role of the US Government

5. Creation of the Children's Global Investment Trust as a separate US government agency empowered to make grants to CBOs working with the most marginalized children and young people
6. Refine agencies within the US government's foreign assistance structure to facilitate funding of CBOs dealing with children's issues. These agencies include, but are not limited to, the Inter-American Foundation, the African Development Fund, the Displaced Children's and Orphans Fund, and the Center for Faith-Based and Community Initiatives
7. Recognize children's issues as a foreign policy imperative
8. Create an Ambassador-At-Large for Children within the US Department of State
9. Create a White House Special Advisor for Children

Strengthening Multilaterals

10. Incorporate CBOs into UNICEF's overriding strategies for funding, strategic development, and public relations
11. Create an Undersecretary for Children and Youth at the UN that would coordinate all UN programs and interventions impacting children

Deepening Academia and Research Institutions

12. Encourage global academic research—evidence-based, cross-sectoral, child-centered, and focused on the work of CBOs—within academia and think-tanks that expands the parameters of traditional thinking concerning the social development of children
13. Leading academic institutions must expand their curricula to embrace systematic study of global children's issues

Representing the Interests of Children and Young People

14. Create a child advocacy organization that represents forcefully the issues of marginalized children and young people from the ground up to policymakers, to philanthropists, to academia, and to the public at large

A Movement for Children—Giving Voice to the Invisible

Too often, we close our eyes to the unpleasant, ugly images that force us to face what we do not wish to see. Human nature compels us to turn away. There is no blame in this; it is who we are.

Children and young people living on society's edges make us uncomfortable. No child merits violence, abuse, disease, hunger, abandonment, or want. No child should be shut off from nurture, aspiration, or hope. But the hundreds of millions of children whose lives are sorely compromised by dysfunctional systems can no longer be ignored.

What we have seen in these pages is a small glimpse of the conditions that dominate so many young lives. We rightly cringe at these images and stories. But we have also seen glimmers of hope. We have seen instances of leadership, creativity, and immense courage. We have seen the resiliency of children and adults who recover from drastic setbacks and find ways to continue moving ahead. We have seen organizations and governments and multilaterals directing resources, thought, and passion to finding ways to alleviate these sad stories. We have seen efficiencies of scale, and the power of small efforts tightly focused. We have seen a way forward.

The recommendations of this blueprint, taken together, create nothing less than a global movement for children. Experience shows us that this can be done. Movements have arisen over the past century on behalf of women, civil rights, those impacted by specific diseases such as HIV/AIDS or breast cancer, and even definable social or economic groups such as organized labor, to great effect. Movements galvanize the assets of a cause, strengthen them, focus their agenda, and give them a voice which must be heeded. Movements change the way societies think and how they behave. They force us to look at things differently.

More children than we can count are consigned to society's corners, lost in the congestion of systems that do not bend and interventions that do not go far enough. We do not see them, and in our collective failure, render them invisible. But they, along with all children, deserve a voice. They deserve a movement of their own, fed by philanthropy, recognized by academia, respected by governments in all parts of the world, and driven by the insights, wisdom, and amazing efforts of those closest to the ground, those at the community level who see these children daily and live their own lives in the conviction that these young people can be given something different.

We can justify such a movement for economic reasons, because these invisible children extract billions of dollars in opportunity costs and program expenses each year. We can justify it on the basis of global security, because low-income societies drain our collective economic and social strength, putting everyone at greater risk. We can justify it on the basis of a collective humanitarian ethos, for nearly every religious or philosophical system of belief compels us to protect our youngest and most vulnerable.

But in the end, we need no justification beyond the simple reality that these children share our time, share our space, and, even if we do not see them, share our humanity. It is, quite simply, the right thing to do.

NOTES

1. See Chapter 2, "Hiding in Plain Sight—Who Are These Children?," for demographics table.
2. http://guidestarindia.blogspot.com/2009/06/how-many-ngos-are-there-in-india.html; *and* http://timesofindia.indiatimes.com/india/India-witnessing-NGO-boom-there-is-1-for-every-600-people/article-show/30871406.cms
3. Sarah Thomas de Benitez, Interview, December 14, 2013, transcript p. 7 (Maya Ajmera and Clare Dreyfus, interviewers).
4. Author Maya Ajmera founded and subsequently led the Global Fund for Children for 18 years, leaving in 2012.
5. http://www.firelightfoundation.org/about/mission
6. Nye, Joseph. *Soft Power: The Means to Success in World Politics* (New York: Public Affairs, 2004) p. 5–7.
7. http://www.foreignaffairs.com/articles/66799/hillary-rodham-clinton/leading-through-civilian-power
8. http://www.theguardian.com/global-development/2013/sep/25/new-development-goals-un-general-assembly
9. http://www.globalallianceforchildren.org/
10. Author Maya Ajmera founded and subsequently led The Global Fund for Children for 18 years, leaving in 2012.

Epilogue

In the relatively short time between the completion of this book's draft and the preparation for its publication, the global landscape for children and youth has continued to evolve.

We have seen moments of triumph and recognition—the awarding of the 2015 Nobel Peace Prize to Malala Yousafzai and Kailash Satyarthi "for their struggle against the suppression of children and young people and for the right of all children to education"[1]—and we have seen more frequently moments of horror, tragedy, and loss—the kidnapping of young girls in Nigeria by Boko Haram; the impact of the Ebola outbreak in West Africa, which kills up to 90% of infected infants and young children while leaving thousands of others orphaned[2]; and the devastation of the war in Syria, which has turned hundreds of thousands of young people into refugees, destroyed their educational system, engaged many as a new generation of child soldiers,[3] and horrified a watching world as the body of a small Syrian refugee child washed up onto a Greek shore. As we look, we see a catalog of similar events that changes and grows almost every day.

The world has not stopped spinning and in its spinning, has not yet found a way to protect its most vulnerable. And while we acknowledge the specific events that captured our collective attention, we recognize sadly that, no matter how current our study, there will always be events that document or underscore the issues raised in these pages.

Nor can we anticipate the new issues that will rise from unpredictable social, political, or economic factors that will conspire to put children at

© The Editor(s) (if applicable) and The Author(s) 2016
M. Ajmera, G.A. Fields, *Invisible Children*,
DOI 10.1057/978-1-137-57838-9

risk. Within the last two decades, we have seen movements percolate from the ground up that use children as the currency of their battles, from the civil war in Sierra Leone where the limbs of young people in the wrong place at the wrong time were summarily severed to the battlefields of the Middle East where the brutalities of ISIS show no regard for age. We cannot guess which new drugs will be crafted that promise release, or ecstasy, or nirvana, and be marketed to the young. We do not know if another economic breakdown will cast hundreds of thousands of young people into harsh or exploitive labor or force them into the streets. We are unable to predict the new diseases that will defy a quick cure while ravaging entire demographics, and especially the weakest and the youngest. We cannot predict the specifics.

And so, in the end, the specifics do not matter. There will be something else, perhaps many things that will thrust young lives to society's edges, beyond our capacity, or our willingness, to see them. Until such time as our collective society derives solutions to the conditions that render millions of children invisible, either through the recommendations offered here or through newer or better ideas, there will always be a need for an Epilogue to bring facts closer to currency in a book such as this.

We look forward to the days when there might be no further need to make any updates at all.

NOTES

1. "The Nobel Peace Prize 2014". *Nobelprice.org.* Nobel Prize Committee.
2. http://www.reuters.com/article/2015/03/25/us-health-ebola-children-iduskbn0ml2kj20150325
3. *Cf.* http://www.bbc.com/news/world-middle-east-32193943 on child refugees; http://www.theguardian.com/world/2015/mar/30/half-of-child-refugees-from-syria-out-of-education-report-save-the-children on the collapse of education; http://www.usnews.com/opinion/blogs/world-report/2015/02/13/the-rise-of-child-soldiers-in-syria on child soldiers.

INDEX

A
Aangan Trust, 185–6
Abdul Latif Jameel Poverty Action Lab
    (J-PAL), 248
Abt Associates, 86
academia and research institutions,
    104–6, 280–2. *See also* siloing;
    specific institutions
addiction. *See* alcohol use by children;
    drug use by children; family
    breakdown
Adolescent Girls Legal Defense Fund
    (AGLDF), 245
Adverse Childhood Experiences (ACE)
    study, 148
advocacy efforts, 182–7, 184, 198–200,
    282–3
Afghan Institute of Learning (AIL),
    129–31, 165, 266. *See also*
    Yacoobi, Sakena
Afghanistan, 22, 94
    invisible children in, 7–8, 47, 53,
        67, 112–13, 119
Africa. *See also* HIV/AIDS; specific
    countries

birth registration in, 20
child soldiers in, 47, 72–3, 206
Ebola outbreak in, 287
foreign aid in, 92, 93
khat chewing in, 56
networking in, 221–2
polio in, 22
school enrollment in, 75
under-five mortality in, 76
youth unemployment in, 41
African American youth, 43, 45, 134–5
African Development Foundation
    (ADF), 237, 238, 271, 272
Aga Khan Foundation, 200, 201
AidData, 83, 85–6
Aide et Action, 216
AIDS. *See* HIV/AIDS
Ajmera, Maya
    academic positions of, ix, 257n68
    education of, viii
    Global Fund for Children and,
        vii–viii, 194, 286n4
    motivations for book, xi, 12
    personal experiences of, viii, 3–6
    as professional lecturer, x

© The Editor(s) (if applicable) and The Author(s) 2016
M. Ajmera, G.A. Fields, *Invisible Children,*
DOI 10.1057/978-1-137-57838-9

in low-income countries, 23, 59, 77,
108–9
WEAVE program, 179
women. *See also* girls
economic impact of, 51
gender gap, 46
initiatives for, 179, 197, 202–4
maternal deaths, 43, 70
World Bank, 49–51, 89, 93–4, 154
World Children's Prize, 166
World Conference on Women
(Beijing), 202–4
World Food Program (WFP), 107,
229, 231
World Health Organization (WHO),
21, 53, 71–2, 229
World Innovation Summit for
Education Award, 165
World Vision, 70, 154, 200

Y
Yacoobi, Sakena, 129–31, 164–6. *See
also* Afghan Institute of Learning
(AIL)
Yemen, 20, 56
Young Lives study (Oxford
University), 58, 59, 105, 247,
250
Yousafzai, Malala, 205, 287
youth. *See* invisible children
Youth bulge, 41, 45
Yugoslavia, 55
Yunis, Muhammad, 175

Z
Zaidi, Anita, 165–6
Zambia, 55, 176–7
Zaya, 215
Zenawi, Meles, 242